THE RESCUE OF THE AGES

by

DIANA LARKIN

The Rescue of the Ages: A Watchman's Journal ©2025 Diana Larkin

Paperback ISBN: 978-1-969202-00-1

Hardback ISBN: 978-1-969202-01-8

Ebook ISBN: 978-1-969202-02-5

Editor: Patty Teichroew and Janet Huxley

Publisher: Light Warrior Publishing, Franklin, Tennessee

Scripture: Scripture quotations marked AMP are from the Amplified® Bible (AMP), Copyright © 2015 by The Lockman Foundation. Used by permission. lockman.org

Scripture quotations marked MSG are taken from The Message, copyright © 1993, 2002, 2018 by Eugene H. Peterson. Used by permission of NavPress. All rights reserved. Represented by Tyndale House Publishers.

Scripture quotations marked (NKJV) are taken from the New King James Version®. Copyright © 1982 by Thomas Nelson. Used by permission. All rights reserved.

Scripture quotations marked (NLT) are taken from the Holy Bible, New Living Translation, copyright ©1996, 2004, 2015 by Tyndale House Foundation. Used by permission of Tyndale House Publishers, Carol Stream, Illinois 60188. All rights reserved.

Scripture quotations marked TPT are from The Passion Translation®. Copyright © 2017, 2018, 2020 by Passion & Fire Ministries, Inc. Used by permission. All rights reserved. ThePassionTranslation.com.

Scripture quotations marked KJV are from The Authorized (King James) Version. Rights in the Authorized Version in the United Kingdom are vested in the Crown. Reproduced by permission of the Crown's patentee, Cambridge University Press

ENDORSEMENTS

The Rescue of the Ages is a precious love offering from a radiant soul whose priceless contribution to society in this remarkable season cannot be understated. Diana's willingness to step out of the safety of comfortable anonymity to share what our God revealed to her in their most intimate moments together has been life-changing for tens of thousands across the globe who have read or tuned into *A Watchman's Journal*. What began as a private journal chronicling conversations between Diana and her Maker, then shared via social media during the years the darkness came at us hardest has now been expanded into this latest gift, sure to inspire multitudes more! Through Diana's entries, the reader's heart will take wings and soar with delight as our God's plan takes clearer form, becoming even more glorious in His golden light! Diana's revelatory courage emboldens us to continue to stand in unification, growing in strength as formidable light warriors in partnership with the God of the Universe! His sweet voice ever assures us; we can do this! The BEST IS YET TO COME!

J. M. Huxley (Janet Huxley), Award-winning author, broadcast news anchor, podcast host

I met Diana through X (then Twitter) at a very difficult time in my life when I was struggling with what our country was going through with COVID-19 and also the constant pressure of wearing masks and taking the vaccine. There were so many opinions, and everyone thought they were right. I would get evil looks when I didn't wear a mask as I knew it wasn't helpful, and then friends and family members disagreed with me about the vax. It was so chaotic. That was when it was like God blew His breath on me through the words God gave through Diana. I was enraptured in God's love as He brought hope and life through Diana's pen. Reading God's promises that Diana heard brought life into my weary soul. It was the breath of life. Once I found Diana, I would read her posts everyday. I often would share them with my friends who were struggling too, and they were encouraged as well. What also amazed me was that not only was I encouraged through God using Diana to share His heart with us, but she supported me in my gifting by inspiring me to share what God was giving to me as well. So I began sharing in June of 2022. I never heard God speak to me everyday before, but He began to do that! Then another event happened to me that blows my mind. I shared with Diana that I had a dream that I worked for her. Her response was, "Well, I need some help. Would you like to?" I immediately said yes. That was November 10, 2023, and now I am a part of the AWJ Team! All this to say, I am so excited to endorse this book to you, and I pray that these words given to Diana by the Father will bring you life, encouragement, and hope just like it did me!

Patty Teichroew, blogger and prayer warrior at
pltprayer.blogspot.com

I have journals full of your words, Diana. They have been such a blessing in my life during these years since the 2020 election. I was new to a life with Holy Spirit, and He led me to you. I don't think you have any idea how many are just like me, and God has used you to guide us and teach us how to live a life listening to and living by His Holy Spirit. I KNOW many join me in thanking our Father and you for all the love, time, and devotion you have given in teaching us. We all love you so much!!

Lisa Griffin

You know that we love you! You have to know how impactful your words from the Father are, and you have made a difference in our lives. The Father's words carry a special frequency. Your Watchman family thanks you for your obedience and faithfulness. We are all better and stronger in faith for having you in our lives. We've learned a lot and have come a long way. This book will be a cherished addition to our library.

Ret. Major General Brett and Janice Cairns

*This book is dedicated to A Watchman's Journal Team
—Patty Teichroew, Ash West, and Callie Simons—
for their faithful support and help in my ministry and their
prayers that saw this book through to completion.
Thank you, my friends*

TABLE OF CONTENTS

DISCLAIMER

The words and messages shared in this book are drawn directly from my personal journals and are the result of my intimate and ongoing relationship with the Father. They have not been copied, adapted, or taken from any other sources. These writings reflect my personal spiritual experiences and revelations and are presented as such. Readers are encouraged to receive them with openness, discernment, and respect for the deeply personal nature of what is shared here.

For clarity, the words of the Father given to me in prophecy are in bold.

INTRODUCTION

This book chronicles our nation and the world in transition from dark to light through the lens of the prophetic words I received from the Father of Lights. It will highlight how the Father AWAKENED us to understand the deep darkness that had taken root in our nation and the nations of the world. The nations hung in the balance, and we were in great JEOPARDY of losing all our freedoms from the widespread net of deception woven over the nations by the lying media, masquerading leaders, and corrupt agencies. These leaders and agencies told people they were working for our good, but secretly they were implementing plans for TYRANNY and POPULATION CONTROL through pandemics, wars, financial slavery, tainted food, water, air, and medications. Behind the web of deception and the death agendas were spiritual forces of darkness empowering deceived people to carry out their plans to steal, to kill, and to destroy. Into the darkness of this war season, the Father's words were beacons of hope and life.

THE RESCUE OF THE AGES

The Father spoke of a RESCUE OPERATION, our induction into the ARMY OF LIGHT, a crash course on SPIRITUAL WARFARE, partnering with the Warrior Hosts and Angels, learning our AUTHORITY as Believers, and receiving a vision for the establishment of GOD'S KINGDOM on the earth—also known as the GOLDEN AGE. The Father painted a picture of an entrance into a time of great creativity, amazing inventions, breakthroughs in science and health, longed-for peace, and abundant prosperity. This vision of hope led us through the DARK STORMS and SHAKINGS, and our courage and faith were built as we saw one promise after another fulfilled. This collection of prophetic words from the Father provides a RECORD of the faithfulness of a powerful God who heard the cries of His children for deliverance from the tyranny and control of those partnered with deep darkness. It is important that we remember these epic battles and realize that evil must be kept beneath our feet and true JUSTICE and RIGHTEOUSNESS must be maintained to preserve our costly victory and God-given freedoms. Welcome to the GREAT AWAKENING AND THE RESCUE OF THE AGES!

CHAPTER ONE

Hearing God's Voice for a Nation

"You are a Watchman." Those words echoed in my spirit, as I realized with wonder that the God of the Universe was telling me my future and the calling on my life. As I lay in the dark one night, I told **Jesus** if He was real, then I was going to lay my life on the altar to Him. If He had given His life for me, then I knew I needed to give my life back to Him. The next morning, the Holy Spirit prompted me to turn in the Bible to Ezekiel 3:17 (NASB) *"Son of man, I have appointed you a watchman to the house of Israel; whenever you hear a word from My mouth, warn them from Me."* There has been a progression in my life as a Watchman: first to my family, then to the Church, and lastly to the Nation and out into the world.

I knew this was a serious call on my life, and I knew it was important for me to learn to hear God's voice so that I could communicate His heart to others. I had grown up in church and was familiar with the Bible, but I lacked a personal relationship with the Lord, and I did not know God's heart. In those days I had a form of religion but no power, and my life bore very little fruit. After I surrendered my life to Jesus, I was surprised and in wonder when I began to hear His voice speaking to me! Nobody in the church I grew up in ever mentioned being able to hear God's voice, so I was unsure about this new adventure that the Holy Spirit was leading me into. What had propelled me into the Kingdom was the untimely death of my dad when he was only fifty-seven. I had to come to terms with the eternal realm—was there a Heaven and did you get there through the Cross of Jesus? My choice to believe in a Savior whose Blood covered my sin and whose Resurrection opened up Heaven to me had brought me into salvation, but what about the things of the Spirit that I was hearing about from a group of Believers who called themselves "Spirit-filled" and who were praying for healing and operating in the gift of prophecy? It drew my spirit, but I wasn't sure it was "safe" to go there.

The Holy Spirit answered that question by giving me a powerful dream. This dream came to me about two weeks after my dad transitioned to Heaven. In the dream, I was walking down a wide hospital corridor. The corridor came to an end, and I had to turn right to continue. As I turned that corner, suddenly, I was face to face with my dad. He looked me directly in my eyes and only said one thing to me: "Trust the things of the Spirit." I received that message from the Lord through my dad who was now part of the Great Cloud of Witnesses. I embraced everything that the Father had for my life in this new realm of the Spirit. That was in the year 1975, and I have never looked back.

Little did I know that the Father would take the next forty-five years to prepare me for my assignment in this uncharted and tumultuous time of the Great Awakening. Over the years, I served in the Body of Christ in women's ministry, prayer counseling, teaching classes, and on worship teams. He taught me through the years how to journal His voice by stilling myself and tuning into the never-ending flow of the Holy Spirit—those rivers of living waters that carry the Father's voice. I would meet with Him every morning and ask Him, "Father, what is on your heart this morning?" When I first began to hear His voice, He would speak to me about my own heart and my family. After some years, He began to speak to me about issues in the Church and His desires and plans for the Body of Christ.

September 30, 2016, He began to speak to me about our nation and about the challenges that we were facing from what He would eventually call the "evil empire." As I heard the Father's voice in the flow of the Holy Spirit, He would emphasize to me that certain words were to be capitalized to draw attention to their importance.

SEPTEMBER 30, 2016: PARTNERING

"Keep partnering with Me for your Nation. Do not look at people or circumstances or you will become discouraged. Can a Nation be born in a day? I AM able to turn the TIDE of DARKNESS in your Nation back to its original purpose and covenant. Keep declaring that My ways would be reestablished in the HEARTS of the people and in the leaders of your Nation and that I would raise up Esthers, Daniels, and Josephs to call your nation BACK to Me. Call this Nation back to Me that it might fulfill its DESTINY in Me."

Packed in that short prophetic word from the Father are familiar themes that will be affirmed over and over. From the very first word He gave to me, He emphasized that we were to partner with Him in the saving of our Nation. We had to keep our eyes on the Father and His strength so that we would not become discouraged by the many schemes the darkness kept sending against us and our Nation. The Father asked us: *"Can a nation be born in a day?"* We find the answer in Isaiah 66:8 (NASB1995) *"Who has heard such a thing? Who has seen such things? Can a land be born in one day? Can a nation be brought forth all at once? As soon as Zion travailed, she also brought forth her sons."* He was letting us know that there would be some sudden happenings in this season. Another repeated theme we were given was the assurance that the Father would turn back the tide of darkness from our Nation and that He would bring us back to original purpose and our covenant roots. In this original word about the future of our Nation, He declared that His ways would become rooted in the hearts of the people and the hearts of the leaders. He promised to raise up Esthers: those who would come boldly before His Throne asking for mercy and grace—no matter what the personal cost might be. Daniels and Josephs: prophetic dreamers and interpreters who would advise leaders with spiritual intelligence and with ways of wisdom. The Father ended this message with an action item for us: we were to use our words to call this Nation back to Him so that we might fulfill our destiny as a Nation.

Before the Father began to speak to me about our Nation, He spoke to me about a heritage of peace that would come through my life. This heritage of peace has become a hallmark of A Watchman's Journal Ministry.

May 24, 2016: Peace—My Heritage

"I have chosen you as a vessel to carry My PEACE. It is My GIFT to you and through you. Do not allow it to be STOLEN from you and don't NEGLECT to CULTIVATE it by RESTING in and ACKNOWLEDGING Me in everything. People will be drawn to this PEACE as to the sound of gently running water. Let My PEACE flow over to all you meet. As you come and are refreshed in Me, so people will be REFRESHED in your presence."

I wasn't sure who the "people" were who would be refreshed in the peace He was giving me to carry because the Father had directed me to lay down every ministry I had been involved in, and my life was hidden away with Him. I had no idea, at the time, that He would call me out of hiddenness, and I would begin to share His words on social media, maintain a blog, and produce videos on YouTube and Rumble where I would share these words from the Father in order to strengthen and encourage those who listened. The comment I hear the most on these videos is that people could feel God's peace through my voice. I am in continual awe of what He does to bless others through our lives.

Here is a sample of other early prophetic words that the Father spoke to me about our nation and this season of great battle. I received these in my journal before I began to share His words publicly.

OCTOBER 5, 2016: CALLING

"Keep turning your heart and your ear to Me, and I will impart My ways and My thoughts to you and give you prayers and decrees to release that will change situations and atmospheres and will bring the Kingdom of Heaven to invade earth and will help to establish My ways and My will into the chaos and destruction. This is the call and the privilege of My Sons and Daughters to help further and to help establish My Kingdom."

Again, in this early word, we see the Father revealing what we were called and commissioned to do in this war season of dark to light. He gave us prayers and decrees that changed things and helped bring His ways and will into the chaos and destruction that came our way. He identified us as His Sons and Daughters called to help establish His Kingdom on the earth.

On October 6, 2016, one month and two days before the historic election of Donald Trump to the presidency of the United States, the Father spoke this to me about that election. The pollsters, pundits, news outlets, and political figures all claimed it would be a landslide victory for Hillary Clinton.

OCTOBER 6, 2016: ASSURANCE

"I have heard the prayers of the saints, and I AM working behind the scenes in this current election. The outcome will be a surprise. Continue to pray asking for My favor and My blessing to return to your nation and for the hearts of its people to turn back to Me."

About two weeks out from the 2016 election, I asked the Father to once again speak to me about this election. This is what I heard:

OCTOBER 26, 2016: THE ELECTION

"You have heard correctly from leaders I have spoken to that Donald Trump is the man I have chosen to lead you through this tumultuous hour for your nation. He will have the inner strength to see your nation through the choppy seas ahead as I set your nation back on its course and its destiny in Me. I have heard the cries of My people, and I will turn this nation back to Me, as My people have humbled themselves before Me and aligned their hearts with My heart, and I will honor their heartfelt cries to return to a covenant nation with Me."

The Father has now confirmed over and over that Donald Trump was His choice to lead our nation out of the creeping tyranny and darkness. The Father promised that He would work through President Trump to restore us to our nation's original covenant with Him.

In the early morning hours of November 9, 2016, the world went into shock when Donald Trump was declared the winner of an election that he was supposed to lose. Our God answers prayers! The media coverage of Donald Trump had been exceedingly negative, and many Christians and the entrenched political establishment in the Republican Party believed or agreed with the bad reports the media kept churning out. One of the first lessons we had to learn in the prelude to the Great Awakening was that the media was not speaking the truth. In fact, they had been almost completely taken over by dark puppet figures who controlled everything that was written in media or spoken on news networks. The morning after the election, the Father spoke this word to me:

NOVEMBER 9, 2016: ACKNOWLEDGE

"Thank you for understanding what I AM doing in your nation and for seeing past surface issues to the heart of the matter of what I AM doing. This man's strong leadership is the answer to the cries of My Church to turn their nation back to Me. Pray for him. Acknowledge him as My choice and watch what I will do."

Leaving the Wilderness for the Promised Land

Over the years, the Father led me through several wilderness seasons where I was stripped of everything and all my branches were pruned back. Although difficult to walk through, I began to greatly value these wilderness seasons because my roots went deep into His heart, and I learned that only He can satisfy and only He can produce true and lasting fruit from our lives. The Father spoke this personal encouragement to me in 2017, as I remained in hiddenness even though I was hearing His messages for our nation.

April 3, 2017: Promises Fulfilled

"I will open up a way in the wilderness, and I will bring you into your Promised Land and the land of your inheritance ... (I) will bring you to a place of great fruitfulness, and you will know My goodness and My power toward you. Watch what I will do on your behalf because I love you and because you have humbled yourself and you have been obedient to My voice and My heart ... You have laid it all down, and you have gained Me."

Because the Father is the Creator, He chooses to speak to us in a multitude of ways. The journal entries I will be sharing came mainly as I waited on Him in the quiet of communion, and I would hear His voice as I tuned into the flow of the River of Life brought by the Holy Spirit. But there were times He chose to speak through other means. Sprinkled throughout this book and showcased as the main theme of Chapter 14, you will read about Dreams, Visions, and Encounters—some in Heaven and some in different places on the earth.

Dreams, visions, and encounters involve your spirit interacting with the spiritual realm. These are not experiences that you can generate; they are initiated by the Holy Spirit, and you must interact with the Spirit to receive clarity about what you have seen, heard, or experienced. That said, this multitude of ways the Father speaks is open to all Believers—not just to a few chosen ones. Much of the Church has, unfortunately, not taught about or valued these spiritual ways that the Father chooses to communicate with us. God is Spirit, and we need to learn His ways of communicating with our spirits.

9

Approximately one-third of the Bible is dreams, visions, and encounters, so that should tell you the value of these ways of the Father communicating with our spirits. Study about these ways of God speaking to us in His Word. They are throughout the Scripture, but you might want to focus on Daniel, Isaiah, Ezekiel, Jeremiah, 1 and 2 Kings (Elijah, Elisha), and Zechariah; the four Gospels contain dreams, visions, trances, encounters, and the book of Revelation is entirely a vision and encounter with Angels and the Most High God. Tell the Holy Spirit that you are willing to have the Father speak to you in these ways, and then value what you are shown or what you hear. Write it down, pray over it, and ask for clarity and wisdom in stewarding what you are being shown. The following is a word from the Father with an invitation to meet Him in the Heavenly realms.

APRIL 28, 2024: ON THE WINGS OF AN EAGLE

"I LONG for you to COME and MEET with Me in My HEAVENLY REALMS. We can know such deep HEART TO HEART fellowship there, and I can show you the WONDERS of that place, and you can TASTE of My great POWER, LOVE, and PEACE. From this PERSPECTIVE, problems and conflicts on earth will not overwhelm you because you will KNOW I can PROTECT you and bring you through ON THE WINGS OF AN EAGLE. You will be in the atmosphere of 'NOTHING IS TOO DIFFICULT FOR ME,' and you will know the POWER of My mighty Hosts and Angels who will join us to bring in the VICTORY. ASCENDING to be with Me (Revelation 4), will QUIET your FEARS and your MIND, and you will be able to receive My DIRECTION and

INSIGHTS for these UNPRECEDENTED days. PRACTICE sitting STILL in My presence, and allow Me to DRAW YOU UP to My heart. I have so much I long to show you, and I want you to keep DRAWING AWAY with Me to Heavenly places even when things are PEACEFUL and My Kingdom has TOUCHED the earth and is being ESTABLISHED there by My Sons and Daughters. You will be STRENGTHENED for each day's challenges, and I will EQUIP and PROVIDE you with all that you need as I carry you ON THE WINGS OF AN EAGLE in My Heavenly Realms."

The Father gave me a vision for my next season that I could hardly imagine—how would He be able to fulfill these wild-sounding promises?

MAY 5, 2017: VISION

"I will give you a vision for your future in the Kingdom that you can clearly see and call forth into being. It will fit you perfectly, and it will be a joy for you to do. It will bring you life and will produce eternal fruit for My Kingdom. I will bring you to a group of like-minded people. You will support each other, grow healthy and strong together, and you will impact the darkness with the love, unity, strength, and glory that you carry. It will be what you've always dreamed of."

It was beyond my wildest dreams to imagine that I would be doing these things in the future, but He has fulfilled every word of this prophetic vision!

A further preparation for being launched into ministry was a Throne Room encounter I had on June 22, 2017. The Father had been taking me to heavenly places for many years in my quiet time with Him. In this encounter, the Father commissioned me as a "burning one." I would pass this commission on to those who began to follow the words the Father was speaking to me in my journal.

JUNE 22, 2017: BURNING ONE

I saw myself in the Throne Room where I was leading worship to the Father of Lights. I was declaring His power, goodness, and His plans done in love. I was asking Him for the harvest that is the reward of His beautiful Son. Jesus then stepped out of the Father, came down the steps of the Throne, and brought me up to the Father who extended His scepter to me. I touched it, and great power flowed through me. Jesus had His hand on my back supporting me. The Father then touched my eyes, ears, mouth, and heart with His scepter, and they all began to burn. I had become a burning one. The Father spoke:

"You have now become My BURNING ONE—full of My FIRE, which is LOVE, PURITY, FOCUS, and DEADLY FORCE against the schemes of the enemy. My FIRE has first of all purged away the dross and false lens of perception in your own heart. Now this FIRE can be released into other people's hearts, and it will enable POWERFUL INTERCESSION ascending to My Throne ... Your prayers are now backed by the FIRE of God, and they will accomplish GREAT THINGS for the sake of My name and My Kingdom."

At the end of my last wilderness season, the Father began to speak to me about posting on social media what I was hearing from Him—beginning with Twitter (now the X platform). This was quite a stretch for me because I had no idea how to post anything online, and I had not a clue how anyone would ever see what I was posting. Never underestimate the power of the Living God!

Nearly two years after the original call to partner with Him for our Nation on September 30, 2016, the Father announced to me on July 26, 2018, "New Season." He said, "Today I AM releasing you to publish My word to you from yesterday. This marks the beginning of a NEW SEASON for you. I'm bringing you out of the shadows of hiddenness and into the light. I AM unveiling My voice to you in a public way. I will be faithful to lead and guide you every step of the way. Look to Me for approval and affirmation and not to man. This is your safeguard and your rest. You are My Watchman, and I AM calling you once again to the front lines."

This is the first journal entry that I posted on X (then Twitter):

JULY 25, 2018: HIS PLANS

"The enemy has set this Nation up for DESTRUCTION, but I have DESTINED it for BLESSING. My plans will be VICTORIOUS. As you stand shoulder to shoulder with Me DECLARING LIFE and LIGHT to your Nation, you will see the sea of darkness and evil PARTED before us, and My righteousness and light will come POURING IN. You will see My SALVATION, DELIVERANCE, and REDEMPTION FLOOD this Land and its people with GOODNESS, MERCY, and PEACE. A DEEP and LASTING UNITY

will invade the hearts of this DIVERSE people who will focus on REBUILDING with EXCELLENCE and who will give back to the world with GENEROSITY. Good days are coming after a HARD-FOUGHT BATTLE. Taste the sweetness of VICTORY."

It is interesting that the Father is already speaking about rebuilding and victory when the battle had just begun! This original entry was seen by at least five or six people! Not an impressive beginning in man's eyes, but the Father honored my obedience and faithfulness by drawing more and more eyes to His words that I was posting. I began posting on other social media sites: Truth Social, Instagram, Facebook, Telegram, and Gab. Somehow, the Father managed to send thousands of followers my way, and we have become an effective Army of Light.

CHAPTER TWO

Houston, We Have a Problem

The astronauts aboard Apollo 13 uttered this phrase, "Houston, we have a problem," when they suddenly discovered they were in grave danger. For many people, there was a sudden and growing realization that this nation was facing huge, life-threatening problems. Johnny Enlow stated on an Elijah Streams Ministry interview on Rumble that the Lord had told him the Great Awakening would be preceded by a Rude Awakening.

Through the Father's words to us, patriot and research channels, uncompromised leaders, and a few unbiased media outlets, we saw that we had been lied to about almost everything —including our history and our modern world. There was a small group of people who had known about the lies for years, but they were discounted by most as tinfoil hat conspiracy theorists. As a watchman for many years, I had observed the steady decline of our nation into darkness and lawlessness. My warnings went unheeded by a Church who scurried into their buildings and slammed the door behind them because it was getting so dark out there! We forgot that we had been called to be the light of the world and to occupy until Jesus returns to the earth in His Second Coming. The Father laid out His plans for our nation.

SEPTEMBER 6, 2017: LIGHT INTO THE DARKNESS

"My plan is to SHINE My LIGHT into the darkness that man's REBELLION and the enemy's schemes have established in your nation. My LIGHT will EXPOSE evil and selfish agendas against the backdrop of My RIGHTEOUSNESS and My LOVE. As darkness reaches its fullness, do not despair, but instead, TRUST My TIMING and ALIGN yourself with My heart, and you will see Me move with GREAT POWER to PUSH BACK the darkness and roll out My LIGHT, GLORY, and TRUTH."

The Father revealed dark lifestyles that I did not know existed and that I found shocking. These people hid their darkness for years. When President Trump and those who backed him came on the scene, they were an existential threat to these hidden lives, their stolen wealth, and dark power.

JANUARY 3, 2018: A HIDDEN WEB

"What is about to be revealed in your Nation's leaders and wealthy ones is A WEB OF IDOL WORSHIP AND PERVERSION that has been HIDDEN from the people of this nation by IGNORANCE and a lack of DISCERNMENT caused by self-centered living. The CORRUPTION AND DEFILEMENT that I AM uncovering will SICKEN people and JOLT THEM AWAKE to their need for God-centered living based on the FEAR OF THE LORD and on My complete and redeeming LOVE. When the DEPTH AND SCOPE of this darkness is revealed, true REPENTANCE will sweep this nation ... I want a powerful Church, CLEANSED AND FOCUSED on Me and on what I AM doing in this hour. Pray for the Son of RIGHTEOUSNESS to arise over your nation with HEALING in His wings. America will once again be BEAUTIFUL, BRAVE, FREE, AND A LIGHTHOUSE to the nations. Come into My Sanctuary to thank Me for what I AM doing and to cry out for a completion of all that I have promised."

I was shocked to learn that educated, sophisticated people were worshiping idols and hiding lives of sickening corruption. How were they able to keep their darkened and selfish lifestyles secret from the public and untouched by the laws of the land? Enter Leviathan (Job 3, 40, 41; Psalms 74, 104), that dark and twisting serpent who had infiltrated our media, our government, our law enforcement, our courts, and the three letter agencies. We were not just facing lying, corrupt people; they were backed by a demonic power who hid truth, spread lies, and twisted people's words. We were fighting a war of words.

MARCH 22, 2020: WAR OF WORDS

"You have heard of World Wars, but I say this season is a worldwide WAR OF WORDS. The enemy is constantly spewing words of FEAR, words of SLANDER, and words that are LIES through those who allow themselves to be used by him. I am combating these evil words with words of HOPE, words of PEACE, and words of TRUTH spoken through those whose hearts are turned to Me. CAUTION: don't allow your communications to align with the enemy's darkness by agreeing with slander, fear, or unproven facts. Make sure you are agreeing with My perspective and check yourself—does your communication bring HOPE, ENCOURAGEMENT, THE TRUTH SPOKEN IN LOVE? I have given you a powerful weapon in this War of Words—your voice, submitted to My truth and love, will break through any lie or threat of the enemy and bring it to nothing. Together we can decisively win this War of Words and release HEALING and HOPE to the nations."

In this word, the Father told us the enemy's tactics with words: he uses fear, slander, and lies. We were to combat the evil sayings with words of hope, peace, and truth. Our voice is a weapon, and we must not use it to align with the enemy by agreeing with slander, fear, or unproven facts. The Army of Light submitted our voices to His truth and love, and we released healing and hope to the nations. Here are two more powerful words that expose the war that we were fighting—from dark to light.

SEPTEMBER 23, 2021: DARK TO LIGHT

"As deep darkness and depravity is EXPOSED to the world, it will bring SHOCK and TRAUMA to people everywhere—their world will be SHAKEN as they gaze upon how EVIL a human heart can become when it partners with DARKNESS. Much of what has been told you of history and current events will prove to be HALF-TRUTHS or outright LIES and MISDIRECTION. It will be a time of outer and inner SHAKING. This is why I have been DRAWING you close, REVEALING My power and love to you, and PURIFYING your hearts and motives. This will result in you being CARRIERS of My LIGHT, and you will be BEACONS of HOPE and SAFETY for those around you. ANCHOR all your hope in Me, and I will KEEP you. As you hear each shocking discovery, LOOSE shock and trauma from your soul and replace it with My PEACE—which is the abiding of your soul in My LIFE and LOVE. Pray shock and trauma off of others, and as they come into My PEACE, they will be able to HEAR My voice and LEAN totally on My love and strength. You REMAIN in My LIGHT, and then you will TRANSFER this light everywhere you go until the LIGHT completely ECLIPSES and OUTSHINES the darkness ... DARK TO LIGHT."

OCTOBER 14, 2021: MAKE NO MISTAKE—THIS IS WAR!

"There may not be troops and guns and tanks lined up against each other, but this is still a very real WAR with CASUALTIES and WOUNDED. This war is being fought for the MINDS and

HEARTS of a Nation using LIES (Leviathan), THREATS (Jezebel), and BIOLOGICAL and PSYCHOLOGICAL warfare (the Destroyer). This is a war of FAITH OVER FEAR and TRUTH OVER DECEPTION. This is cunning, underhanded warfare that seeks to CONTROL and that PUNISHES all who speak out against them. They are a RUTHLESS enemy who have lost the ability to have natural affections, and their hearts are HARD and DARKENED. You must be just as DETERMINED to defeat them as they are to TRAMPLE you to the ground. This is the day for ALL-OUT warfare and PUSHING BACK the darkness and DECLARING the awesome power of your God to defeat His enemies and to TURN THE TIDE from darkness to light. You must RENEW your strength in Me daily so that you stand STRONG in this fierce warfare for the DESTINY of your lives and your Nation. You are not imagining the seriousness of the day nor the heavy warfare you feel. This is why I have continued to strengthen your FAITH and to draw you CLOSE to receive My love and My orders. Be faithful to DECREE what I have PROMISED and march forth with Me to PUSH BACK and to utterly DEFEAT the LYING, STEALING darkness. Make no mistake—THIS IS WAR!"

The Father confirmed to us that what we had been told about our history and current events were half-truths, outright lies, and misdirection. Even though this was not a war like we have known before in history, it was still a very real war for the minds and hearts of a nation. We were being opposed by strongholds of the darkness, including Leviathan the twisting liar. We had to choose faith over fear and truth over deception.

In the buildup to the 2020 Presidential election, we witnessed casualties as many brave truth-tellers on social media were silenced and censored by social media giants who controlled much of the airwaves. Not only were they removed from social media platforms, those partnered with darkness also blacklisted these truth-tellers from electronic funding sites so that they could no longer receive donations for their work. These tyrannical moves proved to us that the truth was powerful and was making inroads into the darkness. Did this stop the Father's plans to combat the dark lies with His shining truth? No way! He inspired alternative social media sites dedicated to free speech. These became platforms for truth-tellers to share the darkness and lies they were uncovering and to rally patriots and Believers to action and prayer. In a victory for the Light, one of the largest censoring social media platforms was bought out by Elon Musk, and it has become a place of free speech—only God!

We discovered the evil empire had jeopardized our health, our financial systems, our security, our government structures, our family unit, and our freedom. Their goal was total domination and control of the world. The Father called them the "arrogant elite." These arrogant elite had infiltrated every area of society with their darkness, lies, bribery, corruption, and perversion. Even as the Father uncovered all this darkness for us to see, He also revealed to us His plan to rescue our nation through His superior power and plans.

MARCH 3, 2023: LIARS, TRAITORS, AND THIEVES

"The arrogant elite have portrayed a FALSE FACE to the world. They present themselves as the SOURCE OF TRUTH, as KEEPERS of DEMOCRACY, and as PHILANTHROPISTS whose

generosity helps those in great need. In REALITY, their darkened hearts do NONE OF THESE. When the FACADE they hide behind is SUDDENLY BROKEN OFF, the world will JOLT AWAKE with HORROR at how DECEIVED and GULLIBLE they have been. When that facade crashes down, the world will see the darkened hearts and lives of LIARS, TRAITORS, AND THIEVES.

The Father continued to reveal to us what the arrogant elite had done, and He was faithful to give us strategies to combat their evil plans:

JULY 22, 2023: REVERSE THE CURSE

"The ARROGANT ELITE have been CURSING you for many years. Whenever the Church's LIGHT GROWS DIM, the DARKNESS MOVES IN and INCREASES LOSS, DEATH, and SICKNESS. My Remnant is now FULLY AWAKE to this CURSED DARKNESS that has INVADED your lands. You can see MAN-MADE DISEASES, TAINTED INJECTIONS, MANIPULATED WEATHER, UNNECESSARY WARS and CONFLICTS, and DIVISION SOWN into your populations. I want to give you a SIMPLE but POWERFUL TOOL to COMBAT all the darkness has released on people. Wherever you see the CURSE of DARKNESS displayed, simply say, 'I REVERSE THE CURSE OF THIS—DISEASE, SHOT, WEATHER, WAR, DIVISION—and I RELEASE GOD'S BLESSING, PEACE, and RESTORATION in the place of the curse.' Your words of BLESSING are more POWERFUL than anything the darkness CURSES. The LIGHT in you will OVERCOME and REMOVE the CURSE through the

POWER of My Son's BLOOD, and BLESSINGS will flow and increase until they FILL your Land. REVERSE THE CURSE!"

In the strongest terms, the Father promised us that He would deal with those partnered with darkness.

APRIL 24, 2022: STRIKE A MATCH

"Reports have begun to surface that the arrogant elite are BURNING DOWN food processing plants in order to create FOOD SHORTAGES. There is no end to their EVIL SCHEMES to STEAL, KILL, and DESTROY because they serve the one who is behind all these WICKED plots and schemes. Their efforts to BURN DOWN your future and your provision will be very SHORT-LIVED. I AM going to STRIKE A MATCH to ALL their ways of receiving ILLEGAL MONEY that they use to try to DESTROY your provision and to ENSLAVE you. I AM burning down and destroying ALL avenues of funding. As their access is INCINERATED, I will DIVERT these funds to My people and to those leaders who have My HEART and who will use the money to BLESS the people. My FIRE will OVERPOWER them and BURN their evil plans to ASHES. Watch Me STRIKE A MATCH!"

FEBRUARY 17, 2025: UNLEASHED: THE FURY OF EXPOSURES

"FEBRUARY FURY is becoming EXPOSURE after EXPOSURE of GROSS CORRUPTION and MANIPULATION of taxpayer funds.

Just wait, the MONEY TRAILS will also be EXPOSED and who benefited from these STOLEN FUNDS and lived EXTRAVAGANT lifestyles on your hard-earned money will be LAID BARE. Oh, the SHAME and EMBARRASSMENT that will fall on corrupted leaders who claimed moral superiority over President Trump while SECRETLY living a LAVISH lifestyle on the backs of hard-working Americans. But that's not ALL that will be EXPOSED. Plots of TREASON to OVERTHROW anyone who THREATENED to EXPOSE these compromised leaders will now come to the surface. CENSORSHIP, SMEAR CAMPAIGNS, CROOKED JUDGES, BRIBED JURIES, MEDIA LIES, ELECTION FRAUD, STOLEN SEATS of POWER will all be UNCOVERED. No PARDONS will work as the arrogant elite's CRIMES AGAINST HUMANITY are UNVEILED. RFK, Jr's BOLD VOICE is now TRUMPETING the DANGERS in the WATER, FOOD, and MEDICINES expressly developed to cause SICKNESS, WEAKNESS, and EARLY DEATH. These exposures will eventually TRACE BACK to the planners and developers of these DEATH AGENDAS. There will be NOWHERE TO RUN and NOWHERE TO HIDE, as the FURY of EXPOSURES IS UNLEASHED. PROPEL these exposures with your decrees and declarations: 'We welcome the February of Fury to expose, expose, expose! Go forth, Angels and Hosts, and accomplish all the Father's purposes in this UNLEASHING OF HIS FURY OF EXPOSURES.'"

We saw the fulfillment of these words as the arrogant elite's illegal and stolen funds were uncovered. Their corruption was brought to the light, and their access to these funds was cut off.

Sometimes the Father would give us a glimpse of what was going on behind the scenes to keep us encouraged that Heaven and patriots were quietly working to take down the darkness.

JANUARY 10, 2024: CRUMBLING FROM WITHIN

"Across all seven mountains of society, EVIL has INSERTED itself. From the outside, it may APPEAR that EVIL is SECURE and HOLDING ONTO their STOLEN territory. But I will assure you that these power bases are CRUMBLING FROM WITHIN. Behind the scenes, leaders are being presented with PROOF of their CORRUPT and PERVERSE behaviors. They are being shown EVIDENCE of their TREASONOUS ACTS. They are being given the option of 'RETIRING' OR 'RESIGNING' from their lofty positions, and in return, they will be given consideration when they are brought before MILITARY TRIBUNALS. Some are taking this offer, but many REFUSE to give up their seats of POWER. Both corrupt groups are looking for deliverance from their DARK and DESTRUCTIVE SCHEMES that they plan to launch. They are hoping to create enough FEAR and CONFUSION so that they KEEP their ILLEGITIMATE POWER from being taken away. Their plots and schemes are IN VAIN because INWARDLY the EVIL POWER STRUCTURE of the mountains is being weakened until a CRITICAL POINT is reached and the mountain CRUMBLES FROM WITHIN. As the plans to BRING DOWN darkness proceed and the CRUMBLING begins, it is your ASSIGNMENT, Army of Light, to remain a STEADY LIGHTHOUSE BEACON of HOPE and FAITH that draws people to the STABILITY of My LOVE and My PROMISES of RESCUE, DELIVERANCE, and RESTORATION. Don't fret because evil still seems to be ruling. Remember, it is CRUMBLING FROM WITHIN."

NOVEMBER 15, 2021: ANGEL INTEL AND A WORD—THE DARK CLOUD OF MY GLORY

I have two Guardian Angels; one watches over my heart to keep it in alignment with the Father's heart, and the other Angel serves as a lookout in both the natural and spiritual realms. He gave me this report: "There is a very large, dark cloud descending on Washington, D.C. It is not evil—it is God's glory, and when the cloud breaks open, the light of His glory will shine forth, exposing all."

The Father speaks:

"A DARK CLOUD of My GLORY is, indeed, descending on Washington, D.C. ... When My cloud descends, it will SUDDENLY break open, and the penetrating light of My glory will suddenly burst forth. My GLORY LIGHT will EXPOSE all the corruption and back room deals, and the world will see the DARKNESS of those who have STOLEN POWER ... Partner with Me in CALLING FORTH My CLOUD OF GLORY over your Nation's capital, and WATCH as My GLORY LIGHT suddenly bursts forth to EXPOSE darkness and bring in My JUSTICE."

The Father revealed to us that exposures were coming for the back room deals, the corruption, and the stolen seats of power. He worked behind the scenes to set them up for exposure, judgment, and justice.

The hardest exposure for everyone was the revelation of the extent of the sex trafficking industry and how children were targets of the greedy, grasping, perverted, arrogant elite. The Father gave us beautiful promises for these precious children. He

26

spoke about the restoration of all the other areas in our lives where stealing had occurred.

DECEMBER 8, 2022: CRUNCH TIME

"The APEX of this battle between the DARKNESS and the LIGHT is approaching—it is what you might call, 'CRUNCH TIME.' It is more important than ever that you allow Me to WEAVE you into Our STRENGTH, our COMFORT, and our JOY. It will PROTECT you, DEFEND you, and cause you to TRIUMPH over every last-ditch, desperate attempt of the darkness to STEAL or to DESTROY. It will keep your DEPENDENCE on Me and your FOCUS on My PROMISED VICTORY and the COMPLETE DESTRUCTION of the enemy's plans to STEAL and DESTROY your Nation. When the deep darkness is revealed against the children, My COMFORT will be WOVEN into you, and I will show you how I HONORED those in Heaven who lost their lives and how My GLORY will fall to HEAL and RESTORE the living victims. There is nothing happening or that has happened in this war of light over darkness that has slipped by My knowing. I SEE IT ALL, I HEAR IT ALL, and I have a PLAN to EXPOSE and CRUSH all darkness and a GLORY-FILLED plan to HEAL, RESTORE, and PROSPER all who choose the light. As you continually PUSH BACK darkness and pray for TOTAL EXPOSURE of all that has been hidden, remember to allow us to WEAVE you into our cord of STRENGTH, COMFORT and JOY, because it's CRUNCH TIME."

May 9, 2023: The Divine Exchange

"This season will be the season of DIVINE EXCHANGE. The HEAVINESS and SORROW you feel for the CHILDREN will be EXCHANGED for EXPECTANCY and JOY as I EXPOSE the evil being done to them and I RESCUE them. Their ABUSERS and CAPTORS will be brought to JUSTICE, and they will be the ones in a PRISON. The FINANCIAL TYRANTS have STOLEN from you and made many LAWS that made them WEALTHY and BLOCKED all you should have been receiving. As I EXPOSE and BRING DOWN these STEALERS and MANIPULATORS, I will EXCHANGE your LACK and your STRAINING to SURVIVE with My ABUNDANCE and with STREAMS of BLESSING that flow to you. Even in My Church I will EXCHANGE DEAD RELIGION that EXCLUDES My Spirit for the FIRE, GLORY, and JOY of My MANIFEST PRESENCE among you. Where Arts and Entertainment have DESCENDED into IDOLATRY and PERVERSION, I will bring a DIVINE EXCHANGE of SPIRIT-LED CREATIVITY that GLORIFIES Me and LIFTS people up. Instead of LYING MEDIA, you will see a RISE of TRUTH-TELLERS who fill the airwaves with the FRESH AIR of TRUTH. I have set in motion a DIVINE EXCHANGE for FAMILIES in STRIFE and DISUNITY to be REUNITED around the TRUTH and My LOVE. Where your HEALTH has been PURPOSELY DEGRADED and ATTACKED, I will bring HEALING and PROTECTION from dark schemes. This season of DIVINE EXCHANGES will find you THRIVING, AT PEACE, and with ALL THINGS RESTORED. HOLD ON while the STORM passes over, and you will receive THE DIVINE EXCHANGE of BLUE SKIES and FRESH AIR."

It comforted our hearts to know that the Father saw the children. He rescued them, restored them, and used them as beautiful lights in the Kingdom Age.

The Rise of Alternative Media

In this war of Dark to Light, we learned to access information through sources other than the mainstream media and controlled search engines. Independent researchers rose to the task and helped provide us with unbiased background and research information. Another surprising and exciting source of information came from an undercover team of Military Intelligence plus a few civilians that called themselves "Q." Q is a high-level security clearance. The Q team first began posting on back channels of the internet (The Wild West of internet land!), where anonymous participants began to try and decode the messages from Q. Patriot researchers picked up the "Q posts" or "Q drops" and published them on public internet channels so that many people could access the messages that would appear any time of day or night.

The Q messages often asked us questions to help us understand that what we had been told about much of our history and our government was not true. The posts often contained cryptic messages in Military Intelligence language that needed to be decoded. Former military personnel stepped up to help explain the possible meanings of the messages. Dedicated patriots also gave themselves to this task of decoding the Q posts. One of the most listened to decoders was Praying Medic (Dave Hayes) who asked the Holy Spirit to help him understand what the Q posts were trying to communicate to us. Newly formed Patriot channels would stop whatever they were broadcasting when a Q drop was posted. All the listeners had ears glued to the new message and began to try and decipher what the post was telling us.

Q informed us of a dark and sinister group of elites who had a plan to control the world through depopulation agendas, propaganda, wars, chaos, and by controlling most of the world's wealth. For many of us, the Q operation furthered our understanding of what had gone wrong in our nation and the world. The Q team encouraged us to learn to research for ourselves and to be bold in speaking and sharing the truth.

I was following a Patriot channel at that time to have an unbiased source of news. They were first called "The Calm Before the Storm," and later changed their name to "Patriot Soapbox." They always read the Q drops as they came through the internet system and attempted to decode the posts in real time. Someone on the Q team was a Believer who often posted Bible passages. In wonder, I watched an organic revival hit this Patriot channel. Broadcasters who had never opened a Bible before would haltingly read the Bible verses, and you could hear in their voices how they were being impacted by the power of the spoken Scriptures that Q posted. Broadcasters and listeners alike began to awaken to a loving and powerful God. Many who had left their faith on the back burner of their lives began to seek Him again. Beautiful testimonies began to fill the airwaves of men and women giving their lives to Jesus. Believers who were on the platform began to help disciple these new Believers, and prayer began to pop up all through the broadcasts and comment feeds.

Q went worldwide and groups of Patriots were formed in many nations. People were emboldened to begin speaking truth and calling for the restoration of our freedoms. A year after Q began to post, the Father surprised me by speaking to me about the Q team.

OCTOBER 28, 2018: WHAT THE FATHER TOLD ME ABOUT THE Q TEAM

"I want you to know that the Q Team seeks Me for WISDOM and TIMING, and they have My HEART for this Nation. They are just men, but they are CONVEYING My heart for this Nation. Their message of JOINING into ONE HEART and ONE VOICE and PARTNERING with Me in PRAYER is giving HOPE to those who are AWAKENED, and it is giving PURPOSE to those willing to FIGHT for the DESTINY of your Nation. Let FAITH ARISE that the LIGHT can and will OVERCOME the darkness and that TRUTH will REPLACE the LIES that now FILL your airwaves. More people are AWAKENING every day, and they are JOINING the ranks of a GROWING ARMY that DEMANDS TRUTH and RIGHTEOUSNESS of all spheres of society and an END to LIES, DECEPTION, and DESTRUCTION of the darkness. Q Team is a TOOL I AM using to PIERCE the DARKNESS and to bring in the LIGHT of My GLORY to SHINE once again on this Nation."

The Q Team last posted on November 27, 2022. It was the 4,966th Q drop! Sometimes Q+ would post, and the Q Team revealed to us that this was President Trump posting to encourage us. The Q team ignited patriots worldwide to stand up for the truth and to work for justice to be restored. Even though they have not publicly posted since 2022, they continue to work behind the scenes to restore our Republic. One of the Q Team's major goals was to help prepare the world for The Great Awakening.

CHAPTER THREE

The Great Awakening

Traditionally, Awakenings have been moves of God that impacted the Church and drew many new converts into salvation through faith in the cross and the resurrection of Jesus. They were marked by passionate preaching, a call to repentance and holy living, and the tangible presence of God in the meetings. The Father shared with us that this was the time in history for another Great Awakening. He also told us that this was not going to be like any other Awakening in the past because this Awakening was going to revolutionize and reform every area of our society!

MARCH 20, 2018: GREAT AWAKENING

"I AM ready and poised to release a GREAT AWAKENING among My people. A FAITHFUL REMNANT has embraced AWAKENING, and I AM ready to build on this FOUNDATION. With AWAKENING comes INCREASED DISCERNMENT that will see through LIES and CORRUPTION. Institutions that promote these things will CRUMBLE and will CEASE TO EXIST because they persisted in their LYING ways and REFUSED TO CHANGE. Trust My ways and My timing. Watch and see what I will do. Keep your heart tuned to My heart and partner with Me in the DELIVERANCE of your nation. These are exciting days."

The Father let us know that this Great Awakening would expose the lies and corruption wherever they were found in our society, and it would uncover the many death agendas being launched against the people of the world.

DECEMBER 4, 2019: LIGHT AND JOY

"My Spirit is moving WORLDWIDE, AWAKENING hearts and spirits to move in concert with My plan to bring FREEDOM AND LIGHT FLOODING into the DARKNESS OF LIES AND CORRUPTION and bringing all those who hear My voice calling to them to come join Me in My Kingdom of LIFE AND LIGHT … My JUSTICE and My MERCY will be fully on DISPLAY before the world, and many will come to KNOW AND SHARE MY HEART … I AM TRUE TO MY WORD, AND YOU WILL SEE MY PROMISES FULFILLED."

The Father informed us that this GREAT AWAKENING was set to go all around the world! It was time to begin to look to the future with hope in His glorious promises.

JULY 26, 2020: AWAKENING AND OPENED EYES

"Remember that the true battle is for hearts and minds to be AWAKENED and flooded with TRUTH and REVELATION from Me. Partner with Me in BINDING deception and silencing its voice and RELEASING My voice of truth. Pray that My truth and revelation will PIERCE and completely remove the VEIL OF DECEPTION over so many peoples' eyes and hearts. Pray that I flood the land with a tsunami of AWAKENED voices crying out as ONE for RIGHTEOUSNESS and for FREEDOM. Instead of wringing helpless hands, join Me in these prayers that will unleash an AWAKENING and will bring about a mass exposure of evil and deception. Then you will see My mighty JUSTICE UNLEASHED!"

This Great Awakening was focused on a battle for the hearts and minds of humanity to be set free from deception that was drawing the world into deeper and deeper bondage. The Father asked us to partner with Him in praying for this Awakening that would expose evil and deception and bring in justice, righteousness, and freedom.

AUGUST 4, 2020: SOUND AN ALARM

"Sound an ALARM across this Nation in the Spirit realm that will jolt the SLEEPING and the APATHETIC awake. Let it RING LOUDLY from sea to shining sea; let it REVERBERATE from mountain to mountain; let it SWEEP over desert and plain; let it FILL the valleys and ECHO across every stream, lake, and river; let its sound FILL every ear and VIBRATE in every heart until all who would seek Me are FULLY AWAKENED to TRUTH and to MY PURPOSES. This is the 'GREAT AWAKENING,' and it will result in Donald Trump being re-elected and in RIGHTEOUSNESS and JUSTICE being restored. Call forth the alarm, and I will RELEASE it!"

NUMBERS 10:9 (AMP), *"When you go to war in your land against the enemy that attacks you, then sound an alarm with the trumpets, so that you may be remembered before the Lord your God, and you shall be saved from your enemies."*

Clearly stated in this word from the Father was that the Great Awakening would result in righteousness and justice being restored. We were called to sound an alarm to awaken the sleeping until we all carried Heaven's frequency that aligned us to truth and to His purposes. This word promised that Donald Trump would be re-elected as the President. This word was given months before the 2020 election, and I assumed that this meant that President Trump would win that election. He actually did win the 2020 election, but it was stolen from him through widespread fraud. The Father in His wisdom ways allowed the stealing so that our cry of alarm would grow. In the fulfillment of this word, President Trump was re-elected in a decisive victory on November 5, 2024.

AUGUST 10, 2020: POWER AND GLORY

"Ready to see My POWER AND GLORY displayed in your Land? I have promised you that I am coming to expose evil and to establish righteousness and justice again. I am coming to set the CAPTIVES FREE! Those caught in the grips of drug ADDICTION, those ENSLAVED by sex trafficking, and those who have been DECEIVED into thinking that evil is good will be SET FREE by My manifested POWER AND GLORY. WELCOME My power and glory, COMMAND it to be manifested across your Land. Be ready to receive, welcome, and disciple the HARVEST that My manifested POWER AND GLORY will awaken. The enemy is sowing VIOLENCE AND DESTRUCTION, so I am sowing AWAKENING AND RESCUE. My POWER AND GLORY can easily overcome any scheme of darkness. FOCUS on what I am doing, and join Me in CALLING it forth."

Not only did the Father expose evil, He laid out plans for His power and glory to be manifested to set the captives of addiction, slavery, and deception free. We were to help call it forth and be ready to disciple the harvest of the Great Awakening.

MARCH 6, 2022: THE SPIRIT WINDS OF SPRING

"My Spirit is STIRRING up the WINDS of Spring that will blow across your Land. My SPIRIT WINDS will serve two purposes: blowing away LIES and VEILS of DECEPTION, and blowing in My REFRESHING, LIFE-GIVING presence and GLORY. I would COUNSEL My people to HOLD LIGHTLY what you have been told about the history of the world. What is about to be UNCOVERED by My SPIRIT WINDS will reveal the LIES and GASLIGHTING you have been told about world events, about wars and rumors of wars. The WEB of LIES spun by the enemy has been WIDESPREAD and the VEIL of DECEPTION has been a SHROUD over the nations. The web and the veil were given place by the WEAKNESS and SELF-ABSORPTION of My Church. But I AM AWAKENING My Bride and filling her with a PASSION for My TRUTH, I AM giving her a heart for My world, and I AM giving her a DESIRE to see My KINGDOM RULE in your midst. When you join Me in My desires for your Nation and the world, then I will give you EYES TO SEE what I AM doing, so you can JOIN Me in bringing it to pass. The heart that is FOCUSED on HEARING from Me will be shown TRUTH. Those whose hearts have been totally SURRENDERED to Me and whom I can TRUST with My SECRETS, I will REVEAL to you the MOTIVES of men's hearts, and you will know whom you can TRUST and whom is CORRUPT and a SELF-PROMOTER. Welcome My SPIRIT WINDS this Spring and be ready to be CLEANSED and REVITALIZED personally and as a Nation."

This Great Awakening was being brought in by the winds of the Spirit and they blew away lies and deception and blew in refreshing, presence, and glory. It served to cleanse and to revitalize a nation that was nearly eclipsed by darkness.

NOVEMBER 6, 2022: HERE COME THE TRUTH BOMBS!

"Your PRAYERS, DECREES, and the TRUTH you believe and share have been WEAKENING the stronghold of TWISTING, LYING Leviathan over the people. I have a plan to FINISH OFF this DECEIVING WEB over your Nation so that the TRUTH can come to the LIGHT, and a GREAT AWAKENING will follow. I have STRATEGIC TRUTH BOMBS lined up to drop that will BREAK THROUGH and DESTROY the web of deception. I AM about to showcase DESPICABLE LIES, CORRUPTION, and GROSS PROJECTION by the arrogant elite. They will be SHOCKED and caught OFF-GUARD that their hastily-FABRICATED STORIES that make themselves out to be VICTIMS and cast FALSE BLAME on others through planted 'evidence' explode in their faces. My TRUTH BOMBS will blow up these lies, and the LIGHT of the explosions will REVEAL the TRUTH. Again, I say, they will be CAUGHT with their pants down and their mouths GAPING in shock because they have been EXPOSED for the FRAUDS that they are. The result of these TRUTH BOMBS DESTROYING their cover will be that the enemy ABANDONS them and leaves them HIGH and DRY, EXPOSED to the world, and with NO HELP from the darkness or from people under them that they BRIBED or BLACKMAILED to help them keep up their FACADE. All the carefully built-up systems that protected their darkened lifestyle will BLOW UP in a moment of time, and the HUNTERS WILL TRULY BECOME THE HUNTED. Keep calling forth TRUTH to REPLACE LIES and for EXPOSURES OF DARKNESS, and you will know your decrees have come to fulfillment when you see THE TRUTH BOMBS DROPPED."

Truth bombs were an effective way to blow up the lies and deception of Leviathan. The Father promised that as the truth was brought to the light, a Great Awakening would follow. We were to partner with the Father by calling forth truth to replace lies and for exposures of darkness.

DECEMBER 9, 2022: WHAT IS BREWING?

"WHAT IS BREWING in the atmosphere? You've heard the many THREATS and INTIMIDATIONS from the darkness about the DESTRUCTION and CLAMPS of CONTROL they have planned for you. Is that all that is BREWING right now over your Nation? I AM telling you to WAKE UP and to SMELL the COFFEE of what I AM BREWING! What I AM BREWING in the atmosphere will TRUMP every plot and scheme of the darkness. They have FOOLED themselves into believing that their schemes are far more reaching and DEADLY than anything I could do to stop them or to bring about a victory. Well, they are in for the WAKE-UP call of their lives, because I AM moving Heaven and earth to answer the HEART CRIES of My people to RESCUE and SAVE a Nation covenanted with Me. This will be a RUDE AWAKENING for those partnered with darkness but also for those who have REFUSED to LISTEN to My VOICE through the prophets. These ones are still under the SPELL of Leviathan. The darkness will awaken to JUDGMENT and JUSTICE. Those who did not believe My REPORT through your voices will awaken to the FEARFUL DARKNESS that almost SWALLOWED them up, and then they'll awaken to the TRUTH that was being shared, and, finally, to My POWER to RESCUE and DELIVER ... WHAT IS BREWING? A RESOUNDING DEFEAT of your enemies and a RICH and FULL VICTORY for My Nation!"

This entry mentioned the Rude Awakening that came to those partnered with darkness and also to those who stubbornly refused to listen to voices speaking the truth. The ones still under the influence of Leviathan's deception had a shocking wake-up call, but it resulted in them being awakened to the truth and to the Father's power to rescue and deliver.

JANUARY 3, 2023: WAY MAKER, MIRACLE WORKER

"Your Nation is in need of a WAY MAKER, a MIRACLE WORKER if it is to SURVIVE. If man could have FIXED the BROKEN CONDITION of your Land, he would have done it by now. Right now, it seems that darkness is going to stay in CONTROL and that their plans of destruction will be CARRIED OUT. What seems like a GREAT DEFEAT will result in a GREAT AWAKENING to your need of Me and the DISCOVERY that I AM the only One who can RESCUE and DELIVER your Land. Your Nation will walk through the VALLEY OF THE SHADOW OF DEATH into a BRILLIANT NEW DAY because I AM the WAY MAKER and the MIRACLE WORKER. There will be a Nation of people who are THANKFUL for the THREAT of darkness because it brought them to their knees, and they found the POWER of My LOVE and My FAITHFULNESS. They will be determined to never be LULLED into believing LIES again, and they will WHOLEHEARTEDLY turn to Me through the blood of My Son, and they will LEARN to DEPEND on My Spirit to GUIDE them into all TRUTH and to keep PASSION for Me BURNING in their hearts. This will be a SICKENING DEFEAT for the enemy —the TOPPLING of his EVIL EMPIRE, and the RISE of My KINGDOM on this earth DISPLAYED through My TRIUMPHANT Sons and Daughters of Light. Get ready, I AM going to reveal

Myself to the world as the **WAY MAKER** and the **MIRACLE WORKER.**"

The Great Awakening came about through the breakthroughs and miracles that the Father did for our nation, and it resulted in an awakened people and a defeated evil empire.

January 24, 2023: Look Out! Heaven's Letting Loose!

"As **EXPOSURES** of the **WEB** of darkness roll out, you will be **STUNNED** at how **WIDESPREAD** and how **INTRICATELY PLANNED** this web was. Fresh **REALIZATION** of how **CLOSE** you came to being **COMPLETELY OVERTAKEN** and **CONTROLLED** by the darkness will wash over you, and you will know that without My **RESCUE OPERATION**, all would be lost lll Being **SHAKEN AWAKE** because something **FEARFUL** is happening is never pleasant. The **PEACE** and **CONFIDENCE** that you've found in Me are **COMFORTS** that you can **RELEASE** to others. That is why I AM drawing you **CLOSER** and **DEEPER** in Me so that you are **STABLE** and **STRONG** when the **SHAKINGS ARE LET LOOSE BY HEAVEN.** Here is your **ASSIGNMENT** (besides drawing aside and resting in Me): you can **RELEASE SUPERNATURAL AWAKENING** to people still lulled into **COMPLACENCY** and **INACTION. My AWAKENING POWER** is **GREATER** than the enemy's power to **SEDUCE** and **DECEIVE** ... As My Sons and Daughters, you have **AUTHORITY** to **BIND** seduction and deception and to **LOOSE** awakening over the people. Take **AUTHORITY** over **SEDUCTION** and **DECEPTION, REMOVE** its power, **SHATTER** the **ILLUSIONS** that hold people captive to lies, UNSTOP ears, and OPEN blinded eyes. LOOSE AWAKENING to the people, and they will join you in seeing all of HEAVEN LETTING LOOSE against the darkness!"

Our assignment was to use our authority to bind seduction and deception and to loose awakening to the people. God's greater power would be shown as people were set free to see and hear truth.

FEBRUARY 24, 2023: AWAKE! AWAKE! AWAKE!

"There is a great need for the world to AWAKEN from LIES and DECEPTION, from the DARK SLUMBER of MORAL DECAY, and from SPIRITUAL APATHY towards Me. I have begun the GREAT AWAKENING by a BREAKOUT of My Spirit on college campuses and in other places. I AM awakening people out of DEAD religion into a LIVING ENCOUNTER with Me—the SOURCE and GOAL of all life. PRAY that this move CONTINUES, DEEPENS, and that these REFRESHING STREAMS become a MIGHTY RIVER of My PRESENCE ... DECLARE FREEDOM to captives, SIGHT to the blind, and DELIVERANCE to the prisoners ... You are EMPOWERED with My LIGHT, My TRUTH, and My LOVE, so begin to EXERCISE your AUTHORITY and INVADE the DARKNESS, TAKE BACK the land, and you will RECOVER ALL. Cry out: 'AWAKE! AWAKE! AWAKE!' and the world will respond."

In a sovereign move by the Holy Spirit, the Great Awakening broke out on college campuses and in worship events. An awakening always breaks people out of dead religion into a living relationship with our God. Deliverance was released from the power of the awakening, and it gave birth to purity and holiness.

MARCH 23, 2023: THE SOUNDS OF SILENCE

"A day will come when I SILENCE the VOICE of the enemy speaking through his PUPPETS, the MEDIA. What will people do when there are not voices telling them what to THINK and how to FEEL? People have grown so DEPENDENT on and MESMERIZED by the LYING MEDIA that they have LOST the ABILITY to THINK THINGS THROUGH or to be able to SEPARATE TRUTH FROM LIES. DISCERNMENT has FALLEN by the wayside because people have been SLOWLY DUPED into depending on others for information rather than learning to SEARCH A MATTER OUT. I want you to PRACTICE your SEARCHING SKILLS and your DISCERNMENT so that you are able to RECOGNIZE PROPAGANDA and SMOOTH LIES. You will be called upon to HELP others LEARN to SEARCH and DISCERN —especially when THE SOUNDS OF SILENCE fill the airwaves. People will be LOST and CONFUSED and will need to learn how to think for themselves again. Teaching people to have a FOUNDATION in My Word will help them learn to separate DARKNESS FROM LIGHT. When you search out things in My Word, you will begin to SEE from My PERSPECTIVE, and you'll IMMEDIATELY RECOGNIZE a COUNTERFEIT. Learn to bring your QUESTIONS to Me, and I will bring you ANSWERS based in TRUTH and RIGHTEOUSNESS. Peoples' 'THINKERS' have gotten LAZY because they have allowed talking heads of MEDIA to do the thinking for them. When I SILENCE

Leviathan's voice and THE SOUNDS OF SILENCE fill the air, be ready to DIRECT people to Me, the FOUNT of all WISDOM and KNOWLEDGE. Part of the Great Awakening is to help people THINK and DISCERN again. This will SPARK CREATIVITY and many new INVENTIONS that will BLESS your world. BREAK FREE from that MINDSET that wants to be TOLD what to THINK and DO, and be ready to EMBRACE THE SOUNDS OF SILENCE, for then a NEW AGE of FREEDOM and PROSPERITY will unfold."

An important part of the Great Awakening was to help people think and discern again because this was the seedbed of creativity and new inventions that brought forth freedom and prosperity.

We were told that shakings were going to be necessary to topple corrupt systems, but also that shakings were needed to bring about the Great Awakening.

April 22, 2023: What Does It Take to Shake the World Awake?

"Because so much of the world (including the Church) has been SEDUCED by Jezebel (self-centered living) and Leviathan (twisting, lying serpent), it is going to take some SHAKING to bring about AWAKENING. Army of Light, I want you to view these SHAKINGS from Heaven's VIEWPOINT. Do not join in the FEAR and PANIC of the world when SYSTEMS, CORPORATIONS, and IDOLS fall. People have been TOLD that their LIVES and FINANCES DEPEND on these systems to SURVIVE. I have shown you these systems are CONTROLLED by the DARKNESS, and they ENSLAVE rather than bring FREEDOM. SHAKING people loose from these systems is not something to FEAR or DREAD. It is something you can CELEBRATE as you have BELIEVED My PROMISES to PROVIDE ABUNDANTLY through NEW SYSTEMS founded on My WAYS and on RIGHTEOUSNESS. DO NOT BE MOVED by the SHAKINGS! Rather, REJOICE that I AM REPLACING BROKEN SYSTEMS with systems RESTORED to RIGHTEOUSNESS and JUSTICE. I have promised to be the STABILITY of your TIMES, and I want you to be the PEACE and STABILITY to those in your circle of influence. WHAT DOES IT TAKE TO SHAKE THE WORLD AWAKE? It takes a LOVING, POWERFUL God arising from His Throne in RESPONSE to the CRIES of the Remnant, to SHAKE the world AWAKE and RID IT of FALSE GODS and ENSLAVEMENT. The SHAKING AWAKENING will bring in many to help you in CELEBRATING BRAND-NEW SYSTEMS founded on FREEDOM, RIGHTEOUSNESS, and JUSTICE."

ISAIAH 33:6 (TPT) *"He will be your constant source of stability in changing times, and out of His abundant love He gives you the riches of salvation, wisdom, and knowledge. Yes, the fear of the Lord is the key to this treasure!"*

This journal entry again gave us a broader view of The Great Awakening other than just reviving the Church. It extended throughout all our systems and all areas of our society. In this next entry, the Father revealed that the Rude Awakening was going to be experienced by the whole world.

AUGUST 18, 2024: RUDE AWAKENING

"The world is going to experience a RUDE AWAKENING. Even those who belong to My Army of Light will experience a MEASURE of this RUDE AWAKENING as the FULL DISCLOSURES of the DEATH AGENDAS are EXPOSED. You know many of them, but you don't know ALL of them. You will be able to STAND in FAITH because you have BELIEVED My POWER to RESCUE and PRESERVE you, and you have seen My hand at work in EXPOSURES and REMOVALS of some partnered with darkness, and you BELIEVE My PROMISE that ALL will be EXPOSED and REMOVED. Still, the RUDE AWAKENING coming to the world will cause some SHAKING in your own life when the DEPTH of DEPRAVITY and EVIL is REVEALED, and who people that you may have TRUSTED really are BEHIND THEIR MASKS will UNSETTLE you for a short time. But I want you to think about the EFFECT the RUDE AWAKENING is going to have on the RELIGIOUS SPIRIT CHURCH and on the UNBELIEVERS and DOUBTERS. They thought they were PERCEIVING TRUTH, but the RUDE AWAKENING will SHATTER almost everything in their WORLDVIEW. I AM COUNSELING you, My Army of Light, to ask for My HELP in QUICKLY PROCESSING the further revelations of DEEP DARKNESS that are shown to you. You need to LEAN ON ME and allow Me to ABSORB your SHOCK and TRAUMA and then receive the PEACE of HEAVEN to HEAL your heart and STABILIZE your thinking. I need you to be POSITIONED to offer SUPPORT and GUIDANCE for those that the RUDE AWAKENING DEVASTATES. Don't throw out comments like, 'I tried to tell you'—not helpful. Come ALONGSIDE them and IDENTIFY with their BROKENNESS. Pull them into your Kingdom view with HUMILITY and UNDERSTANDING. Say to them, 'We all were ASLEEP and DECEIVED, and even though the TRUTH is HARD to HEAR, it is AWAKENING us to FIGHT for FREEDOM and LIGHT.' Share with them that it is your FAITH in Me and My PROMISES for RESCUE and DELIVERANCE that have kept you in PEACE and REST in this TUMULTUOUS season. The RUDE AWAKENING will not be pleasant, but it will lead to a GREAT AWAKENING of who I AM and of a PROMISED VICTORY and stepping into the KINGDOM AGE."

The Great Awakening came by the power of our God, but He invited us to partner with Him in this epic battle of dark to light. He called and commissioned all who would hear His voice to join in the Army of Light.

CHAPTER FOUR

Inducted Into the Army of Light

Because this was an unprecedented season in the history of our world, the Father came alongside His awakened ones to teach us and to counsel us in His ways of spiritual warfare.

OCTOBER 27, 2019: EFFECTIVE WARRIORS

"Such love, such peace, such well-being are available to you in My arms. Rest there often to be strengthened for the battle of light over darkness. This is where you will receive your battle plans, and they will be effective because they will be prompted by FAITH and not FEAR. Don't be an ineffective warrior who only stirs up anger, distrust, and fear instead of standing in My shadow and going forth with truth and faith. These effective warriors know both My gentleness and My greatness, My mercy and My judgment, and My hatred for sin and total love for the sinner. It is those who truly know Me—not just facts about Me—who will be effective warriors in My Army, and they will do great exploits in My name and in My power. Your hope, your wisdom, and your strength are in Me. You will be kept in peace and not ruled by the schemes of the enemy. You will be effective because you will focus your warfare where I am moving and not where the enemy is throwing up distractions and confusion. You will be part of the final blows that take down evil in your Nation. This takedown will send shock waves around the world and great freedom will be the result. Stand FIRM, stand FAST, stay FOCUSED. WE WILL WIN!"

Effective warriors learned to draw their strength from the Father's presence and to battle from faith and not fear. We were in awe that He entrusted us to battle with Him and that we were included in taking down the evil empire. This word gave us three things that caused us to win: stand firm, stand fast, and stay focused in Him. On November 10, 2019, the Father first called us His Army of Light.

NOVEMBER 10, 2019: HEAVEN'S LAUGHTER

"It might help you to remember that I laugh at the roaring and scheming and the dire threats of My enemies. Their power, their plans are puny when compared to My determination to answer the prayers of My Saints who have repented on behalf of your Nation for the evil that was allowed to gain an enormous foothold. I have heard the deep repentance and collected the tears of sorrow over the state of your Land, and I am now moving to expose the evil, cleanse the land, and reestablish My plans and purposes for your Nation. You and many others in My Army are partnering with Me in declaring the fulfillment of My plans and purposes for your Land. No darkness can withstand My unified Army of Light in partnership with Me, the all-powerful, all-knowing, all-wise God. Take heart, take courage, and laugh with Me at a defeated enemy."

Psalm 2:2-4 (TPT) *"Look at how the power brokers of the world rise up to hold their summit as the rulers scheme and confer together against Yahweh and His Anointed King, saying: 'Let's come together and break away from the Creator. Once and for all let's cast off these controlling chains of God and His Christ!' God-Enthroned merely LAUGHS at them; the Sovereign One mocks their madness!"*

The Father assured us that He laughed at His enemies and their puny plans and that our partnership with Him as the Army of Light would defeat the enemy. Our Commander often told us to walk in faith and not fear.

JULY 10, 2020: CHANGING THE ATMOSPHERE

"The enemy can continue to throw DARK SCHEMES and FEAR into the atmosphere, but I AM meeting that darkness with My OVERWHELMING and OVERPOWERING atmosphere of LIGHT and LIFE. My light easily overcomes the darkness. I am looking for My Army of Light to partner with Me in this change of the atmosphere from darkness to My LIFE-GIVING LIGHT. FEAR EMPOWERS DARKNESS. FAITH EMPOWERS THE LIGHT. Look into My eyes of love and receive My complete love, and it will drive out all fear. FAITH and TRUTH are your WEAPONS to change the atmosphere. Go in the strength of My love and power, and SHINE THE LIGHT OF MY TRUTH and LOVE. You will see the darkness receding and the light dawning until the full day."

The Army of Light learned to change the dark and fearful atmosphere that hung over our nation into the Father's atmosphere of life and light. Faith and truth were our weapons that caused the darkness to give way and made way for the dawn of a new day. A whole new world opened up before us as the Father revealed to us that Angels and Hosts were ready and willing to partner with us in defeating the evil empire.

July 27, 2020: Angels

"Aren't angels amazing? Do you understand that I have made provision for ALL of your life in every way? My plans, My creation, My story are all carefully thought out and executed with Divine detail and creativity. That is why there are no IMPOSSIBLE situations because I have already made PROVISION for it. Just call on Me, call on your angels, call on the Host of Heaven—they are at your command as My daughter. As My child and as My friend, you can IMPACT NATIONS with your prayers, declarations, and your command of Heaven's armies. TUNE to My heart when you become aware of a situation, and I will share BATTLE plans with you. ANGELS ARE WAITING FOR MY ARMY OF LIGHT TO UTILIZE THEM. They are prepared and awaiting your commands. What happens in the UNSEEN realm determines what happens in the SEEN realm. Those who affect the unseen realm towards justice and righteousness are HEROES in Heaven forever!"

HEBREWS 1:14 (TPT) *"What role then, do the angels, have? The angels are spirit-messengers sent by God to serve those who are going to be saved."*

Working with Angels and Hosts was new territory for most of us. To state it simply, Angels deliver messages from Heaven to Earth and serve the heirs of salvation, while Hosts are Heaven's Warrior Army. We received battle strategies from the Father. As we decreed and declared His plans, the Angels and Hosts went forth to perform His orders. The Father revealed to us that we were moving towards a showdown between evil and good.

DECEMBER 3, 2020: MOVING INTO A SHOWDOWN

"Quietly, inexorably, I AM moving this Nation towards a SHOWDOWN between good and evil, darkness and light. Your prayers, decrees, worship, and faith have built a highway for My presence to ROLL ACROSS your Land sweeping away evil and corruption and leaving behind My GLORY, POWER, and DELIVERANCE ... I will release a standard of RIGHTEOUSNESS, and the FEAR OF THE LORD will blanket the Nation ... freedom and joy will ring across this Land ... watch Me bring about the showdown."

A showdown came between the darkness and the light, and we were assured that our prayers, decrees, worship, and faith had made a way for the promised removal of evil and corruption and for the restoration of righteousness and the Fear of the Lord.

The battle was more intense and took longer than we had imagined, but the Father understood our hearts and encouraged us to complete the epic battle as His faithful Remnant.

DECEMBER 19, 2021: YOU ARE NOT ALONE

"So far, this EPIC BATTLE against the darkness trying to SWALLOW UP your Nation has been fought by a FAITHFUL and FAITH-FILLED REMNANT who have had EARS to hear My call to join the fight for FREEDOM and who have had their EYES opened to the DARK motives and agendas of those partnered with the enemy. Every day, there are more who are awakening to the TRUTH and the THREAT and are joining the ranks of My Army of Light, but for many of you, this has been a SOLITARY fight with little or no support from family and friends. I know this has been difficult for you, but it has formed you into a WARRIOR who cannot be turned back from the battle. I want to assure you that YOU HAVE NEVER BEEN TRULY ALONE—My presence is with you always, My strength is available for you to receive daily, and My HOST are giving their all to fight for you and with you. My Host hold you in HIGHEST REGARD for staying the course, for continuing to trust Me, and for your surrendered lives to Me. I AM keeping a RECORD of your every prayer, your every tear, your every act of warfare—they will be REWARDED now and in the day of VICTORY. As more evil and corruption are exposed, the ranks of My Army of Light will grow, and you will be thanked for battling for them when they were blind and deaf. For now, My fine and faithful Warriors, know that YOU ARE NOT ALONE."

What beautiful assurances He gave us of being with us, keeping us strong, and maintaining a record of our prayers, tears, and warfare. Rewards awaited us when the battle was won. Many times, He spoke of our promised rewards and how important each of us was in the Army of Light.

January 9, 2022: From the Least to the Greatest

"From the LEAST to the GREATEST in the Army of Light, I have a message for you. Whether you are one of the generals whose names and faces are well known, or whether you are answering My call to battle and hardly anyone knows your name or face, you are ALL an IMPORTANT part of the WAR MACHINE that My Army has become. You are all DANGEROUS to the enemy and his strongholds, and together we are WINNING this war. From the LEAST to the GREATEST you will be REWARDED richly from the spoils of war. JOY will fill your hearts that you heard My CALL to join the Army and that you STOOD in faith and in My STRENGTH until the end. You will hear a resounding 'WELL DONE!' from Heaven! Conversely, from the least to the greatest who have partnered with DARKNESS, you will be met with a HEAVY RECKONING, and you will be required to PAY for all your crimes and corruption. Those who have chosen to LOVE Me, BELIEVE Me, and WALK with Me have chosen WISELY. Enter into My JOY and GREAT BLESSING."

PSALM 37 (TPT) selected passages:

"Don't follow after the wicked ones or be jealous of their wealth ... They and their short-lived success will soon shrivel up and quickly fade away ... Keep trusting in the Lord and do what is right in His eyes. Fix your hearts on the promises of God, and you will dwell in the land, feasting on His faithfulness ... He will manifest as your justice, as sure and strong as the noonday sun ... For one day the wicked will be destroyed, but those who trust in the Lord will inherit the land ... just a little while longer and the ungodly will vanish; you will look for them in vain. But the humble of heart will inherit every promise and enjoy abundant peace ... God laughs at the wicked and their plans, for He knows their day is coming! Even in time of disaster He will watch over them (the godly), and they will always have more than enough no matter what happens ... The godly ones will have a peaceful, prosperous future with a happy ending."

Not only were we called to battle the darkness, we were also called to bring healing and comfort to others.

MARCH 11, 2022: A DEEP BETRAYAL

"As the exposures of darkness become an AVALANCHE, many will be exposed as having BETRAYED this Nation. Some of these will be people you have **TRUSTED** and looked up to. These **BETRAYERS** are leaders in every area of your society—including the Church. Some **BETRAYERS** of your Nation you have known about for a long time, but there will be those whose **UNCOVERING** will be a **GREAT SHOCK**, and you will experience the **DEVASTATION** of deep **BETRAYAL**. There will also be those around you who have believed the **LYING REPORTS** and **FAKE PERSONAS** the media portrayed. For them, the **BETRAYALS** will be many and overwhelming. My Army of Light must be ready to **BIND UP** the wounds of **DEEP BETRAYAL** (including tending to your own heart) that will be widely experienced. **KEY** to healing from **BETRAYAL** is **FORGIVENESS**. Remember how I have **FREELY** forgiven all your sins, and **EXTEND** this forgiveness to your enemies. This takes them off of your 'hook,' but don't worry, it places them on My 'hook' of Divine **JUDGMENT** and **JUSTICE**. Teach people to **LOOSE** the sad feelings and shame of **BETRAYAL** from their souls and to **BIND** to their souls My healing, My life, My trustworthiness, and My wisdom for the future. My **WISDOM** will act as a **GUARD** against being **BETRAYED** in the future. Cast the weight of your life and your complete **TRUST** on Me because I will never **FORSAKE** or **BETRAY** you. I speak **PEACE** and **HOPE** into your hearts even now so that you will be **BUILT-UP** as the **DEEP BETRAYALS** are exposed."

The Father often spoke to us of a day of crisis when everything would change.

AUGUST 30, 2022: THE DAY THE WORLD STOOD STILL

"The SUDDEN REVEAL of darkness that I bring will be so SHOCKING that it will be remembered as THE DAY THE WORLD STOOD STILL. It will be necessary to PAUSE 'life as usual' so that all realize the MOMENTOUS CHANGES that are necessary to SAVE the world from the darkness that THREATENED to SWALLOW IT UP. ALL eyes must be on the REVEAL that I showcase of DIABOLICAL plans of DEATH and DESTRUCTION, and the GREEDY, SELFISH, GRASPING hearts and minds of the arrogant elite and of the fools who served them. THE DAY THE WORLD STOOD STILL will be a day to AWAKEN and to realize how DECEIVED and BLIND they have been. As a new Nation is born out of the FIRES of the wicked and all their corrupted systems, there will be born a VIGILANCE to PRESERVE FREEDOM and to HIGHLY ESTEEM TRUTH and JUSTICE. A FREE and UN-COMPROMISED media will be demanded by the people, and I have been preparing TRUTH-TELLERS who will fulfill this role with INTEGRITY. A beautiful and strong UNITY will emerge because all the schemes to DIVIDE people will be EXPOSED, and everyone will VALUE being an American. They will join together to REBUILD, to RESTORE, and to make BETTER the foundations of this Nation on JUSTICE and RIGHTEOUSNESS. Those who were RADICALIZED will see they were DUPES being used by the darkness. There will be a WIDESPREAD turning to My SON to be CLEANSED and to embrace the beautiful gift of SALVATION. There will be a FRESH START for your Land, and My Army of Light and My Church will JOYFULLY DISCIPLE a Nation. Do not

FEAR or be ANXIOUS, but wait for THE DAY THE WORLD STOOD STILL because it will USHER IN A WHOLE NEW ERA."

The Army of Light was called on to help disciple those who had been shaken awake and to give them hope for a whole new era.

Spiritual intelligence and declarations to stop the dark schemes were given to the Army of Light. Even though voices of doom and gloom were sounding off, we were given a different perspective.

October 11, 2022: A Secret Underground Meeting

"Deep UNDERGROUND in a SECRET LOCATION, evil leaders have quietly gathered to PLOT and SCHEME the DOWNFALL of your Nation. They have plans for WAR, FAMINE, and FINANCIAL COLLAPSE. Because they have LOST all love and natural affection from completely giving their lives to the enemy, they think there is nothing holding them back from carrying out your DEATH and DESTRUCTION. They have gazed at darkness for so long that they have FORGOTTEN the POWER OF MY LIGHT. My LIGHT is set to BREAKTHROUGH all their darkness, and it will EXPOSE their HIDDEN UNDERGROUND HIDEOUTS and their DESTRUCTIVE PLANS. Should you just STANDBY and DREAD all the things they are set to release? Do you just let their plans of war, famine, and financial collapse PLAY OUT? Or have I not called you to DECREE and DECLARE the OPPOSITE OF WHAT THE DARKNESS IS TRYING TO RELEASE? War, famine, and financial collapse are NOT INEVITABLE! Have I not given you POWER OVER THE

DARKNESS through My Son's SHED BLOOD? Rise up, Army of Light, and DECLARE that My LIGHT, My POWER, and My GOODNESS will OVERPOWER all those dark schemes! RELEASE My plans for your Nation and out into all the world of PEACE, PLENTY, and FINANCIAL INCREASE. Where is your FAITH? Is it in the power of DARKNESS to CARRY OUT their plans, or is it in My POWER to RESCUE, DELIVER, and bring ABUNDANCE? What you place your FAITH in is what you will ATTRACT to your life. I SEE ALL and HEAR ALL that is going on in the SECRET UNDERGROUND MEETING, and I have COMMISSIONED YOU and My strongest HOST to DEFEAT every strategy and plan of darkness and to DECLARE My KINGDOM SUPPLY and BLESSING on your Land."

The Father entrusted us with increasingly detailed action items that we decreed and declared as the Army of Light. Believers from around the world joined in praying for America, and we, in turn, prayed for awakening and freedom for their countries. Prayer Poet, a commenter on my Blog, wrote beautiful prayer points for intercessors to use to guide their prayers. Brett and Janice Cairns wrote a multi-page document that they shared with all of us that contained all the different action items the Father had given us. Sara Pounds wrote legal petitions for us to bring to the Courts of Heaven. Countless others contributed in large and small ways to the encouragement of this newly-formed army. The Army of Light was functional and deployed!

MAY 13, 2023: BE BOLD, BE STRONG, BE COURAGEOUS

"Do you see a RISE in EVIL SCHEMES, MAYHEM, and OPPOSITION from the darkness? Then KNOW that I AM EMPOWERING you, My Army of Light, to BE BOLD, STRONG, and COURAGEOUS in the FACE of these ATTACKERS. Know that if the darkness is INCREASING, I AM FILLING you with MORE LIGHT and MORE POWER. DO NOT COWER, DO NOT SHRINK BACK because of their THREATS and INTIMIDATION. You RISE UP and SQUARELY FACE the enemy, knowing that you are dressed in the ARMOR OF LIGHT and My GLORY." (Here is what I'm seeing in the Spirit as the Father speaks: I see a confident person squarely confronting a taunting bully. They take their right forefinger and begin poking the bully in the right shoulder blade, pushing him back, back, back. Finally, the dark bully turns and runs.) "CONFRONT the darkness with the LIGHT of My TRUTH and My PROMISES. DECLARE: 'Your darkness is EXPOSED, your lies are LAID BARE, and the LIGHT of God is PIERCING the WEB of LIES and SCHEMES, and it is EXPOSING and DESTROYING them.' 'Back up!' 'Get off of My King's TERRITORY!' 'You have LOST, we have WON!' I have promised you the VICTORY. Now ACT LIKE YOU BELIEVE THAT and BE BOLD, BE STRONG, BE COURAGEOUS. Carry My promises as BANNERS of VICTORY and TRIUMPH into the battle. WE WIN!"

ISAIAH 28: 5, 6 (TPT) *"In that day, Lord Yahweh, Commander of Angel Armies, will be a crown of glory and a diadem of beauty for the remnant of His people. He will be a Spirit of justice for judges to render right decisions. And He will be strength and bravery for those who turn back the battle at the gate."*

CHAPTER FIVE

The Promise of the Rescue of the Ages

The Army of Light realized we were facing an entrenched, organized, and corrupt enemy who was empowered by dark forces. There was no way we could defeat this enemy on our own. We took heart and rejoiced when the Father shared with us His promise of a Rescue Operation which became the Rescue of the Ages.

OCTOBER 17, 2021: OPERATION RESCUE

"We are launching OPERATION RESCUE. Unprecedented SHAKINGS and OCCURRENCES will happen, but remember I've already told you there will be a HAPPY ENDING. GOOD will triumph over EVIL, LIGHT will outshine the DARKNESS, and JUSTICE will be dealt to the CORRUPT and EVIL. I AM your REFUGE and your STRONG TOWER, and you can bring others who are panicking and troubled into this place of safety. Live in My LOVE and in My PRESENCE. BREATHE Me in and EXHALE any fear or anxiety. I AM your faithful and true Father who has ARISEN to come and fight for His children and for your Land. Let your heart be LIFTED UP knowing that you and your Land's REDEMPTION is very near."

Parameters of this Rescue Operation were laid out for us in increasing detail. The Father assured us that all the areas involved in the creeping darkness over our nation would be rooted out while His protection covered His people.

NOVEMBER 17, 2021: YOU WILL SEE

"You will SEE with your own eyes My WHOLE RESCUE OPERATION unfold for your Nation. It's going to be AWESOME and TERRIBLE. Awesome for the people who have chosen to partner with Me to pursue RIGHTEOUSNESS and JUSTICE, and terrible for those haughty elite who thought they could rule My Land in the power of evil and darkness. You will know for certain that I AM God when you see what I will do to rescue your Nation and SNATCH it out of the GREEDY, GRASPING fingers that were tearing it apart and controlling people through LIES and FEAR. I will dig up and expose CRIMES, BRIBERY, EVIL DEEDS that the wicked thought were buried and forgotten. I will play aloud for the world to hear SECRET meetings with your Nation's enemies to plot and scheme AGAINST the people of your Land. It will leave those partnered with darkness no DEFENSE and nowhere left to HIDE. I will also deal SEVERELY with the media who have allowed themselves to be BRIBED and SEDUCED into COVERING UP evil and spreading LIES about those who are truly seeking JUSTICE and RIGHTEOUSNESS. I HATE LYING and FALSE WITNESS, and they will be called to account, and they will be held responsible for lying and trying to OVERTHROW the rightful leaders of your Land. Heaven and earth are joined together to ROOT OUT and OVERTHROW the entrenched evil, and you will see it, and your PRAYERS and DECLARATIONS will help bring it to pass. You will see a NEW DAY arising for your Land."

That the Father intended to make this Rescue Operation a worldwide event was revealed in His words to us. Many times He told us not to trust what media was reporting but to ask Him for His perspective on people and events.

FEBRUARY 25, 2022: FROM MY HEART

"The GREAT RESCUE OPERATION has begun. My rescue of your Nation involves TENTACLES of EVIL that have spread all around the world and that is why you see CONFLICTS, RUMORS, and CONFUSING EVENTS worldwide. I AM shaking loose the DARK CONTROL these evil ones have established. The rescue of your Land will have a DOMINO effect across the world, FREEING other nations as well. I AM speaking these things to you, My Army of Light, FROM MY HEART because I do not want you CAPTURED BY FEAR or left BLIND and

CONFUSED about what is happening. Come to Me, and I will gladly help you see events from My perspective. DO NOT buy the media's reporting of events—since when could you TRUST what they say? Do not buy the picture they paint of world leaders—remember they UPLIFT those who support DARKNESS and VILIFY those who are on the side of LIGHT. Realize there are going to be many very UNLIKELY HEROES in this war. They may have TARNISHED pasts, but they have PLEDGED themselves to FIGHT for FREEDOM from the darkness that threatens to consume the world. FROM MY HEART, know that this war will end with darkness DEFEATED and LOVE and LIGHT WINNING. Don't let the tumultuous circumstances JERK you around. Instead, flow with Me on My river of life, and we will WIN this war TOGETHER."

Our good and faithful Father revealed to us the dark underbelly of the evil empire that had to be taken down, and He kept His promise to sustain and protect us while these Rescue Operations were being carried out.

July 18, 2022: The Shaking, The Breaking, The Awakening

"Sometimes a RESCUE OPERATION can look, on the surface, like CHAOS. I want you to be aware of this so that you don't LOSE HEART or fall into FEAR and DOUBT. My rescue operation involves SHAKING LOOSE the foundations of IDOLATRY that were established in your Nation by the darkness. The shakings will include EXPOSURES of the shedding of innocent blood and the trafficking of humans to gratify PERVERSIONS and to AMASS FORTUNES. It will UNCOVER financial theft established by the elite. It will SHOWCASE medical fraud, media lies, and political theft. After the SHAKING exposes these evil roots, I will then BREAK their power and their hold on America. This will mean temporary crashes of whole systems that people thought they depended upon. It is at this point that your FAITH in what I AM doing and your HOPE being firmly anchored in My promises, will cause you to be a LIGHT that guides others through the AWAKENING process. The SHAKING and the BREAKING will clear away evil in order to REBUILD on new foundations. My people will be KEPT like the Children of Israel were kept in the land of Goshen. SHARE FREELY with those in fear and need—share your FAITH and CONFIDENCE in Me and My future plans, and share PROVISION with those in lack. The more you GIVE AWAY, the more I will PROVIDE. My Army of Light is KEY to AWAKENING people to My GOODNESS and POWER. I will walk with you every step of the way through THE SHAKING, THE BREAKING, and THE AWAKENING."

Even though our Great God was the force behind the Rescue Operation, we were still called to partner with Him, and we were given action items to help defeat the enemy's desperate schemes.

OCTOBER 26, 2022: CANCELING THE ASSIGNMENTS OF THE ENEMY

"I REVEAL the dark plans of the enemy, not so you can HIDE from them, but so you would CONFRONT them in your AUTHORITY as My BLOOD-BOUGHT Sons and Daughters. How do you RESPOND to THREATS of nuclear war, assassination attempts, food shortages? I AM revealing these evil schemes to you because I want you to RISE UP and CANCEL THE ASSIGNMENTS OF THE ENEMY. When you arise and SPEAK OUT your authority over the darkness, it throws them into CONFUSION and PANIC. For years there has been LITTLE RESISTANCE from the sheep against their POWER GRABS and their dark plans to cause FEAR and DESTRUCTION to your Land. They are SHOCKED and PERPLEXED to witness a UNIFIED, POWERFUL remnant speaking BOLDLY the TRUTH and DEMANDING true JUSTICE and RIGHTEOUSNESS be restored. My Army of Light, as you continue to SHINE My LIGHT OF TRUTH and to CANCEL THE ASSIGNMENTS OF THE ENEMY for your Nation, your families, and your personal lives, more and more people will JOIN your ranks as they see the plans of darkness FAIL and your own lives SHINING with My GLORY and DELIVERANCE. When you join Me in CANCELING THE ASSIGNMENTS OF THE ENEMY, you are helping make a WAY for My RESCUE OPERATION to come to its STUNNING FULFILLMENT."

Defiling traps from the darkness were carefully inserted into a sleeping nation, and many people fell for those defiling schemes and were taken captive by them. The Father spoke to us about partnering with Him in setting these people free and bringing down the defiling corruption.

APRIL 12, 2023: THE DEFILEMENT OF A NATION

"The darkness has carefully planned for years to DEFILE THIS NATION. Their WICKEDNESS and CORRUPTION knows no bounds, and they have LOST their ability to love. Their GOAL is to DEFILE and CORRUPT this Land that I love, and this goal knows NO bounds. When I raised up a Cyrus to LEAD your Nation OUT OF DARKNESS AND BONDAGE, it caused those partnered with evil to DOUBLE-DOWN on their plans to completely DEFILE and OVERTAKE the people and the Land of this Nation. Their FRANTIC MOVES are serving to UNCOVER their DARK AGENDAS, and I will completely EXPOSE and OVERTURN all their wickedness. I will CUT OFF the TRAFFICKING of human lives and the STEADY SUPPLY of ADDICTING DRUGS, but what about the CONSUMERS of these DEFILING TRAPS? Even some of My people have FALLEN for these DEFILING SCHEMES; it has brought DARKNESS and SHAME to them, and it serves to CUT THEM OFF from My PRESENCE and from being a FORCE for the LIGHT. As you partner with Me in BRINGING DOWN the DEEP DARKNESS, also PARTNER with Me in SPEAKING FREEDOM for the CAPTIVES to the SCHEMES OF DEFILEMENT. Declare that a WAVE OF REPENTANCE would SWEEP the Land CLEAN; then decree a MOVE of My Spirit of FIRE to CLEANSE HEARTS and BREAK the POWER of BONDAGE. Release My LOVE to CONSUME those hearts and to WASH them CLEAN of DEFILEMENT and SHAME. SUDDENLY, the Army of Light will GROW by leaps and bounds as these FREED ones GLADLY join the ranks of My Army to DEFEAT darkness and to CLEAN UP the Land. This is also a part of My RESCUE OPERATION. It will

COMPLETELY COUNTERACT the carefully planned DEFILEMENT OF A NATION. FREEDOM will RING across your Land and in the HEARTS of the people."

A brilliant plan was laid out for us by the Father that involved converging Heaven and earth into the spectacular Rescue Operation.

DECEMBER 14, 2023: MY ARROW OF RESCUE

Mind. Officially. Blown. I was shown a little glimpse of how God's rescues work. I saw a large tip of an arrow in the sky and received the understanding that it was somehow bending time—like a tesseract (a way of visualizing the concept of time in a four-dimensional universe, also known as the fifth dimension.). God was inserting something into our time. It is what we might call a "defining moment," "fullness of time," or a "Kairos moment." It focuses something from the eternal realm into our present time. It is capturing all the spectacular turning points, rescues, and bravery from history and converging it into changing a present dilemma. Eternity interjects itself into our time.

From the Father:

"My RESCUE OPERATION will be SPECTACULAR. Because I AM outside of time, I have determined to gather together all the GREAT VICTORIES of the past, all the GREAT HEROES and displays of VALIANT COURAGE, and all the Angelic and Host's ACTIVITY and POWER. I will CONVERGE them into the TIP OF AN ARROW that I will SHOOT from eternity, and it will RIP THROUGH all the layers of time and ERUPT into your present time. It will cause a **BOOMING SOUND** that the whole world will hear. The **EVIL** will lose control of their bodily functions, and the **RIGHTEOUS** will **LIFT A SHOUT** because they know the **TRIUMPH** of their God is here. My Army of Light will **ARISE** covered in all the past **VICTORIES** and **BRAVERY**, and they will do **EXPLOITS** and display **VALIANT FAITH**. Don't **WASTE** your time magnifying or rehearsing what the enemy is doing. Instead, **MAGNIFY** Me and look for My **ARROW OF CONVERGENCE** to **SPLIT OPEN** the heavens and come to your **RESCUE**. You will see My **FOCUSED POWER** on **DISPLAY** like never before. You will see **MY ARROW OF RESCUE**."

The Arrow of Rescue word mentioned a "booming sound" that would be heard around the world. It reminded me of the shot heard round the world from the Revolutionary War. The Father spoke of this in a journal entry before I began posting on social media.

August 5, 2017: Change

"**CHANGE** is coming. **CHANGE** is in the wind. Those who oppose My will and My ways think that the **CHANGE** will establish their agenda and will bring them into power. They are **BLINDED** by their own desires for **POWER** and **CONTROL**, and they do not perceive that the **CHANGES** that are coming will sweep away their ungodly, man-centered agenda. They are so focused on personal gain and power that they have lost perspective nor do they see things objectively but through a **DISTORTED** lens of selfish ambition. Their **COLLAPSE** will be great, and it will be **HEARD AROUND THE WORLD**, and it will

71

affect governments far and wide. I AM patiently waiting until they finish building the GALLOWS they plan to hang those that they see as obstructions to their plans. But My plans will prevail, and it is they who will hang themselves, be brought low, and be brought to nothing. The flood of righteousness that I release will be My people crying out for their nation and joining their hearts to Mine and calling forth My plans and My purposes for their nation. Keep aligning with My heart and keep declaring and calling forth My purposes and plans for your nation."

Another repeated theme in the Father's words to us was a question: "Can a nation be born (changed or saved) in a day?" Isaiah 66: 8 (TPT) "Who has heard of such a thing? Who has seen such things? Can a land be born in one day? Or can a nation be brought forth in a moment? As soon as Zion was in labor, she also brought forth her sons."

The following entry is, again, before I began to post publicly.

AUGUST 18, 2017: STAND FAST

"Just as I saw Satan fall like lightning from Heaven, you will SUDDENLY begin to see leaders come to an END—permanently losing their positions of INFLUENCE, and in some cases, losing their lives as they turn on one another. CAN A NATION BE CHANGED IN A DAY? Only by My POWER and My PLANS being executed in righteousness and justice. The unrighteous magnifying lens that has been put on this President is about to be FOCUSED on his adversaries, and the TRUTH about them and the POWER behind them will be brought to a PAINFUL CLARITY for them ... The LIES will SUDDENLY CRUMBLE, and the hypocrisy will be laid bare, and in that day I will raise up a standard of righteousness in your government and in your people that will FLOOD the land with My Kingdom and My power ... STAND FAST in Me, keeping joined to My heart."

Following are excerpts from additional journal entries with this theme of a sudden rebirth of our nation. It was heartening to see that His promises remained the same whether He was speaking just to me or to the people who read His words when I began to publish them on social media.

SEPTEMBER 28, 2021: BEHIND THE CURTAIN

"Behind the curtain of the illegitimate administration, there's a whole lot of FRANTIC MOVEMENTS and INSECURE PEOPLE ... What was once a UNIFIED, DRIVING FORCE of evil is CRUMBLING from the inside out. I want to give you this report from BEHIND THE CURTAIN so that you will be encouraged that your prayers are working and know that the Host of Heaven have been deployed to carry out My Word spoken through your prayers. If a nation can be BORN in a day, then a FAKE power structure can also COME DOWN and be DESTROYED in a day. Keep watching and waiting and hoping in Me—My Kingdom will prevail in your Nation."

NOVEMBER 13, 2021: YOUR PATIENCE WILL BE REWARDED

"I have asked you to TRUST My words and My promises above the destruction and evil agendas you see playing out in the natural realm. I have asked you to SEE circumstances through My eyes and to look at what I AM doing in the spiritual realm. My goal has been to STRENGTHEN your faith and to open the WONDERS of the Spirit realm to you ... Your PATIENCE to see My promises unfold, PUSHING THROUGH the doubts and fears back into FAITH, and your increasing love for and dependency on Me have made you a SHINING LIGHT—one of My LIGHT-BEARERS. So, here we stand on the PRECIPICE of faith ... answer these questions in your heart: 'Is the great I AM coming as a Hero to rescue your Land?' 'Can a nation be born in a day?' Let your FAITH SHINE as you watch Me do these things for you and your Nation!"

OCTOBER 16, 2022: AFTER THE SUDDENLY, THEN WHAT?

"I have promised you a SUDDENLY for your Nation. I have spoken of a nation being BORN IN A DAY. I have said that in ONE DAY an evil empire will be EXPOSED and BROUGHT DOWN and righteous leaders will be RAISED UP ... You have done VALIANTLY on the frontlines of this war, My Army of Light! Now, you will move into a CLEANUP and a REBUILDING assignment ... Your Nation will be TRANSFORMED before your eyes ... Receive My GLORY and SHINE for Me in your Nation and as a LIGHT OF HOPE for the rest of the world."

DECEMBER 15, 2022: THE DARKNESS WILL GIVE WAY TO A NEW DAWN

"No matter how DARK it may look for the LIFE of your Nation, I AM assuring you that a NEW DAWN is coming … I have been FORMING a NEW Nation in the HEARTS of My people. You are each CARRYING an IMPORTANT PART of this new Nation that I AM creating. Will I bring it to fullness and then not allow it to be BIRTHED? Will I allow the enemy to take its life or PREVENT it from being BORN? A nation can be born in a day, but realize I have been preparing it in HIDDENNESS, out of the SIGHT of the enemy, and he will be DUMBFOUNDED when I bring this new Nation to BIRTH. What I have done in HIDDENNESS will be REVEALED before the world, and WONDER and AWE will fill hearts as THE DARKNESS GIVES WAY TO A NEW DAWN."

MARCH 11, 2023: BEFORE THE DAWN BREAKS, IT WILL ALL BE CHANGED

"Can My LIGHT SUDDENLY BREAK THROUGH the deep darkness in such a POWERFUL way that when MORNING DAWNS, a Nation has been BORN AGAIN? In the middle of one night, do I have the POWER to completely CHANGE the COURSE of a Land CAPTURED by darkness? Can a Nation be REBORN IN A DAY? … Can a TRUTH BOMB be so BIG that when it is dropped, it will BLOW UP and COMPLETELY EXPOSE the deep darkness? … Your enemies think they have gotten away with their SCAM, but I AM coming with JUDGMENT in one hand and

HEALING in the other ... you will be PAID BACK all that was STOLEN from you. Can this happen that BEFORE THE DAWN BREAKS, IT WILL ALL BE CHANGED? You'd better BELIEVE it!"

MAY 8, 2024: A SPECTACULAR RESCUE

"There will be a SUDDEN and SPECTACULAR WORLDWIDE RESCUE that delivers nations IN A DAY and that showcases My SUPERNATURAL and POWERFUL RIGHT ARM. Illegitimate thrones of power will be SWEPT AWAY, systems that ENSLAVED you will CRASH and BURN, the places of HIDDEN SECRETS and MASSIVE STASHES of supplies will be BURST OPEN, and everything will be EXPOSED. It will take people MONTHS to PROCESS all the LIES they have been told for many years, and they will take hold of TRUTH and FREEDOM and will EMBRACE and VALUE them. The AWE and WONDER of who I AM will fill the Land as people realize that going their own way led them to be DUPED and ENSLAVED. You can welcome them HOME to My heart through the BLOOD of Jesus, and My Kingdom of Light will grow in NUMBERS and in POWER as you become KEEPERS of TRUTH, FREEDOM, and LOVE. It will come ... A SPECTACULAR RESCUE."

One of the most powerful messages I ever heard from the Father came in an unusual way. It was like I was thrust into the trailer for an epic adventure movie, and I felt like I was present on the intense battlefield.

DECEMBER 22, 2024: WHEN TIME STANDS STILL

"There is often a PAUSE, a STILLNESS before a GREAT CHANGE happens. The world seems to HOLD ITS BREATH waiting to see what is coming next. Will darkness WIN or will the Light TRIUMPH? All of Heaven is ON HOLD, eyes FASTENED on the One on the Throne, WAITING for His SIGNAL to be given. The darkness MISTAKES the STILLNESS for WEAKNESS, and their evil plan is about to be released. For My Army of Light, TIME WILL SEEM TO STAND STILL as they wait for the FINAL CLASH to begin. Their eyes are FIXED on Me, My PROMISES REPLAY in their minds, and under their armor, their HEART BEATS AT THE SAME FREQUENCY OF HEAVEN. The darkness is so SELF-FOCUSED that they think the Army of Light has GIVEN UP, but they are not looking at the STEELY-EYED RESOLVE and TIGHTLY GRIPPED SWORDS. F L A S H ! ! ! R O A R ! ! ! The SIGNAL comes from Heaven, and both armies CHARGE onto the field. Where STILLNESS REIGNED a second ago, the air is now FILLED with BATTLE CRIES, CLASHING SWORDS, and the ground is SHAKING as the Hosts of Heaven SLAM into the earth to FIGHT alongside the Army of Light. The evil empire is DESPERATE and RUTHLESS, but they are beginning to TREMBLE. They have never seen such a MASSIVE DISPLAY of Heaven's POWER CONVERGED with the VALIANT, BLOOD-BOUGHT WARRIORS who have laid down their lives to win back JUSTICE and RIGHTEOUSNESS. The evil empire is being SURROUNDED and DEFEAT is near. A BURST OF LIGHT and CRIES OF VICTORY FILL THE AIR! And then, another STILLNESS comes, but it is the stillness of PEACE. After My Army of Light SAVORS the moment, a GREAT TIME of

CELEBRATION will arise. Then it will be time for SWEET VINDICATION and My REWARDS that will be given to My Beloved Army of Light."

As the Rescue Operation was carried out, we were protected, provided for, and kept safe.

JUNE 20, 2024: SAFE HARBOR

"I AM your SAFE HARBOR in the days ahead of GREAT CHANGE and UPHEAVAL. From your place of SAFETY and PEACE in Me, you will observe the CHANGES, and I will help you ADAPT your life to the New Kingdom era that emerges from the ASHES of the evil empire. Those whose hearts are ALIGNED with Mine will receive an ABUNDANCE of FINANCES. These finances will continue to GROW and MULTIPLY as long as you are WILLING to ABUNDANTLY SHARE with others what FLOWS to you. In a SHORT AMOUNT of TIME, the Rescue Operation will DRAMATICALLY TRANSFORM your world and your life. Do you believe I AM POWERFUL enough to INSTIGATE, OVERSEE, and COMPLETE this TUMULTUOUS TRANSFORMATION while keeping you at PEACE and PROTECTED in My SAFE HARBOR? I AM. For the sake of My people who are CRYING out for DELIVERANCE from the TYRANTS who think they are gods, I will make this a SUDDEN and DRASTIC CHANGE. The world will be REELING from the EXPOSURES of EVIL PEOPLE and DEATH AGENDAS. You are to WELCOME the SHOCKED and FEARFUL into My SAFE HARBOR of salvation, deliverance, and healing. Their lives will be BORN AGAIN as the world is BORN AGAIN into the KINGDOM AGE. Settle yourself NOW in My SAFE

HARBOR so that you are positioned there to WELCOME the FEARFUL, LOST, and BROKEN into My SAFE HARBOR."

The promised Rescue of the Ages will take its place in history as an unparalleled and powerful deliverance by the hand of the great I AM.

CHAPTER SIX

The Trumpet

The Father is always a strategic planner, and the man chosen to lead our nation through the rescue of the ages and into a whole new era was carefully prepared and chosen during the first six decades of his life. Donald John Trump became a master builder of hotels, golf courses, and skyscrapers that were known for excellence, innovation, and for getting the job done in spite of many obstacles. His mother and his great aunts in Scotland were involved in the Hebrides Revival before his mother immigrated to America. President Trump's mother brought a Bible from that revival in Scotland that he inherited, and it has marked his presidency.

Throughout the Bible and history, the Father has used men and women to spearhead what He was doing in the earth. We remember the lives of Moses, Joshua, Abraham, Deborah, Gideon,

Cyrus, Esther, and David. President Trump was uniquely equipped to plow through all the roadblocks the evil empire put in his way, uncover their corruption, bring them to justice, and rebuild a nation into greatness again. President Trump knew that God's hand was upon him as he was saved from assassination attempts, fraudulent lawfare, and dark forces trying to destroy our nation. Prophetic voices began to speak of the Trumpet or Trump years before he decided to run for the office of the Presidency of the United States in 2015. The Father often spoke to me of President Trump as the one He had called to serve our nation at this pivotal time in its history. The following journal entry describes in a nutshell the call on his life, the obstacles thrown in his way, and what the Father had purposed to accomplish through his leadership.

FEBRUARY 12, 2025: DESTABILIZE

"The evil empire has been working for years to DESTABILIZE your GOVERNMENT, ECONOMY, and FAMILY STRUCTURES. They played DARK and DIRTY with a COMPLACENT population and an APATHETIC Church. Only a few WATCHMEN saw the SHADOWS of DEATH that were being released by the deep darkness. Few would LISTEN to the voices of the watchmen who were SOUNDING the ALARM. People IGNORED or marginalized these voices that were crying out: 'They are INFILTRATING every area of our lives, and they are DESTABILIZING our way of life and our security.' And then, I RAISED UP MY TRUMPET, and he began to BOLDLY ANNOUNCE and EXPOSE what the evil empire was doing to TEAR our nation APART. The ALARM began to be heard and more were AWAKENED to the efforts of the darkness to DESTABILIZE and to take TYRANNICAL CONTROL of the world. I have raised up My Trumpet because the AWAKENED REMNANT has CRIED OUT for RESCUE and for a return of JUSTICE and RIGHTEOUSNESS. My Trumpet has been anointed to be a BULLDOZER, a WRECKING BALL, and a THRESHING MACHINE. He has been called to DESTABILIZE the evil empire by CLEARING OUT the ROADBLOCKS set up to keep society from PROGRESSING and from coming together in UNITY. My Trumpet is DISMANTLING structures that DIVERTED WEALTH to the wicked, that SOWED FILTH and PERVERSION into society, and that BRIBED and COMPROMISED leaders in order to ensure that CONTROL and TYRANNY could be established. My Trumpet has released a THRESHING MACHINE to DIG UP all the DARK SECRETS, UNDERHANDED DEALINGS, and GROSS PERVERSIONS of those partnered with darkness. Don't FRET if things look a bit MESSY for a while as My Trumpet DESTABILIZES the DESTABILIZERS. Their mouths now resemble GAPING CODFISH who can't believe that their DIRTY TACTICS are being EXPOSED and used AGAINST them. Army of Light, keep BACKING UP the Trumpet who has been called to DESTABILIZE the darkness that had EMBEDDED itself into your nation. Back him up with your PRAYERS, DECREES, and DECLARATIONS. Join Me in LAUGHING at your enemies' BEWILDERMENT that every dark structure and scheme is being DESTABILIZED. The TIDE HAS TURNED against them, the TABLES have FLIPPED EXPOSING their underhanded ways, the BOOMERANG EFFECT is in full swing as their DARK SCHEMES and DEATH AGENDAS come back upon them. THANK

Me that My Rescue Operation is in full swing to DESTABILIZE the DESTABILIZERS."

Revealed in this powerful prophetic word were the plans of the evil empire to infiltrate every area of society with their dark plans and death agendas that would result in their tyrannical control of the world. Most of the world remained asleep to the creeping darkness that threatened to consume us. The Remnant had been crying out for a rescue and for justice and righteousness to be restored. The Father raised up His Trumpet with an anointing to be a bulldozer, a wrecking ball, and a threshing machine. The Trumpet began to boldly expose what the evil empire was doing to destroy lives and nations. The Bulldozer cleared out roadblocks to growth and unity set up by the darkness. The Wrecking Ball brought down structures that were created to steal our wealth, break apart our family units, and sow perversion into society. The Threshing Machine uncovered those partnered with darkness, perversion, bribery, blackmail, and treason. The Trumpet's work flipped the tables of the evil agendas, turned the tide from injustice to justice, and boomeranged their dark schemes back upon them. The Army of Light partnered with the Father's anointing on President Trump's life by backing him up with prayer and sharing the truth wherever our voices could be heard.

In the following word, the Father fleshes out more of His call on President Trump's life in the Rescue of the Ages and in the good future that had been promised to us.

SEPTEMBER 14, 2022: MY EYE IS ON THE TRUMPET

"The darkness has TARGETED the one I have CHOSEN and ANOINTED to REBUILD your Nation on the principles of My JUSTICE and RIGHTEOUSNESS and to make your Nation a FORCE OF GREATNESS to the world. Yes, you will be PROSPERED and bring forth GOOD FRUIT, but it will not be just for you; it will be so that you can BLESS the WORLD with your ABUNDANCE. My TRUMPET will be a FATHER TO THE NATIONS and will TEACH LEADERS to be STRONG in Me and to BUILD their nations on My principles and to SERVE their people and not think they should be SERVED and be made WEALTHY from the people. This is a MIGHTY CALL I have placed on the TRUMPET'S life, and he will need your PRAYER SUPPORT to accomplish it. Now, do you see why the darkness is so DETERMINED to KILL him or to bring him DOWN with FABRICATED EVIDENCE and OUTRIGHT LIES? Don't FEAR if it looks like they are CLOSING IN on him. Realize this is PART OF THE TRAP I laid that will result in THEIR DOWNFALL. The world will see that everything they ACCUSED My TRUMPET of were CRIMES THEY COMMITTED. The world will be angry at how they were DUPED by these ARROGANT ELITE, and the people will DEMAND JUDGMENT and JUSTICE be released against them. Everything they planned for My TRUMPET will FALL ON THEM. These PROUD HAMANS will hang on their own gallows; so DO NOT FEAR. MY EYE IS ON THE TRUMPET."

The Trumpet was called to rebuild our nation as a force for greatness to bless the world. The Father declared that President Trump would be a father to the nations and would teach leaders how to govern their nations well. Our part was to provide the prayer support he would need to fulfill this call on his life. The Father often spoke of the "traps" He was laying for the darkness and that what the evil empire had planned to do to the Trumpet would come "back" upon them.

The following is a dream that the Holy Spirit gave me about three-fourths of the way through President Trump's first term in office. He had endured attack after attack from a desperate evil empire, and this dream gave hope for a happy ending.

AUGUST 19, 2019: DREAM

I saw a circular pool with a high wall around it and men in dark suits were completely lining the edge of the pool. These dark-suited men reminded me of the mafia. They were throwing a man between them like a ball. I recognized the man as being President Trump. Their end purpose was to drown him. The men had parked their cars—all large, black cars—along the street outside the pool fence. Someone called the police, and they surrounded the wall while an officer wrote down all the license plate numbers from the parked cars. When the police were in position, they realized the man was weakening and ready to drown. They all popped up around the pool wall with their guns aimed at the men in black. The police ordered the men out of the pool. Handcuffs were put on each of the men. The man was saved.

Dream Interpretation:

I am an observer or a watchman in this dream. A nationwide or worldwide "ring" of evil, powerful men is determined to "throw" everything they can at President Trump in order to weaken, silence, and get rid of him. The true law/justice/ enforcers have surrounded the dark men, and their "license" to do evil has exposed them. With powerful, authoritative words (guns) these evil men are ordered from their positions of power, bound, and on their way to jail. I believe the Army of Light was part of this group of "enforcers," and we used our prayers, our spiritual warfare, and our words of truth to call out and defeat the dark schemes of the enemy. What these men tried to do to President Trump happened to them.

About a month after this dream, the Father spoke a word confirming the dream's interpretation, and He asked us to call forth His plans and purposes for the Trumpet.

OCTOBER 11, 2019: NO WORRYING, NO FRETTING

"Do not worry and do not fret over the lies, slander, threats, and intimidation of the enemy. I am allowing them to completely out themselves to those with eyes to see and ears to hear and to name their own crimes and punishment. What they threaten the President with will fall back on their own heads, and it will completely expose their crimes and their hypocrisy. I will allow the enemy to push them too far, and it will result in their ruin, takedown, and jail time for many. Those guilty of treason will face execution. President Trump will be fully vindicated and will receive the honor that is due him. Keep calling forth My purposes, My ways, and My timing, and rest in My faithfulness and My immense power to carry out My word."

This entry from 2020 reaffirms this theme of constant attacks that were overcome by the counterattacks from Heaven.

JANUARY 14, 2020: COUNTER ATTACKS

"As you see plot after plot and scheme after scheme released against your President, be aware that I knew of these evil plans before they were hatched. I HAVE ALREADY LAUNCHED COUNTERATTACKS to bring down these schemes. Not only will I bring them down, I will expose those who planned them and those who attempted to carry them out. They will be brought to justice. Just as they attempted to connect President Trump to made up crimes, so I will expose their real crimes, and the world will see that they were smearing the President in order to keep their corruption from being exposed. DON'T BE DISCOURAGED at the length of the battle and don't rely on your own strength to fight. Lean on My strong right arm, and we will battle together. Take the time to refresh and recenter yourself in My love. Ask the Holy Spirit to reveal to you My power and glory that are resting on this Nation and on you."

The Father consistently prophesied two terms for President Trump.

January 22, 2020: Hold Fast. Stand Firm.

"Hold firm. Have faith that I Am is in control of the destiny of your Nation. The evil plans of destruction and usurpation have been cancelled, and President Trump will serve his full two terms in office. The conspirators who plotted and schemed in the shadows will now have the full light of exposure shined on them, and full justice for them has been released from Heaven. They are about to encounter a terrible day of reckoning, and there will be no place to hide. Even in My great wrath against those who gave their lives to evil out of greed for wealth and a lust for power combined with a willingness to sacrifice and use innocent lives for their own benefit, I will show mercy to them if they repent, turn to Me, and tell the truth of all their vile deeds and plans. They will not escape justice, but I will promise to be with them and to see them through until they come home to Me. Even in My wrath, I will remember mercy for those who repent, but nothing and no one will stop the day of reckoning that is on this group of evil-doers who are being completely brought down. Hold fast. Stand firm, and see the salvation of your God."

This entry carries the same theme as the dream with evil canceled, the schemers exposed, and full justice released to President Trump. It clearly states that the Trumpet would serve his two terms in office. We did not see ahead to his two terms being separated by an illegitimate administration, but God allowed this to happen in order to uncover more evil-doers and to awaken more sleeping citizens. The Father plainly shared what His opinion was of those who stole their way into power.

FEBRUARY 27, 2022: I AM AGAINST USURPERS

"I will reaffirm to you today that I AM against USURPERS. Usurpers are those who use ILLEGITIMATE powers and bribes to WEASEL their way into positions they were never intended to fill. Because these are STOLEN positions, USURPERS do not have My ANOINTING and WISDOM to fulfill the position they have illegally grabbed. I AM AGAINST USURPERS because they are focused on their OWN gain and not on how they can BENEFIT those this position was meant to SERVE. Usurpers open doors to EVERY EVIL thing because their rise to power was fueled by GREED, LAWLESSNESS, and LIES about the rightful person I had chosen for that position. Let Me be clear, I AM speaking of positions throughout all seven mountains of influence where DARKNESS has fueled USURPERS—and that includes positions in the Church. My focus today, though, is on the HIGHEST SEAT of power in your Land that has been STOLEN by a gang of completely CORRUPT and RUTHLESS people. This ILLEGALLY INSTALLED PUPPET WILL NOT STAND. I AM coming to REMOVE him with My own righteous right arm, and what is BURIED will be EXPOSED. I AM sounding a TRUMPET throughout your Land, and your RIGHTFUL leader will ARISE to take his place with My ANOINTING and My BLESSING."

Proving what the Bible says about reaping what you have sown, Joe Biden had the candidacy stolen right out from under him, and he wasn't even allowed to run for the office of the president again. The Trumpet overwhelmingly won over Kamala Harris and took his rightful place as President of our nation.

Amazing prophetic promises were given about the Trumpet's two terms in office.

JUNE 20, 2020: THE GREATEST REFORMATION OF A NATION EVER

"There will be a collective WAKE-UP CALL like millions of ALARMS ringing at the same time, and a Nation will be CHANGED and UNIFIED. President Trump will have FREE REIGN to bring about government reforms that will bring a greater FREEDOM to this Nation, and the people will be responsible to uphold their part of this government by and for the people. This will be known as the GREATEST REFORMATION OF A NATION EVER IN HISTORY! REJOICE!"

JULY 21, 2022: INVITATION, DECLARATION, PROCLAMATION

From the Father of Lights:

*INVITATION: THE GLORY TRAIN

"Get on board My GLORY TRAIN! My train is not confined to run on tracks that restrict where the train can go. My GLORY TRAIN runs on the BREATH OF MY SPIRIT carrying it where heartfelt prayers are asking for it to come. Ask for My GLORY to fall, and then get on board the GLORY TRAIN because it will come to you. It will be THE RIDE OF YOUR LIFE through uncharted territory ... MIRACLES, DELIVERANCE, and RESTORATION like you've never seen! ALL ABOARD!

*DECLARATION: HEAR MY TRUMP!

"Hear My TRUMP that I AM blowing! I declare to you that darkness will FALL, and My light will PREVAIL! My Trump will SPLIT the atmosphere, and darkness will fall to the earth, SHATTERED and EXPOSED. My light will SHINE FORTH bringing TRUTH, JUSTICE, and FREEDOM. Get behind My trump and DECLARE your freedoms come from Me and that darkness must GIVE WAY."

*PROCLAMATION: I AM WHO I SAY I AM

"I proclaim to you that I AM who I say I AM, and that I will DO what I have said I will do. America will be SAVED, My Trumpet will RETURN, and all that has been STOLEN will be RESTORED. My judgment against the wicked and My justice released to My people will come in FULL FORCE that nothing and no one can turn back. DARKENED and FOOLISH days will give way to My LIGHT and My WISDOM. THE BEST IS YET TO COME!"

PROMISED AND FULFILLED:

*Reformation of a nation

*Changed, unified

*Darkness will fall and be exposed

*Light will bring truth, justice, and freedom

*The Trumpet will return

*America will be saved

*What has been stolen will be restored

*Light and wisdom will overtake the darkness

*The Best is Yet to Come! (A promise spoken often by the Father and also by the Q Team)

Because the Father is the Creator, He used creative ways to speak of His winning plans.

MAY 5, 2023: WHO HAS THE WINNING HAND?

"The ARROGANT ELITE thought they were playing a game of POKER with Me, and they thought they had a WINNING HAND that I could not OVERCOME. They were BLINDED to the fact that I held TWO UNBEATABLE CARDS: My TRUMP CARD and My CARD OF FURY. I AM laying down those cards on the table, and the world will see My TRUMP CARD TRIUMPH and My CARD OF FURY being UNLEASHED against those of darkened hearts and DEATH AGENDAS. Righteousness and glory will fill the Land as we REBUILD together on LIGHT and LIFE. Truly, the AWE of who I AM will fill the atmosphere, and My PROMISES will be FULFILLED."

NOVEMBER 11, 2024: THE TRUMP CARD

"The darkness has been playing a DEADLY game to establish their COMPLETE CONTROL over the world. They thought they had ALL the WINNING CARDS to play: SICKNESS, INTIMIDATION, FEAR, DESTRUCTION, RIGGED ELECTIONS, and BRIBED and BLACKMAILED GATEKEEPERS. How could they

LOSE?? The TASTE of fresh blood was in their mouths as they anticipated their DARK VICTORY and the SNUFFING OUT of any LIGHT or FREEDOM. They thought I had NOTHING left to play against them. They knew I had a card that could DEFEAT them, but they thought they could DESTROY this card. Well, I have had this card PROTECTED under the shadow of My wings, and it has become even MORE POWERFUL and ANOINTED as it stayed in My presence. The time has come to play My TRUMP CARD, and the world will CHANGE. I AM laying it on the table for the world to see, and the darkness will FOLD their cards and try to ESCAPE. I have all the exits BLOCKED by the military and My FIERCE HOST. NO ONE WILL ESCAPE. They will be held ACCOUNTABLE for all their CHEATING, LYING, and MURDERING WAYS. Those who FOOLED much of the world will now become the CHIEF FOOLS. Their CORRUPTION and PERVERSION will be on DISPLAY as I play My TRUMP CARD. Those who played to win the world to satisfy their GREED for POWER and WEALTH will now be the world's BIGGEST LOSERS. It's time to lay it down for the WIN—My TRUMP CARD."

What a faithful, powerful God who brought about the Rescue of the Ages! As we close out this chapter on the Trumpet, we remember that we are all just men and women, but our great God chose to use us to fulfill His purposes in our nation and in the world.

DECEMBER 15, 2024: THE BIG CONCEAL WILL BECOME THE GREAT REVEAL

"A day is coming when ALL the evil empire has CONCEALED will be REVEALED. The GREAT REVEAL of TRUTH will SHAKE AWAKE those who have CLUNG to the LIES that media and education told about CURRENT EVENTS and HISTORY. Even My Army of Light will have some SHOCKS at what is UNCOVERED and brought to the LIGHT. Even WORLD MAPS will CHANGE as the BIG CONCEAL BECOMES THE GREAT REVEAL. Make sure your HOPE and your TRUST are firmly ANCHORED in Me so that the GREAT REVEALS do not cause you to FALTER because you were TRUSTING in certain people that turn out to be TRAITORS. Keep your FOCUS on Me, and SUPPORT the one I have chosen as your leader—Donald Trump—as you transition from DARK TO LIGHT. I AM with him, and I AM speaking to him, and his heart is to FULFILL all I have given him to do for your Nation and for the world. He is just a man, but I have his 'yes' to fulfilling My LIFE PURPOSES for him. The same is true for you, My Army of Light. I have called you, and you have said 'yes' to the BLUEPRINTS for your life in Me. Donald Trump's AGREEMENT with Me and your AGREEMENT with Me are the SOURCE of your GREAT STRENGTH, and I will perform My WONDERS and My PURPOSES through your lives. Hold LIGHTLY and don't get DISTRACTED by THEORIES and OPINIONS on what is TRUTH or what is happening BEHIND THE SCENES. Stay anchored in Me, My Word, and My prophets, and you won't be caught OFF GUARD or DISAPPOINTED when THE BIG CONCEAL BECOMES THE GREAT REVEAL."

CHAPTER SEVEN

Natural and Supernatural Signs

FLOODS, TSUNAMIS, AVALANCHES, VOLCANOES, FIRES, WEATHER, TIDES, ECLIPSES, EARTHQUAKES, SIGNS AND WONDERS

Floods, tsunamis, avalanches, volcanoes, fires, weather, tides, eclipses, earthquakes, signs and wonders, oh my! The Father spoke to us of these natural and supernatural phenomena as witnesses of the Rescue of the Ages coming to pass. Some occurred in the natural realm, but He also used them as symbolic actions that were happening in the spiritual realm in reaction to what was going on in the natural realm. We will look at entries where these events were spoken of symbolically and naturally.

NOVEMBER 2, 2019: VICTORY

"Victory is on My heart today. I am seeing the victory of light over darkness for your Nation. It is surely coming as a TSUNAMI of righteousness and justice FLOODS your land. It is coming as sure as the sun will rise in the morning, and nothing will stop this CRIMSON TIDE from pouring over your Nation. My eyes are upon those who concoct evil plans to defeat My purposes, and I am exposing these evil plans and unmasking the perpetrators for all to see. A day of total reckoning is very close at hand. Stand firm in My power and My plans. Join your heart to My heart, and we will bring down the evil empire that sought to control the world. A day of JOY and VICTORY is on the horizon—keep focused on calling that forth."

NOVEMBER 29, 2019: NO TURNING BACK

"No turning back. Press ahead pushing darkness out before you. Be fearless. Be confident. Be bold in your declarations of a sure victory in Me because what I have promised you is now going to unfold before your eyes and the eyes of the world. As corruption and treason are exposed and dealt with, the SHOCKWAVES will go around the world setting off TSUNAMIS all over that will result in rooting out darkness and evil motives."

JUNE 19, 2020: BEHIND THE SCENES

"Quietly, behind the scenes, a TSUNAMI is building. It will be released at just the right moment, and it will CHANGE THE WORLD ... the time is approaching when the tsunami of REVELATIONS will be released. Truth will crash in with great power that NOTHING and NO LIE CAN STOP. Even the lying media will not be able to spin the truth away. The MOUNTAIN OF TRUTH will be released like a powerful AVALANCHE that nothing can stop ... A collective sigh of relief will be released in your Nation that will be heard around the world, and HOPE will increase in other Nations that they too can be FREE and GOOD. Stand with Me and see My saving, redeeming, mighty right arm be released for your Land."

OCTOBER 8, 2021: THE HUSH OF WAITING

"REMIND yourself of all My PROMISES—let them fill your thinking and not fear and anxiety. This HUSH OF WAITING will be broken—the other shoe will DROP, the EARTHQUAKE will come, the VOLCANO will erupt, the TSUNAMI will roll, the AVALANCHE will thunder down, and JUSTICE will PLOW the evil under your feet. Be still and know that I AM God."

OCTOBER 22, 2021: THE VOICE OF THE LORD THUNDERS

"Amidst the dark and troubling plots and schemes those partnered with darkness will attempt to carry out during these LAST, DYING DAYS of their rule, you will hear MY VOICE OF THUNDER. My voice will THUNDER through natural and spiritual shakings. The natural shakings will be SIGNS AND WONDERS in the heavens and on the earth—volcanoes, earthquakes, winds, fires, strange weather systems. My VOICE OF THUNDER awakens the earth to respond in this way. These are not My judgments; they are the earth REACTING to all the evil that has been done by those serving darkness. These natural occurrences will AWAKEN people to the seriousness of the hour, and they will begin to seek Me and run to My LOVE and PROTECTION. My VOICE OF THUNDER in the spiritual realm will release EXTREME EXPOSURE, the HAMMER of My JUDGMENT, and My system of JUSTICE into the earth. The evil schemes and My thunderous plans will release SHOCKWAVES, so it is imperative that you find your REFUGE in the shelter of My wings, CLOSE to My heart, and I will see you through to a VERY HAPPY ENDING."

JANUARY 18, 2022: MY JUSTICE: A HAMMER OR A REWARD

"My JUSTICE is falling like an IMPENETRABLE CLOUD over your Nation. NOTHING will block the descent of this cloud of JUSTICE. It will completely cover this Land, and NO ONE will escape it. My JUSTICE comes to MAKE THINGS RIGHT, and ALL things will be made right in your Nation as a result of My cloud of JUSTICE. To those who have STOLEN, CHEATED, LIED, MURDERED, and PLOTTED DESTRUCTION, My justice will come down like a HAMMER, smashing open every HIDDEN darkness and bringing a GUILTY verdict and requiring them to PAY BACK their victims. To those who have been stolen from, lied to and about, and stripped of liberty and freedom, My JUSTICE will bring you VINDICATION and REWARD. It will be a GREAT REWARD, beyond your expectations, and the BATTLE you have fought against the darkness will seem small in comparison to your GREAT REWARDS. You have already begun to see a trickle of justice in favor of the LOWLY and against the seemingly UNTOUCHABLE, but it will become a FLOOD. (This will be pictured in the natural with floods.) You will know My JUSTICE CLOUD is lowering when you see Royals being EXPOSED and brought to JUSTICE. My JUSTICE is a HAMMER or a REWARD."

FEBRUARY 2, 2022: THE WITNESS

"I call Heaven and earth today to WITNESS that what I have PROMISED, I will INDEED DO. You may think that the SIGNS, WONDERS, and SHAKINGS that are happening are extreme, but they are only acting as a WITNESS of what I will do in the supernatural realm. I AM shaking AGE-OLD POWERS of darkness out of their seats of CONTROL, and all those who served them in the natural realm will also be SHAKEN out of their seats of POWER and CONTROL. The cold weather in unusual places is a picture of FREEZING and immobilizing BIOWEAPONS that were planned to be used against you. The extreme warm days are a picture of Me making things TOO HOT for the corrupt to handle. They will be DRIVEN out of their overheated hiding places, and they will be EXPOSED in My hot light. TIDES changing, RIVERS running backwards, FLOODS, WINDS, are all a picture of My mighty hand over My creation and My POWER to change the TIDE OF EVENTS in your Land and to FLOOD OUT and BLOW OUT the corruption until the Land is clean. See unusual events as a WITNESS to what I AM doing to FULFILL My words and promises to your Nation."

FEBRUARY 16, 2022: PROPHETIC INTEL IN THE NIGHT

3:34 a.m.

"The top will blow off from a completely DORMANT VOLCANO —a mountain people did not even know was a volcano."

4:56 a.m.

"From ICEBERGS to TSUNAMIS to unusual TIDES to the discovery of a large SEA MONSTER, My hand will be SEEN as I stir up the waters, and people will know that I AM GOD."

The Father adds: "You may wonder why I chose to speak to you in the night season to give you spiritual intelligence. I sometimes choose to release REVELATIONS that would be hard for your rational mind to accept, so I speak to you at night when those defenses are lowered. This is a season of SIGNS and WONDERS from My hand, and a season where I have chosen to make Myself known to your world as the

RESCUER and DEFENDER of RIGHTEOUSNESS, JUSTICE, and TRUE FREEDOM. You will say, 'Great and marvelous are Your works, O Lord! Just and true are Your ways! I worship and love You with all of My heart!' Good days are ahead for the nations of the earth, but those who have stood in FAITH with Me will be DOUBLY BLESSED. Your hearts of faith in the midst of giant ADVERSITY have deeply touched My heart, and I gladly pour out My POWER and STRENGTH to RESCUE you."

JUNE 4, 2022: THE NATURAL THINGS SPEAK OF THE INVISIBLE

"I AM using NATURE to speak LOUDLY where peoples' ears are CLOSED or RESISTANT to My voice. EARTH, WIND, and FIRE are speaking a WAKE-UP CALL to the nations. These NATURAL signs—earthquakes, tsunamis, great winds, heat, and fires are CONFIRMING the messages of My prophetic voices and SPEAKING LOUDLY to those who have not used their SPIRITUAL EYES AND EARS. To you who hear My voice and are learning to know My heart, I will give INSIGHT into the natural occurrences. Deep earthquakes will be used to UNCOVER SECRET HIDING PLACES and STASHES of supplies the selfish ones had for themselves. Winds, storms, and fire will be used to DESTROY their monuments erected in REBELLION to Me. BLESSED are you with STABILITY and HOPE who hear My voice and what I AM speaking through My prophets. To those who REFUSE to hear My voice, the NATURAL THINGS SPEAK OF THE INVISIBLE, and they will know that I AM GOD."

January 17, 2023: My Tsunami Will Reveal All

"In spite of the DESPERATE moves made by the darkness to DISTRACT and DESTROY you, MY TSUNAMI is coming, and it will REVEAL ALL. My TSUNAMI of TRUTH will EXPOSE all the HIDDEN plans of destruction, all the perverse and corrupt lifestyles, and all the hidden places of hoarded supplies and incriminating evidence. Your enemies are so DECEIVED, they think they are launching deadly attacks that will STOP MY TSUNAMI from coming. But I have REVEALED their plans to My prophets who were allowed to HEAR what the darkness is PLANNING in their SECRET MEETINGS. I have directed you, My Army of Light, how to take AUTHORITY over these dark schemes, BRING THEM TO NOTHING, and BLOW THEM BACK into the enemy camp. My prophets, My Army, and My Host are JOINED together as an UNSTOPPABLE, UNBEATABLE FORCE against the invading darkness. When My TSUNAMI REVEALS ALL about those partnered with darkness, they will be left HIGH and DRY and COMPLETELY EXPOSED before the world ... They will NEVER be in a place to launch them again after I send MY TSUNAMI that will REVEAL ALL. Partner with Me in CALLING FORTH THE TSUNAMI that reveals all. Watch JUSTICE and RIGHTEOUSNESS come rolling in."

October 15, 2023: Keeper of the Cosmos

"The sun, the moon, the planets, and the stars are under My CONTROL. I HUNG them in space, and it is My POWER that keeps them there. I MOVE them around at My WILL to TELL

My STORIES, to PROPHESY coming events, and to DISPLAY My WONDER. If I can keep the WHOLE COSMOS TOGETHER, don't you think I can HANDLE the affairs and the FUTURE of a nation? If you would spend a LOT MORE TIME GAZING into the WONDER of who I AM, WORRY and ANXIETY would FALL OFF of you like WATER off a duck's back. The MORE you WORSHIP Me, the MORE your FAITH will GROW because I REVEAL Myself to those who MAGNIFY My name. I know what a DIFFICULT season this has been for you, and that is why I AM creating SIGNS and WONDERS in the skies. I AM PAINTING RAINBOWS where they don't belong. I AM sending FLAMES of FIRE into your SUNSETS and SUNRISES to DISPLAY My FIERY POWER before your eyes. You will now WITNESS KINGDOMS FALL and KINGDOMS RISE; you will WATCH as LEADERS FALL and LEADERS RISE; you will SEE MOUNTAINS FALL and RIVERS CHANGE their COURSE. My MIGHTY POWER will be on DISPLAY before your eyes because I AM coming to RESCUE you and your Land out of the GRIP of darkness and into My Kingdom of LIFE and LIGHT, PEACE and PLENTY. STUDY My POWER, GAZE on My LOVE, and you will FIGHT by My side with CONFIDENCE and BRAVERY. There is no doubt about our VICTORY. The KEEPER OF THE COSMOS is by your side."

For several years, I hosted videos sharing photos sent in by my viewers of the signs and wonders they were being shown in the skies and in their surroundings. Rainbows did begin to appear where no one had seen a rainbow before. Double and even triple rainbows appeared all over the world! The mighty Host of Heaven began to show us they were there in the skies by cloud shapes that revealed their spiritual form. What an exciting time to be alive and to witness the majesty and faithfulness of a good, good Father who was giving us signs and wonders to confirm His words to us!

NOVEMBER 14, 2023: VIOLENTLY SWEPT AWAY

"Your eyes have been OPENED to the DEVASTATION that CHOOSING DARKNESS brings into their nations. They see the FLOODGATES of EVIL being opened throughout the land as people COOPERATE with the darkness through COMPROMISE, IDOLATRY, and SELFISH LIVING. These focuses DULL your spirit's PERCEPTION and DISCERNMENT until righteousness and justice have FALLEN by the wayside. But you, My Remnant, have AWAKENED to My LOVE, My BEAUTY, and My RIGHTEOUSNESS and JUSTICE. You can CLEARLY SEE your world's need for a RESCUE OPERATION and for FOUNDATIONS to be re-established on My Kingdom of LIGHT. The POWER of your AGREEMENT with Me is VERY GREAT ... Because evil became so ENTRENCHED, it must be REMOVED FORCEFULLY. The VIOLENCE and the SUDDENNESS will AWAKEN those still UNDER THE CLOUD of DECEPTION and DENIAL. As darkness and Light CLASH, the earth will respond by SHAKING, SPLITTING OPEN, and VIOLENT STORMS. A RUDE AWAKENING is much better than being lulled into PERMANENT SLAVERY. The areas where darkness has had SEATS of POWER will have the HARDEST SHAKINGS as the clash of war between dark and Light INTENSIFIES. I AM able to KEEP My own no matter where they are. Don't LOSE HEART when you see things VIOLENTLY COLLAPSE because it will CLEAR the WAY for My KINGDOM to be established and My GREAT BLESSINGS to FLOW FREELY to the people of your Land."

MARCH 1, 2024: RUMBLE, RUMBLE, RUMBLE!

"GET READY TO RUMBLE, FORCES OF LIGHT! The darkness is MOUNTING their forces and all their DESTRUCTIVE schemes to come against mankind. Let My BOLDNESS, My COURAGE, and My STRENGTH RUMBLE through your inner being and AWAKEN the WARRIOR in you. DECLARE to the enemy and all his schemes, 'You WILL NOT STAND nor will your plans SUCCEED! The Forces of Light have come to OPPOSE you and to OVERPOWER you in the NAME of the Most High God!' I AM ready to RUMBLE, and you will see My RUMBLINGS go forth into the earth, the sea, and the skies. The response to My RUMBLINGS will be EARTHQUAKES, VOLCANOES, TORNADOES, TSUNAMIS, CRACKS in the ocean floors, and SIGNS in the heavens. My RUMBLINGS will produce SHAKINGS, SHIFTINGS, and REMOVALS of CORRUPT people and things ... RUMBLE, RUMBLE, RUMBLE!"

Eclipses are one of the most observed natural phenomena in the world. The Father used eclipses both as a natural sign and also as a metaphor for how He was going to overcome the darkness with His superior Light. The following word was given several weeks before the total solar eclipse in 2024. It is very interesting to note that a lunar eclipse happened in 2025 on March 13-14th—a year after this word was given.

MARCH 16, 2024: THE ECLIPSE FROM DARK TO LIGHT

"The ECLIPSE on April 8th is a MARKER in time for this BATTLE of DARK to LIGHT over your Nation. The battles being fought in the heavenly realms will now become CLEARLY SEEN BATTLES in the earthly realm. Those who have been ASLEEP to the spiritual battle that has been RAGING will SUDDENLY be CONFRONTED with a DISPLAY of the UNDERBELLY of DARKNESS. Those who partnered with evil think their plans to UNLEASH CHAOS, DEATH, and FEAR will work to their ADVANTAGE and will lead to the people handing over CONTROL to these PUPPET MASTERS. Forces of Light, it is up to you to PARTNER with Me to BRING ABOUT A DIFFERENT OUTCOME. Declare that these dark plans will ONLY SERVE to EXPOSE those who set them in motion. Say, 'I REMOVE the POWER and the DEATH out of these agendas, and I say they will BACKFIRE on the darkness.' Where CHAOS, RIOTING, and PAID FOR DEMONSTRATIONS BREAK OUT, release My PEACE and My PRESENCE to CHANGE the ATMOSPHERE. Declare that My LOVE WILL ECLIPSE ALL THE HATRED that is being released. These are the battles that you have been TRAINING for. Now, PUT ON your ARMOR of LIGHT and RESPOND to My COMMANDS, not to the voices of FEAR and COWERING. Inside of you is the same SPIRIT that BROODED over darkness and chaos and brought forth a BEAUTIFUL earth. It is the very SPIRIT that BREATHED RESURRECTION LIFE into the Son. This is the same POWER that BLEW OPEN the waters of the Red Sea to DELIVER Israel and then to cause them to POUR DOWN on the enemy. DO NOT FEAR the enemy because HE FEARS YOU WARRING AGAINST him in your COVENANT AUTHORITY and HOLY SPIRIT EMPOWERMENT. Rise up Forces of Light. THE ECLIPSE OF DARK TO LIGHT HAS BEGUN."

CHAPTER EIGHT

Heaven's Warfare Strategies

The brilliance of our Mighty Creator and Lord was manifested in the varied warfare strategies employed in the Rescue of the Ages. Let's take a look at some of these awesome plans.

THE FALL OF THE FALL

SEPTEMBER 23, 2018: FALLING

"This day on the calendar marked the beginning of the Fall, and it also marks the beginning of the FALL of those OPERATING in DARKNESS. What has been happening BEHIND CLOSED DOORS to INVESTIGATE and EXPOSE the darkness will now be laid bare in the PUBLIC arena for all eyes to see, and both courts and public opinion will agree on JUSTICE coming to those who have been involved in BREAKING the law and in DEEDS of DEEPEST DARKNESS. FALLING, FALLING, their carefully crafted schemes are FALLING, and they will face JUSTICE for all their deeds and crimes and selfishness. Once the FALL begins, it will proceed RAPIDLY until all is EXPOSED and DEALT with. Look up, REDEMPTION draws near for your Nation, and it will spread WORLDWIDE. The time of ACCOUNTABILITY you have been longing for is here."

AUGUST 26, 2021: THE FALL OF THE FALL

"The darkness can only hold back the TSUNAMI of TRUTH for so long; they can only release a limited amount of attacks meant to bring FEAR, DESTRUCTION, and designed to turn the ATTENTION AWAY from their EVIL and LIES because My Army is DEFLECTING and DIMINISHING these attacks with their AUTHORITY and DECLARATIONS and because I am DRYING UP their resources to pay for these attacks ... This next season will be known as the GREAT FALL of the Fall, and the world will see the EVIL AGENDAS that have ruled it as I pull back the curtain and reveal ALL. These who were STRONG, PROTECTED, and RICH will find themselves STRIPPED of all three, and when they cry out for mercy, they will find none because they gave none. Let the FEAR of My great name sweep the Land as you watch the FALL OF THE FALL. To those who fear My name, it will bring REPENTANCE, CLEANSING, and FREEDOM."

Every time the Father mentioned the "Fall of the Fall," we assumed it would be the current Fall season. However, we came to realize that the "Fall" was His name for the group of arrogant elites and that this whole war season could be characterized as the season of the "Fall."

OCTOBER 30, 2021: THE FALL IS FALLING

"The ARROGANT ones who have partnered with darkness think of themselves as the 'High and Mighty,' but I think of them as the 'FALL' because PRIDE goes before DESTRUCTION and a HAUGHTY spirit before a FALL. These evil plotters and schemers thought of themselves as UNTOUCHABLE and ABOVE any of man's laws. Indeed, they had placed GATEKEEPERS all throughout the JUSTICE system who would STOP any uncovering of their deeds and who would HALT any justice proceedings. However, now they are dealing DIRECTLY with Me, the GOD OF JUSTICE, and they are beginning to FALL. As they FALL, they will set off a DOMINO effect that will bring down all those under them—including their carefully placed gatekeepers. Their arrogance BLINDED them to the fact that I have been setting them all in a row (an intricately formed trap), and when I cause them to FALL, all those beneath them will be FALLING as well. It takes a LONG time to set up an elaborate domino pattern, but it goes down in SECONDS. Your PATIENCE, your PERSISTENCE, and your FAITH will be GREATLY REWARDED. Watch as I display My setup of the FALL IS FALLING."

OCTOBER 10, 2022: STRIPPED BARE

"Do you see the Fall leaves being BLOWN from the trees? Soon, they will be STRIPPED BARE and all their branches will be EXPOSED. This is a picture in the natural of what I AM releasing from the Spiritual Realm. My Host are bringing to earth the EXPOSING WINDS of Heaven. You are seeing leaders FALL here and there, and soon it will be like it's RAINING FALLEN LEADERS as I STRIP them from their positions and I EXPOSE who they really are. Just like a Fall leaf cannot REMAIN on its branch INDEFINITELY, so these darkened leaders will be coming down in the FALL OF THE FALL. You will see them STRIPPED BARE before the world, EXPOSED for all their EVIL DEEDS and PLOTS, and they will meet the JUSTICE I released from Heaven on this earth."

THE HOUSE OF CARDS, DOMINOES, AND CHESS

Both the darkness and the Light were playing to win, and the Father used game metaphors to describe what was playing out on the world stage. We will take a look at the earliest entry where some of these games were mentioned. This post has never been published before. It was in my journal from a date before the Father called me to begin posting on Social Media sites.

JULY 28, 2017: HE HAS HEARD OUR CRIES

"I have HEARD and I AM HEARING THE CRIES of My people for this nation. I AM DISMANTLING the carefully-crafted schemes of the enemy. They look overwhelming and powerful, but they will fall like a HOUSE OF CARDS and like a carefully-placed set of DOMINOES. I AM set to return RIGHTEOUSNESS and ORIGINAL INTENT to your nation, and no power of the enemy or of man can STOP Me. I will faithfully answer your cries for your nation, and I will HONOR your prayers for its leaders in every sphere of society. Do not listen to the ROARING of the people who have been DECEIVED by the enemy and by their PRIDE in thinking they are godlike. Instead, listen to My voice, ask for eyes to see what I AM doing and pray for those in darkness to be ILLUMINED by My light and My love."

OCTOBER 17, 2022: I WILL WIPE THE CHESSBOARD CLEAN

"You have been watching an EXTENDED CHESS MATCH between the DARKNESS and the LIGHT. To the eye of natural man, it will look like the darkness has had the UPPER HAND and that they are CLOSING IN to WIN the match. This is why so many people are ANXIOUS and AFRAID right now. But you have chosen to LISTEN to My VOICE and to LOOK with the eyes of your SPIRIT at what I AM doing behind the scenes. You know that I ALLOWED them to think they were WINNING, all the while, I was SETTING TRAPS for EVERY PIECE on their side of the CHESSBOARD. When My powerful TRUMPET voice cries out, 'CHECKMATE!', you will see My strong right arm come, and I WILL WIPE THE CHESSBOARD CLEAN. None of those who PLOTTED and SCHEMED to STEAL a Nation or those who helped them in their dark plans will be LEFT STANDING ... Wait for the TRUMPET CRY of 'CHECKMATE!' and then watch My arm WIPE THE CHESSBOARD CLEAN!"

OCTOBER 27, 2022: KING OF THE AGES

"I AM the KING OF THE AGES, and I have WALKED the earth in this HARVEST season. I have put My MARK upon those who have chosen to serve the darkness and to further the EVIL AGENDA of the enemy ... What I have MARKED for JUDGMENT will be JUDGED FULLY and will result in JUSTICE for the people. Remember all the pictures I've given you of this RESCUE SEASON: an AVALANCHE, a TSUNAMI, a great SHAKING, a row of DOMINOES, a fallen HOUSE OF CARDS, a FLOOD, an empty CHESSBOARD. One day things will appear to be the same as always, and the next day, everything will be CHANGED ..."

BIBLICAL PATTERNS OF DELIVERANCE: THE RED SEA, GOSHEN, NOAH AND THE ARK, QUEEN ESTHER, LAZARUS, AND THE CROSS

There are many accounts in the Bible of Divine rescues, protection, and resurrections. Some of these supernatural accounts were used by the Father to describe the Rescue of the Ages that He was bringing.

MAY 9, 2022: YOU AIN'T SEEN NOTHING YET!

"Until the waters of the Red Sea came CRASHING down on the soldiers and powerful chariots of Egypt, Pharaoh thought he and his gods were more powerful than Me. He thought I was BLUFFING and that I would never carry through with My PROMISE TO DELIVER Israel out of his hand. His PRIDE and ARROGANCE and DISREGARD for human life made him a SELF-FOCUSED TYRANT, and he did not think he could be brought down. Same enemy FEEDING these same DELUSIONS to the PRIDEFUL TYRANTS of your day. Just like Pharaoh, they think I AM bluffing and that they will be able to LIE and use DARK POWERS to get their way. They have turned their backs to My offers of REPENTANCE and MERCY, and now they will see who I AM in JUDGMENT and JUSTICE. They will be SHOCKED when I arise with SUDDEN VIOLENCE against their wickedness. The violence of the Red Sea was against one nation and one ruler. The evil regime in your day is WORLDWIDE, and so My response will be FAR GREATER than the Red Sea. It will SHAKE the world until evil thrones are TOPPLED and FREEDOM is established. Think about the POWER of the Red Sea and realize—YOU AIN'T SEEN NOTHING YET! I AM your RESCUER and DELIVERER!"

FEBRUARY 8, 2023: RESURRECTION DAY IS COMING

"As EMPIRES TUMBLE, LEADERS FALL, and SYSTEMS FAIL, it is very important that you COMBAT FEAR of the FUTURE or FEAR of DEFEAT by speaking My promise: RESURRECTION DAY IS

COMING! Keep REHEARSING examples of DEATH to LIFE I have laid out in My Word. There is the OPENING and CLOSING of the Red Sea, the CALLING FORTH to LIFE of Lazarus who was dead —really dead for four days—and the ULTIMATE RESURRECTION from death to life EVERMORE of My Son. I can DO IT AGAIN! Are you afraid of LACK? Remember how I FED the nation of Israel in the wilderness, Elijah at the stream when he was hiding from Jezebel, the widows SUPERNATURALLY fed and provided for through Elijah and Elisha, and the FEEDING of the multitudes through My Son's hands. Am I able to PROTECT and PROVIDE for My children when My JUDGMENTS FALL? Think about Noah and his family in the ARK, Israel PROTECTED from My judgments in the land of Goshen, Israel PROTECTED from Egypt and other surrounding enemies in the wilderness, My Son KEPT and PROTECTED as the enemy sought to take His life many times. When My Son died, it was because He GAVE His life away as a RANSOM for many. As shakings come, keep these words in your mouth, 'RESURRECTION DAY IS COMING!'"

MARCH 16, 2023: GIVE ME YOUR TIRED, YOUR POOR ...

I was surprised to hear the Father quote part of the poem inscribed on the base of the Statue of Liberty. Questions have been raised about the statue being based on a false god. However, as I researched the author of the poem on the base of the statue, it seems God's hand was placing seeds of deliverance for our Nation on the questionable statue. The poet's name was Emma LAZARUS;

her parents' names were MOSES and ESTHER LAZARUS. Mind officially blown!

*The Father speaks:

"Seeds of DESTRUCTION and seeds of LIFE were sown into the foundation of your Nation. It is now HARVEST time, for those seeds have reached the MATURE crop stage. Those whose eyes I have OPENED can see the DARK HARVEST of EVIL and TYRANNY and the HARVEST of LIGHT and GLORY that My hand has inspired. My Army of Light has chosen to partner with Me in MOWING DOWN and TRAMPLING the DARK harvest that evil men have planned for centuries, and My Army is joining Me in CALLING FORTH the harvest of LIGHT and GLORY, and they are JOYFULLY bringing in the sheaves. Yes, DARKNESS was sowed into your foundation, but so was My LIGHT, and My LIGHT always OVERCOMES the darkness. The ARROGANT elite thought they were so clever at planting the Nation with DARK SEEDS that the UNDISCERNING GULLIBLY ACCEPTED. In their PRIDE, they DISDAINED the SMALL SEEDS of LIGHT that I planted at the same time. This PRIDE will prove to be their DOWNFALL. They always UNDERESTIMATE the POWER of My GOODNESS. I AM going to INFUSE these words, 'Give me your tired, your poor,' with My RESURRECTION POWER, and this Nation will be brought through the Red Sea (Moses), resurrected from death (Lazarus), secure the defeat of those who tried to destroy you, and take your place ruling and reigning by My side (Esther). REJOICE that My HARVEST of LIGHT is coming to OVERPOWER the dark harvest."

TRAPS, WINDS OF CHANGE

Some of these entries speaks of the traps of the evil empire, but most of the words revolve around traps that the Father was setting for the enemy to be captured.

APRIL 29, 2020: CLEAN SWEEP

"My broom is poised over your Nation, and at just the right time, it will touch the earth and sweep out all the darkness and filth. It will begin with the leaders, and then it will move out among the people, sweeping away the ugly traps these evil rulers unleashed by their alliances with darkness. My powerful broom will sweep away pornography, human trafficking, drug abuse, idolatry, and occult fascination and worship. What do you do before you sweep? YOU TURN ON THE LIGHTS! I am turning a huge searchlight on your Land, and it will expose all darkness. People will be forced to see darkness in their leaders and darkness in themselves. Then My broom will accomplish a clean sweep—those who repent will receive mercy and a place in My Kingdom. Those who do not will receive My justice, and they will be forced to carry the weight of their wickedness. Allow My searchlight on your own heart now to show you any areas of darkness. Repent of these areas, let the blood of My Son cover them, and welcome My Holy Spirit to transform them into areas of LIGHT and STRENGTH. My clean sweep is coming."

November 26, 2021: The Rat Trap

"I have set up an elaborate, worldwide RAT TRAP and in the coming months, you will see many rats all over the world CAUGHT in this well-laid TRAP. Those rats were all given opportunities to repent and to come into the LIGHT, but they chose to remain partnered with DARKNESS, and now the darkness will be their PORTION as they face JUDGMENT, JUSTICE, and some DEATH. Weep that they have chosen to remain in darkness and to live outside My LOVE and LIGHT, but do not give them UNSANCTIFIED MERCY—that is giving mercy where I AM bringing judgment. Even in My judgment, as they suffer the consequences of their choices, there will yet be an opportunity to repent and come to Me for forgiveness. It would be a GREAT VICTORY against the darkness if those heavily partnered with it became BORN AGAIN and came into the Light. They will still receive judgment and justice for their RAT-LIKE behavior, but My GRACE and COMFORT will see them through, and light will TRIUMPH over the darkness in their lives. I AM declaring to you that My RAT TRAPS are set and that JUSTICE is coming."

May 28, 2022: Taken to the War Room of Heaven

My lookout guardian Angel invites me to visit the War Room of Heaven, and I take his hand, and we're off flying through the sky above earth's atmosphere where dark skies and shining stars streak by. A little breathless, I arrive at the door of the War Room. I'm so aware of the intense battle we are waging for our Nation right now that the mood in the War Room catches me off guard. It is an atmosphere of relaxed conversation, smiling faces, and in front of each Elder is a piece of cake! No one is eating yet; they are patiently waiting for a signal to begin the celebration in earnest.

*The Father speaks: "You may be surprised to see Heaven's Council so relaxed and smiling when all on earth seems CHAOS and threatened DESTRUCTION. I wanted to bring you up here to give you HEAVEN'S VIEW of this war in order to STRENGTHEN your FAITH and HOPE in My POWER and My PROMISES. The enemy is well known for his WEBS of DECEPTION and LIES that he entraps people in to defeat their faith and obscure My voice. While the enemy and those partnered with him were planning your DEFEAT, I was quietly behind the scenes, setting up an INTRICATE TRAP for every SCHEME and every PERSON involved in darkness. This INCREDIBLE TRAP will SPRING all at once and will EXPOSE their DARKENED HEARTS and their EVIL SCHEMES. There will be a LOUD TRUMPET in the heavens when My TRAP springs SHUT, and heavenly and earthly THRONES will come CRASHING DOWN. Heaven can REST because they know all that is left is for the TRAP to be SPRUNG, and My finger is POISED to do that. This is as sure as pushing the first domino in the set-up will cause ALL the dominoes to fall."

JULY 16, 2022: LIKE A STEEL VISE TRAP

"I want you to know that when I set a TRAP, there will be NO ESCAPE from it. My TRAPS are like STEEL VISES, and when they are clamped tight, NOTHING can get free. The ones partnered with darkness are so focused on themselves and on launching their DESTRUCTIVE schemes that they did not notice they were standing in the OPEN JAWS of My STEEL VISE TRAP. As they frantically launch every effort to defeat you, I have been QUIETLY CLOSING the JAWS of the TRAP. Quite suddenly, they will feel the steel close in on them, and NOTHING they try will get them out of My STEEL VISE TRAP. None of their old ways of escaping judgement and justice will work—no MURDERS for hire, no CROOKED JUDGES, no SLICK ATTORNEYS, no LYING MEDIA will free them from My STEEL VISE of JUDGMENT and JUSTICE. Take heart, My Army of Light; they are not going to WIGGLE OUT of this one ... no one escapes My STEEL VISE TRAP. The day of RECKONING is here."

It was the Father's wisdom and skill that set these traps for the wicked, but He did call us to partner with Him in becoming part of the trap that was closing in on the wicked.

JULY 20, 2022: ROUND 'EM UP!

"'ROUND 'EM UP!', declares the Most High Sheriff of heaven and earth. 'It's ROUNDUP TIME!', decrees your God. I laid traps that your enemies, in their GREED and in their ARROGANCE, walked right into. They did not notice that they had entered a large CORRAL, but I have continued to PUSH them into smaller and smaller ENCLOSURES, and some of the wicked have SUDDENLY REALIZED they are NOT in control and that they are SURROUNDED. I AM in the process of moving them into smaller and smaller PENS where I have SHACKLED them (in the shackles they meant for you), and there is NO WAY of

ESCAPE. For some of the evil ones, these pens will become PRISON BARS, and for some their place of DEATH. This may seem harsh, but you must understand that they are REAPING what they have SOWN—this is the result of their choices to partner with DARKNESS and GREED instead of trusting My LIGHT and My GOODNESS. Do you know what the CORRAL and PEN FENCES are made of? They are made of My FIRE, My HOST, and My ARMY OF LIGHT. When you PARTNER with Me and ALIGN yourself with My purposes, you become part of the FENCE that keeps narrowing in on the enemy. Your FAITH-FILLED decrees and declarations place you in the GAP, and it DRAWS the HOST to surround you and to strengthen you. Keep PRESSING in, My Wranglers; it's time to ROUND 'EM UP!"

This one is particularly satisfying!

AUGUST 16, 2022: TRAPPED

"The ARROGANT ones LAUGH behind closed doors as they plot DEATH and DESTRUCTION for you and your Nation. They have NO REGARD for anyone's life except their own. Their UNITY was built on their PRIDE in being the 'ELITE' and on their GOAL of gaining CONTROL over you and the earth's resources. In their HASTE to reach their goal of WORLD DOMINANCE, they did not realize they were RUSHING HEADLONG into My TRAP. When they SUDDENLY hear the TRAP snap shut, their 'UNITY' will be shattered, and the RATS will turn on each other to save themselves. You will see them BITE and DEVOUR each other in their FRANTIC QUEST to save their LIVES and their FORTUNES. Those who portrayed themselves as NOBLE,

GOOD, and TOLERANT will be EXPOSED and HIGHLIGHTED for who they really are—GREEDY, GRASPING, LYING pawns of a puffed-up enemy. The TRAPS they laid for you will become the TRAP that catches them, and there will be NO ESCAPE. Let this PICTURE of the darkness being TRAPPED carry you through these FINAL DAYS of the GREAT BATTLE over your Nation. My Army of Light, PUT AWAY criticism of and strife with your brothers and sisters, as those are TACTICS sown by the enemy to WEAKEN your ranks. I'm giving you this STRONG PICTURE of your enemies being TRAPPED so that you will not fall prey to the WEARINESS, the DEPRESSION, or the DOUBT the enemy is sending against you. Place yourself FIRMLY by My side with the SPIRITUAL WEAPONS I have given you and your SHIELD OF FAITH protecting your heart. Watch, as your enemy is TRAPPED."

OCTOBER 4, 2024: THE PIT IS GETTING DEEPER

PSALM 9:15-16 (TPT) *"For the nations get trapped in the very snares they set for others. The hidden trap they set for the weak has snapped shut upon themselves! Yahweh is famous for His justice. While the wicked are digging a pit for others, they are actually setting the terms for their own judgment. They will fall into their own pit."*

"THE PIT IS GETTING DEEPER that the wicked have dug for the DESTRUCTION of anything GOOD or anything RIGHTEOUS. They are FRANTIC to cause great DESTRUCTION and great FEAR. In their haste to take back CONTROL, the SCHEMES they use and their HIDDEN MOTIVES are being RAPIDLY

UNCOVERED. The darkness is ANGRY that people are not GIVING UP and COWERING in FEAR, but instead they are PULLING TOGETHER and PLANNING to REBUILD. Every evil, destructive scheme they release is DIGGING THE PIT DEEPER FOR THEM TO FALL INTO. In the end, you will see them SUDDENLY FALL to their DESTRUCTION into the DEEP PIT they dug for you. They will have NO HOPE of ESCAPE or RESCUE. I have PROMISED to RESCUE you out of ALL their PITS, NETS, and TRAPS, and you will see them CAUGHT in their own NETS and TRAPS and THROWN into the PIT THEY DUG FOR YOU. CALL OUT for those who were DECEIVED by the darkness into their NETS and TRAPS of STOLEN IDENTITIES and ADDICTIONS—CALL OUT for their RESCUE and DELIVERANCE, and DECLARE that the NETS and TRAPS would COME BACK on the darkness. Don't be fearful of the DEEP PIT DIGGERS because their TIME IS SHORT, and the PIT they dug is OPENING ITS MOUTH WIDE to receive them. I will be faithful to RESTORE LOSS and DAMAGE BEYOND what you can think or imagine, and the DEEP PIT DIGGERS will see all they tried to DESTROY THRIVE and be BEAUTIFUL AGAIN. Continue to PUSH BACK on their DEEP PIT SCHEMES and know that when they FALL in the PIT that they dug for you, they will LOSE EVERYTHING, and you will GAIN EVERYTHING. I AM JUSTICE, and you will see it DISPLAYED in the earth."

Filled with promise and power, this word speaks of the worldwide traps and a sudden rescue.

DECEMBER 6, 2024: POWER, MIGHT, AND MAJESTY

"You will SEE with your own eyes, and there will be NO DOUBT that I AM God when I show up in POWER, MIGHT, AND MAJESTY to RESCUE your Nation out of the GREEDY CLUTCHES of the DEEP DARKNESS. The rescue of your Nation will TRIGGER RESCUES of nations around the world. As the HUGE TRAP I have set for those partnered with darkness SPRINGS SHUT in your Nation, it will TRIGGER the SPRINGING of My TRAPS that have been set all around the world. Just like a row of DOMINOES falls, those partnered with EVIL, GREED, and CORRUPTION will FALL, one after another. The world will go to bed one way and AWAKEN the next to a day of RESCUE and LIGHT as I move in POWER, MIGHT, AND MAJESTY to CRUSH the darkness that tried to RULE My world. Army of Light, you have been POWERFUL in OPPOSING and EXPOSING the darkness, and you will see Me respond to your prayers, decrees, and declarations with My POWER, MIGHT, AND MAJESTY. The world will respond with SHOCK and AWE, and all will say, 'GREAT IS OUR GOD!' The REWARDS of your faith and your faithfulness will be GREAT."

WINDS OF CHANGE

The Winds of Change were from the Holy Spirit and often directed through His Angels.

June 18, 2022: Stir Up, Stir Up!

"Let these words be on your lips, 'STIR UP, STIR UP, oh WINDS of GOD!' Then send these SPIRIT WINDS to accomplish My will and to carry out My plans:

*STIR UP the camp of the enemy with STRIFE, PANIC, SUSPICION, and CONFUSION.

*STIR UP the Army of Light with RENEWED VISION for VICTORY and STRENGTH to finish well.

*STIR UP the Host of Heaven to FULFILL their orders with complete FIERCENESS and BRILLIANT LIGHT to MOW DOWN the forces of darkness.

*STIR UP the Court of Heaven to begin RELEASING their GUILTY VERDICTS into the earth where they will MANIFEST in the courts on the earth.

*STIR UP the UNCOVERING WINDS that will reveal HIDDEN DOCUMENTS and SECRET MEETINGS where great evil was planned.

*STIR UP the winds that will BLOW AWAY the spirit of DELUSION that has BLINDED the masses.

*STIR UP the winds of PASSION in people's hearts to KNOW Me and the POWER of My Kingdom.

*STIR UP the WINDS OF CHANGE to usher in a brand-new day of LIFE, PEACE, and RIGHTEOUSNESS. STIR UP, STIR UP, Oh WINDS of GOD!"

APRIL 21, 2023: THE ANSWER IS BLOWING IN THE WIND

The night before I heard this word from the Father, this folk song from the '60's by Bob Dylan began going through my head. I looked up the lyrics and found it was a cry to mankind to stop war and bring freedom to all men. This song was sung at the event where Dr. Martin Luther King, Jr. delivered his famous speech, "I Have a Dream."

The Father shared:

"This song is about to come FULL CIRCLE in your day. As DEEP DARKNESS and DEATH AGENDAS are EXPOSED, people will be CRYING OUT for ANSWERS. I AM telling you that the ANSWER to all DEATH schemes and agendas to STEAL IDENTITIES, WEALTH, and HEALTH are going to be found BLOWING IN THE WIND. This WIND is the WIND OF MY SPIRIT BLOWING AWAY INJUSTICE and CORRUPTION and BLOWING IN CLEANSING, FREEDOM, and GREAT CHANGE. My Remnant, My Army of Light are AWAKENED to the deep darkness, and they know that I AM the ONLY One who can RESCUE and BRING LASTING CHANGE. You have been given eyes to SEE My Kingdom, and you have been PREPARED to HELP BRING My Kingdom in ALL ITS GLORY and POWER to ALL areas of society. My SPIRIT WIND WILL BLOW through you with KINGDOM POWER to TRANSFORM the world around you. Every act of LOVE, OBEDIENCE, ENCOURAGEMENT, GIVING, RELEASING HEALING, will result in My Kingdom EXPANDING. This is not 'Church' activity; it is the WAY YOU LIVE YOUR LIFE. The world is looking for answers, and you have the ANSWERS and the

POWER to bring CHANGE as you YIELD to My Spirit winds. THE ANSWER IS BLOWING IN THE WIND."

JULY 16, 2023: STIRRINGS AND WHISPERINGS IN THE WINDS

I was walking in Heaven with the Father on one of my favorite forest paths. Suddenly, a breeze sprang up and began swirling around us, and I could feel a stirring and hear whispering voices in the wind.

"A SUDDEN wind is moving through the trees. This is both a SPIRITUAL WIND and a WIND you will SEE in the NATURAL. PAY ATTENTION when a SUDDEN BREEZE SPRINGS UP—I AM sending you WHISPERINGS of things TO COME so that you are prepared and so that you know it is TIME to WORSHIP and EXALT Me. What is the wind WHISPERING? What are those voices COMMUNICATING to you? Here are some of the WHISPERINGS: 'CHANGE, CHANGE, winds of CHANGE are blowing.' 'CRASHING, CRASHING, Babylon's systems are CRASHING.' 'FALLING, FALLING, ancient THRONES of EVIL are FALLING.' 'GONE, GONE, the EVIL is SWEPT AWAY in a POWERFUL GUST of the WIND of God.' CHAOS and DARKNESS for the WICKED, but LIGHT and PEACE for those in Goshen.' 'OVERPOWER, OVERPOWER, the SCHEMES of DARKNESS by your WHOLEHEARTED PRAISE!' 'NEW DAY, NEW DAY, a new day is DAWNING.' 'LOOK UP and REJOICE, your RESCUE DRAWS NEAR.' As you feel the STIRRINGS in the wind and hear these WHISPERS, DECLARE them back into the atmosphere as ARROWS of TRUTH. SING them out as VANQUISHING WARRIORS, and see them UNFOLD before you. WORSHIP Me as

EVIL SYSTEMS CRASH, and EXALT Me as you see the NEW DAY DAWN. Pay attention to the STIRRINGS AND WHISPERINGS IN THE WINDS."

FEBRUARY 28, 2024: THE WINDS OF CHANGE ARE BLOWING

"THE WINDS OF CHANGE ARE BLOWING, and they are blowing in the PROMISED SEASON OF DELIVERANCE. Some of these WINDS OF CHANGE will be quite STRONG, and they will leave what LOOKS LIKE a path of DESTRUCTION. However, what BLOWS OVER in this season NEEDS to COME DOWN and to be RE-ESTABLISHED on RIGHTEOUS and TRUE FOUNDATIONS. The enemy is trying to BLOW in their STORM of DEATH and DESTRUCTION in a desperate attempt to TAKE BACK CONTROL. Ask Me for DISCERNMENT to know if this is MY WIND or if this is an ENEMY STORM. CALL FORTH MY WINDS OF CHANGE, and PUSH BACK and BREAK APART the ENEMY'S STORMS. Be in AWE of My WINDS OF CHANGE, and use your AUTHORITY to DEFEAT and DEFANG the enemy's STORMS. You have the most BRILLIANT COUNSELOR to walk you through this season of THE WINDS OF CHANGE. Because this is an UNPRECEDENTED season, and because all the systems you have RELIED on must be BROUGHT DOWN, you must RELY on the Spirit's WISDOM WAYS and His COUNSEL to see you through the DRASTIC CHANGES on the horizon. MOVE IN THE PEACE THAT HE GIVES TO YOU, and DO NOT make decisions BASED ON FEAR OF LOSS. Living in the UNFORCED RHYTHMS OF GRACE means you NEVER make a decision from FEAR OF

LOSS, or from ANXIETY, or from PRESSURE by people to follow their advice ... I want to be your ADVISOR, your PROVIDER, and your PEACE. Come to Me, lean on Me, and I will move you through THE WINDS OF CHANGE with GREAT GRACE and PEACE. This is your HERITAGE as a COVENANT Son or Daughter of the Most High King. Tell the STORM of FEAR and UNCERTAINTY in your heart to BE STILL AND KNOW THAT I AM GOD."

CHAPTER NINE

Whack-A-Mole and Other Unusual Tactics of War

From serious to humorous, the Father unfolded unusual tactics of war. While He was deadly serious about winning the war against the evil empire, He reminded us that He laughs at His enemies. Psalm 2:1, 4 (TPT) says, *"How dare the nations plan a rebellion. Their foolish plots are futile! ... God-Enthroned merely laughs at them; the Sovereign One mocks their madness!"* Following are both serious entries and entries with humor in them.

ANGEL OF DEATH, BOOMERANGS, AND BATTERING RAMS

The seriousness of the hour was highlighted by the Father mentioning the Angel of Death.

FEBRUARY 26, 2022: TARGETED FOR REMOVAL

"I want to share with you, as My friend, that I have MARKED many rulers and influential people around the earth for REMOVAL. I have placed My TARGET on them, and they are now OPEN GAME to be HUNTED, CAPTURED, and some completely DESTROYED by the Angel of death. Does this seem harsh to you? Remember that My MERCY far outweighs yours, and know that I have given these corrupt people opportunity after opportunity to REPENT and turn to Me, but they have REFUSED My love and HARDENED their hearts towards seeking to CONTROL and USE you for their gain and their selfish pleasures. I will ARISE to PROTECT and DEFEND My children and My people, and I will RIP the stolen wealth out of the hands of the wicked and RETURN it to My people. My people will be BLESSED with abundance, and they will be a blessing to the broken world. Most of the corrupt will become aware that a TARGET has been put on them, and they will begin to PANIC as they FRANTICALLY look for someplace to HIDE and they SCRAMBLE for additional resources to try and PROTECT themselves and their wealth. NONE OF IT WILL WORK. The MARK that I place on a man cannot be REMOVED, and they will be EXPOSED and brought to JUSTICE. Know that you are MARKED by Me with My PASSIONATE and FIERY LOVE, and it marks you for FULFILLMENT and BLESSING. You will RISE, and the darkness will FALL because I have TARGETED IT FOR REMOVAL."

APRIL 5, 2023: APPLY THE BLOOD

"The BLOOD of a spotless lamb applied to the doorways of the children of Israel's homes saved them when the DEATH ANGEL of My JUDGMENT PASSED OVER the land. This is another season of HARVEST and RECKONING—this time it is a WORLDWIDE move of the death angel. He is being released against the STUBBORN, ARROGANT ones who have REFUSED to let MY PEOPLE GO from SLAVERY and into the FREEDOM I created them to live in. These PROUD, HARD-HEARTED ones will come FACE TO FACE with My JUDGMENT released through My ANGEL OF DEATH. They will be STRIPPED of all their WEALTH and their POWER, and some will LOSE their lives. Because you have received the BLOOD of the FINAL and PERFECT PASSOVER LAMB, My Son, your life is FOREVER MARKED with His SAVING, PRESERVING, DELIVERING, HEALING, and PROVIDING sacrificial BLOOD. This may be hard to wrap your mind around that you really are going to see My DEATH ANGEL released to SAVE My people and My Nation, but I assure you IT IS GOING TO HAPPEN. As an act of FAITH (not out of FEAR or PANIC), I want you to APPLY THE BLOOD over your life, your family's lives, and over your homes and all that you have been called to steward. The PASSOVER BLOOD will PROTECT and DEFEND you. The BLOOD is forever over your lives, but I want you to ACTIVATE it in this PASSOVER SEASON so that all I have ENTRUSTED to you will be PRESERVED and PROSPERED. The BLOOD of My Son, the PASSOVER LAMB, is the MOST POWERFUL FORCE in the Universe, and it is yours to apply. APPLY THE BLOOD."

JULY 1, 2023: EXPLOSIONS, IMPLOSIONS, DEMOTIONS

"As July HEATS UP, expect to see more EXPLOSIONS of TRUTH, witness more IMPLOSIONS in the ranks of the wicked, and observe a string of DEMOTIONS to continue to happen. Oh, the darkness still has some BIG CARDS to play to try and SCARE the people into SUBMISSION. These are DARK and DESPERATE schemes of GREAT WICKEDNESS meant to STEAL, KILL, and DESTROY. Your assignment is to DISEMPOWER these schemes. In other words, I want you to use your AUTHORITY to REMOVE the DEATH, the STING (poison), and the DARK POWER behind these plans. Declare these will be CUT OFF and OVERPOWERED by the LIGHT within you. I will ALLOW these plans to go forward because these are the FINAL STEPS into the JAWS of My TRAP and because many people still need to be AWAKENED to the darkness that has STOLEN and CHEATED its way into POWER. Some of the IMPLOSIONS in the ranks of the darkness will come about because COMPROMISED, BLACKMAILED ones will come to realize they are going to be EXPOSED and LOSE everything. They will CONFESS and THROW themselves on My MERCY. Their CONFESSION will further UNCOVER the DEEP WEB of LIES and DARKNESS spun by the ARROGANT LIARS and CHEATERS. The darkness will SHUDDER when they realize their IRON GRIP on people is being BROKEN by their victims saying, 'Enough!' of being CONTROLLED by FEAR. A STRONG DESIRE to have a CLEAN CONSCIENCE will OVERPOWER their FEAR of EXPOSURE. The enemy always UNDERESTIMATES the POWER of My LOVE to TOUCH and CHANGE hearts. Pray for those you know to be COMPROMISED that they will FEEL My LOVE and be given the COURAGE to COME CLEAN. You will see many be DEMOTED from their positions of power by EXPOSURES and by the ANGEL OF DEATH being LOOSED on the earth to REMOVE those steadfastly committed to promoting their DARK agendas—especially those against the CHILDREN. Through it all, My Army of Light, remain STEADFAST in My PROMISES, My POWER, and My JUSTICE being displayed on the earth."

Boomerangs were a constant theme throughout this war of Dark to Light. It was a prophetic picture of all the evil being sent against us, returning back to those who sent the dark and deadly schemes—it was a boomerang of sowing and reaping.

MARCH 5, 2022: HOPE DAY—I AM YOUR STRONG SAVIOR

"I AM your STRONG SAVIOR! I see what the enemies of your Nation and your RIGHTFUL President are doing. I AM well aware of every LYING SCHEME and every DESTRUCTIVE PLOT they have contrived; but know this: I have SET THEM UP—in their ARROGANCE they have failed to see they are walking into MY TRAP. All their LIES will be EXPOSED as their plans for your destruction BOOMERANG back into their camp and BLOW UP in their faces. You, My Light-Bearers, represent Me on the earth. When they LIED to you and about you, when they MOCKED My prophets, when they SMEARED My chosen leaders, when they STOLE finances and ENSLAVED you, they were not just attacking you—they were attacking Me. Their window to repent has CLOSED, and My right arm of POWER is now bared, and they will receive the CRUSHING BLOW of My judgment and justice. I have spoken, and I will arise as your STRONG SAVIOR."

JULY 27, 2023: REMEMBER THIS: WHEN IT LOOKS LIKE THEY ARE WINNING, THEY ARE ACTUALLY LOSING

"Your enemies may begin to CROW with DELIGHT thinking their lawsuits against your rightful leader are SUCCEEDING and that his FALL is imminent. I want you to REMEMBER THIS: WHEN IT LOOKS LIKE THEY ARE WINNING, THEY ARE ACTUALLY LOSING. They are FOCUSED on the TRAP they have laid for My CHOSEN LEADER. Their ARROGANCE has BLINDED them to the fact that all their ACCUSATIONS against your rightful leader are things THEY HAVE DONE; and SUDDENLY, all these accusations will BOOMERANG back onto them. They have walked into My HUGE BEAR TRAP, and EVERYTHING and MORE that they accused My chosen leader of will COME BACK on them with a VENGEANCE. SNAP! Goes the TRAP that I QUIETLY LAID behind the scenes, and the darkness will find itself CRUSHED in its JAWS. The DOWNFALL they planned for My leader and for you will become THEIR DOWNFALL— complete EXPOSURE, Leviathan media REVEALED as one BIG LIE, and all that was STOLEN will be UNCOVERED and

RETURNED. Don't CAVE IN to FEAR and ANXIETY when it looks like they are winning. Remember that My TRAP is BIGGER than their trap, and My trap SNAPPING SHUT on them will be a HUGE SHOCK and SURPRISE to the darkness. Continue to UPHOLD TRUTH and LIGHT; release My GLORY into LIES, CHAOS, and FEAR; declare 'YOU LOSE, WE WIN!' REMEMBER THAT WHEN IT LOOKS LIKE THEY ARE WINNING, THEY ARE ACTUALLY LOSING."

JUNE 18, 2024: WINDS OF CHANGE, TSUNAMIS, AND BOOMERANGS

"A season of CONVERGENCE is unfolding before you as I work out My Rescue Operation. You will see the WINDS OF CHANGE blowing in the natural, and you will feel them in the Spirit realm. These winds are SHIFTING the ATMOSPHERE by BLOWING OUT darkness and RELEASING the Light and the FREQUENCIES of Heaven. This makes a way for the TSUNAMIS of TRUTH to FLOOD the Land, and you will see EXPOSURE after EXPOSURE that NOTHING CAN STOP and the LYING media will not be able to SPIN. As the atmosphere SHIFTS and the TRUTH FLOODS in, all the dark schemes and agendas will BOOMERANG back onto those partnered with EVIL. This three-pronged STRATEGY of the Rescue Operation is UNSTOPPABLE because My POWER and your DECREES and DECLARATIONS are calling forth My powerful WINDS OF CHANGE, the flood of TSUNAMIS of TRUTH, and the BOOMERANGS of EVIL SCHEMES BACK into the camp of the darkness. Do not fret if it LOOKS LIKE the darkness is

SUCCEEDING in their evil plots. I AM ALLOWING them to position themselves to be OUT IN THE OPEN in an IDEAL PLACE to be taken SUDDENLY DOWN by the CONVERGENCE of the WINDS OF CHANGE, THE TSUNAMIS OF TRUTH, and the BOOMERANGS OF JUDGMENT AND JUSTICE."

AUGUST 27, 2024: FOOLHARDY DECISIONS

Foolhardy: unthinking recklessness with disregard for danger.

"The enemy camp has spent years ASSESSING the MINDSETS of the people. They have STRATEGICALLY LAUNCHED LIES and DISINFORMATION that have convinced people to GIVE UP their RIGHTS and FREEDOMS in order to be 'protected.' Of course, the IRONY is that those who proclaim they want to 'protect' you are the VERY ONES trying to DESTROY you. It is time for My Army of Light to become STRATEGIC. The time is RIPE for you to ASSESS the TEMPERATURE of the enemy's camp. Where once they were FOCUSED and UNIFIED in their purpose to SUBJUGATE and CONTROL the masses, they have become DOUBLE-MINDED. One minute their ARROGANT PRIDE asserts itself, and they are sure their DARK, DESTRUCTIVE SCHEMES will bring you under their CONTROL. The next, they realize that everything around them is SHAKING and THREATENING to PULL APART at the seams. What they fear most—THEIR EXPOSURE—is BREATHING DOWN their necks and THREATENING to DESTROY their GREEDY, SELF-FOCUSED LIVES. Now, it is TIME for you to SOW FOOLHARDY DECISIONS into the camp of the enemy. Ask My Host to make the BAIT of FOOLHARDY DECISIONS IRRESISTIBLE to the CONFLICTED

DARKNESS. Ask My Angels to WHISPER SUGGESTIONS into the enemy's camp that make FOOLHARDY DECISIONS very APPEALING. Send ARROWS of FEAR of the FUTURE, FEAR of FAILURE, FEAR of LOSS into the enemy's camp. These are the ARROWS they shot at you, but you are sending these ARROWS as BOOMERANGS back into their camp. RISING FEAR will set the stage for FOOLHARDY DECISIONS that will result in their COMPLETE EXPOSURE and DOWNFALL. This is your STRATEGIC WEAPON to LAUNCH into the enemy's camp: FOOLHARDY DECISIONS."

BATTERING RAMS

Battering rams may not be high technology, but they can be very effective at opening locked or barred doors!

APRIL 26, 2022: THE BATTERING RAM

I saw a battering ram—a HUGE log cranked back as far as it would go—suspended, waiting to be released. I heard the Father say:

"My BATTERING RAM is hoisted, and it is ready to be DEPLOYED. When it strikes, it will BRING DOWN THE WHOLE EVIL EMPIRE crashing to the ground that the enemy worked so long to construct through the DARKENED hearts of men. It will turn it to RUBBLE, and all that is HIDDEN will be EXPOSED in the LIGHT of My TRUTH. This BATTERING RAM is composed of many WHISTLEBLOWERS whose testimonies I have been saving up and HIDING from the enemy. The enemy felt safe—

thinking they'd been SILENCED through threats or by the LYING MEDIA covering up their stories. The BATTERING RAM will come as a SURPRISE to those in darkness because I have BLINDED them to what I have been building behind their backs. My BATTERING RAM will not miss! It will hit DEAD CENTER to do MAXIMUM DAMAGE, and you will see leaders all over the world come FLYING DOWN. Even HIDDEN PUPPET MASTERS will be EXPOSED and brought DOWN. The reign of darkness is DONE, and My REIGN OF LIFE AND LIGHT will begin to expand all over the earth. Call for My BATTERING RAM to be released at just the right moment. Pray COURAGE, SAFETY, and ALIGNMENT for My WHISTLEBLOWERS. Just to let My Army of Light know—there is also a SECRET ingredient in My BATTERING RAM that no one else knows about. Kaboom!"

We will re-visit this journal entry about "The Battering Ram" in a later chapter to explain an astonishing confirmation.

NOVEMBER 17, 2022: AN ALL-OUT WAR AGAINST LEVIATHAN

"The MAJOR REASON so many people are still ASLEEP to the DEEP DARKNESS that THREATENS this Nation's survival is the LYING VOICE of the LEVIATHAN MEDIA. This stronghold TWISTS THE TRUTH and declares that GOOD IS EVIL and that EVIL IS GOOD. This stronghold has taken DEEP ROOT in your Land because so many people (including many churches) no longer VALUE the WORD OF GOD, nor do they SEEK Me, the SOURCE OF TRUTH. This has left them OPEN to this DECEIVING, MESMERIZING stronghold of darkness that has

CAST A SHADOW over your Nation that has BLOCKED people from SEEING and HEARING the TRUTH. Will you join Me in a LIGHT-FILLED, POWERFUL, OFFENSIVE PUSH that will WEAKEN and BRING DOWN this BLINDNESS that keeps so many in BONDAGE? Partner with Me, and we will mount A WORLDWIDE WAR AGAINST LEVIATHAN. I want you to get AGGRESSIVE in your WARFARE against this MIND-NUMBING SPIRIT. COMMAND that every LIE Leviathan speaks will be TURNED BACK into their camp. Send forth BATTERING RAM Angels to BREAK OPEN the fortresses of this BOASTING, ARROGANT voice. SEND the Host to SHINE MY LIGHT OF EXPOSURE on all their LIES, BRIBERY, and CORRUPTION. SEND forth those who carry My Spirit of Truth to REPLACE the lies with what is TRUE. SEND forth UNCOVERING and DELIVERING Angels to REMOVE BLINDERS from peoples' eyes and to OPEN THEIR EARS to hear My truth. I AM coming with a SUDDEN REVEAL that will bring SHOCKING TRUTH TO THE LIGHT, and people will be CONFRONTED with the truth. This REVEAL will be more effective if My Army of Light and My Host have MAJORLY WEAKENED the stronghold of Leviathan by your OFFENSIVE move against this stronghold. LET'S GO! Let the Spirit of Truth and the Kingdom of God PREVAIL!"

HUMOROUS AND QUIRKY

Even in the midst of confronting deep darkness and being exposed to their evil schemes and death agendas, the Father wove His amazing sense of humor throughout the serious war strategies. Laughter is the best medicine, and the joy of the Lord is our strength. His ability to laugh at His enemies kept us from losing our joy, renewed our faith in His promises, and awakened hope within us once again.

HUMOROUS

WHACK-A-MOLE

NOVEMBER 27, 2022: A GIANT GAME OF WHACK-A-MOLE

"The enemy's camp knows that this is 'MAKE IT OR BREAK IT TIME.' Either they establish their CONTROL NOW, or their plans will be PUSHED BACK a hundred years or more. Therefore, I want you to know that they have lined up a SERIES of VERY EVIL SCHEMES to bring about DEATH, DESTRUCTION, and GREAT FEAR with the ultimate goal of their DOMINATION of the world. As these schemes begin to POP UP, you may feel like you are playing A GIANT GAME OF WHACK-A-MOLE. Do not let this DISCOURAGE or DISMAY you, because this INTENSE SEASON won't last much longer, and I have given you a DIVINELY POWERFUL HAMMER to beat down every scheme that raises its head. Do not allow the enemy to make you feel OVERWHELMED or INTIMIDATED by the multitude of evil plans. Instead, TURN your face to Mine and feel My STRENGTH filling you up with POWER and LIGHT. Every time you WHACK-A-MOLE with your powerful hammer, sparks of LIGHT fly off and release LIGHT into the darkness. The BLOW you strike directly on the enemy plan will cause that plan to go RIGHT BACK ONTO THOSE who sent it. As long as your FAITH REMAINS in Me and My promises, and as long as you keep coming to Me to be STRENGTHENED, you will be a

142

FORMIDABLE WHACK-A-MOLE player who SMASHES the enemy's schemes BACK into their camp. HAMMERS READY, Army of Light? LET'S GO!"

POP GOES THE WEASEL

JUNE 4, 2023: POP GOES THE WEASEL!

"Ahhh ... look! The RATS are turning into WEASELS! Frantic to SAVE themselves, the RATS are seeing that behind the scenes their GRANDIOSE schemes to RULE OVER you are DISINTEGRATING. Their PROTECTIONS are being TAKEN DOWN, and soon NOTHING will stop the FLOOD of EXPOSURES of all their EVIL, PERVERSION, AND CORRUPTION. The very SELFISHNESS and GREED that brought them together in a UNIFIED PURPOSE to KILL, STEAL, and DESTROY you will now TEAR them APART as SAVING themselves becomes their ONLY GOAL. RATS turned into WEASELS are NOT to be trusted, but their TESTIMONY AGAINST the other RATS can be very USEFUL in CONVINCING the STILL ASLEEP that all is NOT as the LYING MEDIA portrayed it. WEASELS are facing a CRISIS in their lives, and your INTERCESSION will turn some of their HEARTS and LIVES to Me. From RATS to WEASELS to My SON or DAUGHTER—now that's a TRANSFORMATION! Pray PROTECTION over the WEASELS as they provide FIRSTHAND testimony of the DARK and DEPRAVED lives that the RATS have been living. These WEASEL TESTIMONIES will VALIDATE what My TRUTH-TELLERS have been saying for years, and more will AWAKEN to the reality of what has been happening to your Nation and how the LYING MEDIA has had a great role in HIDING the DARK AGENDAS and in MOCKING and SILENCING those speaking TRUTH. This is another SURPRISE move in My orchestrated TAKEDOWN of darkness. The Rescue Operation is in full swing as the RATS become WEASELS. POP GOES THE WEASEL!"

PIN THE TAIL ON THE DONKEY

SEPTEMBER 6, 2022: PIN THE TAIL ON THE DONKEY

"Remember that childhood party game where you are given a DONKEY TAIL with a pin, BLINDFOLDED, SPUN around, and left to WANDER trying to find the donkey to PIN HIS TAIL ON? This is a picture of the ENEMY'S CAMP right now. They are CLUTCHING those TALL 'TALES' they've been trying to PIN on those fighting for JUSTICE and RIGHTEOUSNESS. They are BLINDFOLDED because I have REMOVED most of their MOLES who were feeding them INSIDE INFORMATION from your camp. They have been SPUN AROUND as plot after plot and scheme after scheme BACKFIRES on them, and they are left CONFUSED and DESPERATE. You are going to WITNESS scheme after scheme of DESPERATE ATTEMPTS to make any ACCUSATION or LIE stick to My chosen leader or those close to him. This is why you should not PANIC or REACT to these LYING SCHEMES because they WILL NOT STICK on the wall of accusation. They will all FALL to the ground. Oh, did I mention that the WHOLE TEAM of arrogant evil ones is now BLINDFOLDED? That is why they are not seeing the Host I have sent to PICK UP all the fallen TALL 'TALES', and he is sticking them to the donkey. And, what do you know, the donkey was THEM ALL ALONG; everything they LIED and ACCUSED others of will be STUCK TO THEM. They will BEAR THE WEIGHT of their own CORRUPTION and EVIL, and I will declare them THE BIG LOSERS. You are invited to PARTICIPATE in this party game that will unfold—every TALL 'TALE' you hear trying to be pinned on the Light, you pick it up and FIRMLY PIN it onto them. This will be a POWERFUL PROPHETIC ACTION that you will see played out in the natural realm. WELCOME the TRUTH and LIGHT to come FLOODING in, and ILLUMINATE the PINNED DONKEY."

POKING THE BEAR

SEPTEMBER 29, 2023: POKING THE BEAR

"How do you DISTRACT a VICIOUS BEAR who is CLOSING IN on an INNOCENT PREY? Plans were formulated in the War Room of Heaven for just this moment in history. My Host have received their ORDERS, and I have SHARED My plans around the world with those SEEKING My HELP and My WISDOM. The first phase is to POKE THE BEAR in order to DISTRACT him from CLOSING IN on the INNOCENT. These 'POKES' take the form of COUNTER-LAWSUITS and INDICTMENTS of those so busy INDICTING INNOCENT people. Don't be DISAPPOINTED if these 'POKES' do not have the RESULTS you'd like to see. Their VALUE is not JUSTICE, but it is in the POWER of BREAKING the enemy's FOCUS while GREATER PLANS are being prepared

BEHIND THE BEAR'S BACK to be unleashed at just the RIGHT TIME. If you understand what I AM doing right now in POKING THE BEAR, you won't put your HOPES in those plans that are meant to DISTRACT the BEAR. Don't FOCUS on PLANS—FOCUS on Me, and you won't be DISAPPOINTED because I will OPEN your EYES to see the COMPLETE PICTURE. As the BEAR is DISTRACTED by all the POKING, behind his back I have AMASSED INNUMERABLE TROOPS—the Host and My Army of Light—and when the BEAR does look behind him, he will realize his DOOM is CLOSING IN. Hear the call to MUSTER with My Host, OBSERVE Me POKING THE BEAR, and WAIT for My SIGNAL to CLOSE IN and CAPTURE the BEAR."

QUIRKY

THE COMEUPPANCE

JUNE 15, 2023: THE COMEUPPANCE

Comeuppance began as a term that meant "present oneself for judgment by a tribunal."

A deserved rebuke or penalty.

"Does it seem like the WICKED, ARROGANT ones are CONTINUING to GET AWAY with MURDER? Who is STRONG enough, COURAGEOUS enough, and POWERFUL enough to bring them THE COMEUPPANCE they DESERVE? I AM, AND I WILL BRING THEM THEIR DAY OF COMEUPPANCE. This COMEUPPANCE will not be a SLAP on the wrist or a FINE; it will require FULL PAYBACK of STOLEN resources and COMPLETE JUSTICE for all their CRIMINAL actions. Some of their COMEUPPANCE will come DIRECTLY from My HAND, worked out through My mighty Host. THE COMEUPPANCE for some will be a LOSS of their lives—their BREATH will be taken from them. THE COMEUPPANCE from My HAND will COLLAPSE buildings, monuments, and systems tied to their EVIL empire. I have placed My COURAGE, DISCIPLINE, and TRUE JUSTICE into your MILITARY TRIBUNALS, and they will render JUST decisions, DESERVED penalties, and DEATH sentences for HIGH TREASON and the MURDER of innocent lives. When the day of COMEUPPANCE arrives, you will no longer WONDER if JUSTICE will ever come. That day of COMEUPPANCE will SLAM into them like a FREIGHT TRAIN and ROLL over them like a TSUNAMI—NOTHING WILL STOP THE COMEUPPANCE. The world will once again know the FEAR OF THE LORD and will learn WISDOM WAYS to walk in. Don't get DISCOURAGED, My Army of Light; the day of THE COMEUPPANCE is at hand."

RUCKUS

AUGUST 25, 2024: OCTOBER RUCKUS

Ruckus: a noisy fight or disturbance, a commotion in which many people are angry or upset.

"There will be a BUILD-UP of events in September that will lead to an OCTOBER RUCKUS. Those partnered with Me will become MORE UNIFIED in their fight to RESTORE LIGHT and JUSTICE to your Land. Those serving darkness will continue their SLIDE into CHAOS, as DESPERATE and ABRUPT MOVES are made to try and SAVE their POWER POSITIONS and to STOP the EXPOSURES of their evil. It will become more and more OBVIOUS that they are FOCUSED on trying to PRESERVE their PERSONAL DYNASTIES, and that will DISPROVE their HIGH-MINDED public statements about being for the people and for 'democracy.' The IN-FIGHTING and RECKLESS MOVES to PRESERVE POWER will result in an OCTOBER RUCKUS BREAKING OUT among those who have been LIED to, ABUSED, and USED by POWER-HUNGRY, CORRUPT leaders. There will be an OCTOBER RUCKUS in NEWSROOMS as it begins to DAWN on them that they were convinced to COMPROMISE their INTEGRITY for a BOGUS CAUSE. BITTER PILLS will be taken in October, and the result will be an OCTOBER RUCKUS. This will be DEVASTATING to the darkness as that UNSEEN, POWERFUL MAGNET (held by My hand) PULLS them to the PRECIPICE of DESTRUCTION. They will feel the PANIC, FEAR, and SHEER TERROR that they wanted you to experience as they try to unload all their DEATH AGENDAS against you. Here is how I'd like you to partner with Me: SOW more CHAOS and CONFUSION into the enemy's camp, SOW DIVISION and SELF-PRESERVATION into their midst, CALL FORTH the BUILD-UP to the OCTOBER RUCKUS; DECLARE that many more BLIND EYES will be OPENED to the LIES and TREACHERY from CORRUPT leaders. DECLARE that the Army of Light will become MORE FOCUSED and MORE UNIFIED around TRUTH, JUSTICE, and RIGHTEOUSNESS. PRAY that the BITTER PILLS of TRUTH and EXPOSURE coming out in the next few months would result in MANY TURNING to the LIGHT, finding their ANCHOR in Me, and JOINING the ranks of the Army of Light. Watch for it and call it in—the OCTOBER RUCKUS."

BUFFOONERY

JANUARY 1, 2025: BUFFOONERY

Buffoonery=foolish actions or behavior, acting like a clown

"Welcome to 2025, My Army of Light! Are you ready for a year of EXPOSURE, JUSTICE, and RECOMPENSE? That is Heaven's AGENDA for your year. The evil empire is now in a GREAT DITHER over the way the TIDE HAS TURNED in FAVOR of the Light, and they will now LAUNCH all their SCHEMES to keep your rightful leader from being SWORN into his office. If they can't STOP that from happening, they have PLANS to SABOTAGE his administration from WITHIN and WITHOUT. I have seen the FLURRY of SECRET MEETINGS where those of darkened hearts have plotted these schemes to DEFEAT DJT and the WHOLE FREEDOM and JUSTICE MOVEMENT. The enemy is DESPERATE as he sees his WORLDWIDE CONTROL PLAN being DISMANTLED piece by piece, so he has convinced the planners of these plots that they are CLEVER PLANS and that they will SUCCEED. Will you join Me, Army of Light, in DECLARING EXPOSURE of all these schemes, DECREEING that they will SELF-DESTRUCT, and that the perpetrators will be shown to be BUFFOONS? PRAY that their BUFFOONERY will be SHOWCASED worldwide. You will see them MOCKED and LAUGHED at, and they will be DISQUALIFIED from their positions. In the end, My anointed leader will take his rightful place, and the BUFFOONS and all their evil plans will be EXPOSED. They will be required to DRINK the BITTER CUP of DEFEAT and bear the world's MOCKING at their BUFFOONERY."

RILED UP

FEBRUARY 1, 2025: RILED UP!

"A person can be RILED UP in a NEGATIVE WAY or in a GOOD WAY. RILED UP in a negative way is to be ANGRY, DEFENSIVE, and AGITATED by something or someone. If you allow the enemy to RILE YOU UP about something that has come against you or that has come against the truth, you will REACT from your flesh, and it will result in ANGRY WORDS that cause further DIVISION, PUSH BACK, and your PEACE will VANISH. Realize the enemy is DESPERATE, and he is STIRRING UP LIES, DISINFORMATION, and FEAR about your new leadership. People who have been DECEIVED into BELIEVING LIES are NOT going to be CHANGED by your RILED UP ARGUMENTS. Deception is not countered by FACTS and ARGUMENTS. It is countered by a REVELATION of the TRUTH, and that can only come from the Holy Spirit, the Spirit of Truth. Instead of getting RILED UP against people, get RILED UP against the enemy and his DECEPTIVE ways. This is the POSITIVE RILING UP of EXCITEMENT and STIRRED EMOTIONS against the LIES being spewed by the darkness. Let excitement for the coming RELEASE of TRUTH and the coming GOLDEN AGE move you to take your FLAMING SWORD and to WHACK and BURN the enemy's LIES and DECEPTIONS. This kind of RILING UP will TAKE DOWN the enemy's LIES and his Leviathan-controlled platform. Expend those RILED UP feelings against the enemy and his evil empire, and DO NOT speak to people with ANGRY WORDS that you will come to REGRET. The enemy is greatly RILING UP the deceived, so don't take the BAIT of reacting IN

KIND. Direct your WARFARE against the camp of the enemy, RELEASE Angels of Deliverance to bring REVELATION to the deceived, and RETURN to the River of Life where you will be at PEACE and REST in Me. Choose the good RILING UP!"

Coupled with unusual tactics of warfare, the Father revealed to us that we were journeying a road that we had never traveled before.

CHAPTER TEN

You Have Not Been This Way Before

In preparation for the Army of Light to be able to negotiate this uncharted season, the Father gave us directives that would open our understanding of His character and of His ways so that we would partner successfully with Him towards the great victory of Dark over Light.

The Father wanted to clarify to us which voices we should listen to in order to be in alignment with His purposes.

JULY 3, 2020: BE CAREFUL WHO YOU LISTEN TO

"In this tumultuous transition season, it is especially important that you GUARD what you HEAR and who you

LISTEN to. Guard against listening to ANGRY voices that stir up more STRIFE. Remember that the anger of man does not achieve the righteousness of God (James 1:20). I have given you civil authorities to appeal to for justice. If man does not hear and act on your behalf, you have the COURTS OF HEAVEN and the BLOOD OF JESUS to come before and to ask that JUSTICE and RECOMPENSE would be released. Dwelling in unresolved anger is TOXIC for you and solves nothing. Appealing to authority in a wise and respectful way is much more powerful, and you always have access to My Courtroom to plead your case and to ask for justice for yourself or for others who have been wronged. I am the most POWERFUL JUDGE in the Universe. When you hear prophetic words, dreams, and visions that stir up FEAR, HOPELESSNESS, and IMPENDING DOOM— these revelations are not from Me but are pictures of what the enemy wants to accomplish. Those who are convinced I AM angry with this Nation and that I'm releasing judgment against it will receive this type of revelation. What I am judging in this season is the darkness and evil unleashed for generations to destroy this land. Any who are aligned with these evil schemes and who refuse to repent will fall under My judgments. But My plans are to RESTORE, PRESERVE, and PROSPER your Land as a force for LIGHT, RIGHTEOUSNESS, and JUSTICE in the earth. ALIGN with words that point you in that direction. Fight with Me to defeat darkness and overcome evil with good. Be My Sons and Daughters of LIGHT."

AUGUST 9, 2024: SHELTERED FROM THE STORM

"A STORM is coming to ALL AREAS of your society. Those of the darkness had a STORM of COMPLETE DESTRUCTION planned for you, but your PRAYERS, DECREES, and DECLARATIONS have POSITIONED mighty Host to SURROUND that STORM and to bring it to NOTHING and of NO EFFECT. This is your assignment: continue to CANCEL OUT the enemy's STORM and be BRAVE and CALL IN My STORM. My STORM will be the MOST DEVASTATING STORM the world has ever seen. However, I want your hearts to be at PEACE and COMPLETELY RESTING in My LOVE because I have PROMISED that you will be SHELTERED FROM THE STORM. This STORM is a GREAT DISPLAY of My POWER. To those partnered with darkness, this STORM will EXPOSE them, BLOW AWAY all their LAYERS of PROTECTION, and DESTROY all their EVIL WORKS and SYSTEMS. To those who only know Me in a SUPERFICIAL WAY, they will STRUGGLE with FEAR and ANXIETY, not knowing that the systems they thought were SUSTAINING them were actually STEALING, KILLING, and DESTROYING them. To you, My Army of Light, you have SUNK your FAITH ROOTS DEEP in My HEART, and you have BELIEVED My PROMISES to TEAR DOWN all the DEMONIC STRONGHOLDS in your Land and to REBUILD with Me on GOOD foundations of JUSTICE and RIGHTEOUSNESS. You will EXPERIENCE the STORM in My SHELTER where I will KEEP YOU IN PERFECT PEACE, where you will be SUPERNATURALLY PROVIDED FOR, and you will REST BY MY RIVER OF LIFE and be SATISFIED. The KEY to how you go through this STORM in PEACE is to KEEP CONNECTED to My heart, ASK for My GUIDANCE IN EVERYTHING, TRUST MY

DIRECTIONS FOR YOU, and be CAREFUL to LISTEN to voices that BUILD YOUR FAITH and not YOUR ANXIETY LEVEL. I AM YOUR SHELTER IN THE STORM."

PROVERBS 1:33 (TPT) *"But the one who always listens to me will live undisturbed in a heavenly peace. Free from fear, confident and courageous, that one will rest unafraid and sheltered from the storms of life."*

We were clearly told that the planned judgment was for those partnered with darkness and that His plans for our nation were to release His Light into us so that we would become a force for righteousness and justice for the whole earth. He supplied us with battle strategies, and one of the strategies was to declare the victory by faith before it came into being.

NOVEMBER 6, 2020: DECLARING THE VICTORY

"It is important that you align your heart with Mine right now and begin to DECLARE that the VICTORY has been WON over the darkness in your Nation. Even though your physical eyes do not see the fulfillment of this victory; nevertheless, I am telling you that it has been won in the HEAVENLY REALMS, and as you align with My declaration and SPEAK IT into the physical realm, you will see it displayed in the EARTHLY realm. Your declaration of what I say becomes FAITH that moves the mountains in the physical realm and ushers in the FULFILLMENT of what I have declared. This is one of the ways you can partner with Me in bringing forth My purposes and plans for your Nation."

MARCH 28, 2021: FLIPPING THE SCRIPT, TURNING THE TABLES, PULLING THE RUG OUT

"Are you ready for an ADVENTURE with Me? Don't you love stories where the SCRIPT GETS FLIPPED and the true motives of the bad guys are REVEALED, and the plots where DOOM seems inevitable and suddenly the TABLES ARE TURNED ... or the arrogant evil one has the RUG PULLED OUT from under his feet? How about you partner with Me in seeing all three of these scenarios played out against the darkness that is threatening your Nation and your own life? Join Me in DECLARING these three scenarios will be played out against the evil ... I AM the HERO who will accomplish these miracles, and all of you who have clung to My PROMISES and who have continued to SHINE A LIGHT on the darkness will also join Me in the ranks of HEROES ...."

FEBRUARY 22, 2022: ALL HEAVEN IS ABOUT TO BREAK LOOSE

"Hell thinks it has GREAT and DESTRUCTIVE plans for this day, but I say HEAVEN IS ABOUT TO BREAK LOOSE into your world. My mighty right arm is SMASHING down on the wicked leaders, and when it STRIKES like a huge HAMMER blow, the earth will SHAKE, and the wicked will SUDDENLY tremble in great FEAR and BEWILDERMENT. How did the tables get SUDDENLY TURNED on them? How did they go from being the POWERFUL HUNTERS to the ones now being HUNTED by a FORCEFUL POWER that strikes TERROR in their hearts? Who

157

UNCOVERED their hidden SECRETS and who SHINED the blinding light of TRUTH on their multitude of LIES? I AM has met you on the BATTLEFIELD, and you corrupt and wicked ones are FINISHED. My faithful Army of Light, CALL FORTH and CELEBRATE our GREAT VICTORY before you see it. You will WITNESS all HEAVEN BREAK LOOSE in your favor, and you will join Me in celebrating and in rebuilding on the foundation of JUSTICE and RIGHTEOUSNESS. I have spoken, and I will do it."

PSALM 22: 24, 30, 31 (TPT) *"For He has not despised my cries of deep despair. He's my first responder to my sufferings, and when I was in pain, He was there all the time and heard the cries of the afflicted ... His spiritual seed shall serve Him. Future generations will hear from us about the wonders of the Victorious Lord ... And they will all declare, 'It is finished!'"*

Continually, the Father told us we had never been this way before, but we could depend on Him to prepare us for this road and to direct our steps.

DECEMBER 12, 2021: EPIC BATTLES, EPIC VICTORIES

"You have been in an UNPRECEDENTED season of EPIC BATTLES. They have tried your soul and your endurance, but you are still STANDING! You have not GIVEN IN or BACKED DOWN, nor have you UNFAIRLY judged My heart of love. WELL DONE, good and faithful servants! Your LAID-DOWN lives, PERSEVERANCE, and UNYIELDING faith are BEAUTIFUL to Me and TERRIFYING to the enemy. You may not perceive it, but you are SHINING brighter and brighter in the spiritual realm, and your collective light is OVERPOWERING the darkness. These EPIC BATTLES will result in EPIC VICTORIES, and you will be REWARDED above and beyond what you can imagine. Shine on, LIGHT-BEARERS, we are taking back your Land!"

JANUARY 11, 2022 : THE BLESSINGS OF ABRAHAM

"The BLESSINGS OF ABRAHAM will be on this generation of Believers who have heard My CALL to their hearts to leave their COMFORT zones and come on this perilous journey through UNKNOWN territory. You have faced HOSTILE conditions and people in this EPIC journey to save your Nation. You have experienced loss and very uncomfortable conditions. If you'll look back, you'll see that I was ALWAYS with you, that I KEPT you, PROTECTED you, PROVIDED for you, drew you CLOSE to My heart, and COVERED you with My LOVE and My Son's BLOOD. Along this barren and rocky road that you have been fighting your way through, I have been your WATER OF LIFE and the BREAD that satisfies. Now, I AM bringing you into a land of PROMISE and FULFILLMENT with rich REWARDS and days of PLENTY. Don't FALTER at these last days when perilous events are THREATENED. STRENGTHEN yourself in Me and PRESS ON to the FULLNESS of ABRAHAM'S BLESSINGS for your life and for your Nation. The best is yet to come!"

MAY 15, 2022: IT'S READY TO BLOW!

"The EVIDENCE and EXPOSURES of LIES and WICKED SCHEMES are building, building, and the VOLCANO of TRUTH is about to EXPLODE. The force and the magnitude of DARKNESS and DEATH SCHEMES that shoot out will cover so many WICKED people and CORRUPT institutions that the FALSE MEDIA will be forced to play whack-a-mole, and they won't be able to COVER-UP nor SPIN everything that POURS OUT. These scandals will be just like LAVA—too HOT to touch, and those who try to stop the hot lava exposures will be BURNED UP and TAKEN DOWN. The darkness UNDERESTIMATED My ability to CHANGE peoples' hearts. My LOVE can TRANSFORM any heart, and the darkness will be SHOCKED at who turns over EVIDENCE of their many CRIMES and TREASONOUS BEHAVIOR. Do you see darkness throwing everything they can into the battle? Don't be AFRAID! It is actually YOUR PRAYERS PARTNERING with Me to PUSH BACK DARKNESS that have forced them to act PREMATURELY, and their decisions to try to save their dark agenda will BACKFIRE and lead to the EXPLOSION of the VOLCANO OF EXPOSURES. The darkness is being pushed in their desperation toward CROSSING A RED LINE that will activate your military. This will be an UNPRECEDENTED time of change in your Nation, but know I AM behind it. Remember My good promises and help others NAVIGATE the changes with the STABILITY I've place in you. Get ready —IT'S ABOUT TO BLOW!"

OCTOBER 23, 2022: I AM IN YOUR FUTURE

"You may not know what your FUTURE HOLDS because these are days like you have never walked in before. When will the darkness LAUNCH their big attack? When will My RESCUE come rolling across your Land? When will TRUTH finally be spoken over the airwaves? When will your RIGHTFUL leader be restored? So many UNKNOWNS are facing you, and you could easily slip into FEAR and ANXIETY; but I have called you to LIFT YOUR GAZE HIGHER and look into My eyes of LOVE and FIRE and to settle this in your heart that I AM IN YOUR FUTURE. If I AM IN YOUR FUTURE, then you have it ALL, because I AM your TRUE SOURCE of LIFE, PROVISION, SAFETY, and LOVE. You can look to the future with HOPE because I AM THERE, and I AM your SURE HOPE and your ANCHOR. You are totally LOVED and CARED for, so REMAIN IN MY PEACE."

JUNE 29, 2023: YOU ARE MY WITNESSES

"You who have walked this difficult road of FIERCE BATTLE and an UNKNOWN FUTURE are My WITNESSES that what I have promised will come to pass. You chose to BELIEVE My words spoken through the prophets that VICTORY, BREAKTHROUGH, and a GOOD FUTURE were just around the corner. You FOLLOWED Me through the CLAMOR and the DANGER of the battle. You could not see ahead because of the SMOKE that filled the air from FIRES and EXPLOSIONS the enemy set off. And yet, you FOLLOWED ME STILL in BLIND FAITH because you had felt My LOVE and I had PROVED My

FAITHFULNESS to you through the CROSS and through PROMISES kept to you. When the GREAT DECEPTION FALLS, and I bring in the LIGHT OF TRUTH and FULFILLMENT, people who MOCKED and SCORNED you will realize you were HEARING and FOLLOWING Me, and they will come to you for WORDS OF TRUTH. You will be MY WITNESSES, and you will declare My GREAT DEEDS and MIGHTY ACTS that I have performed, and you will show them the GOOD PATHS to walk on. Instead of SCORN, you will be HIGHLY ESTEEMED, and because of the HUMILITY you wear, you will FOCUS people on ME, and you will show them the path of LIFE. DO NOT TURN ASIDE from the BATTLE because the SMOKE is thick and the enemy is SCREAMING THREATS. PRESS ON close behind Me, and we will SUDDENLY BREAKTHROUGH into the prophesied VICTORY. Be MY WITNESSES of My POWER and My FAITHFULNESS."

July 30, 2023: Behold, I Am Here!

"The most IMPORTANT PREPARATION that you can make for the days of bringing down the evil empire is to KNOW WHO I AM, to REHEARSE My PROMISES to you and your Nation, and to EXPERIENCE My LOVE for you. These goals will STRENGTHEN you and POSITION you to RECEIVE My ABUNDANT PROVISION and My SUPERNATURAL PROTECTION. The Holy Spirit will be your FAITHFUL GUIDE in all these things. ASK every day for His GUIDANCE and His REVELATION of who I AM and who you are in Me. ASK Him to KEEP the FIRES of PASSION BURNING in your heart with LOVE and DEEP

SURRENDER to Me. ASK Him to let you FEEL the LOVE that I have for you. I want you to KNOW, to FEEL, to EXPERIENCE how much I LOVE you because then you will be SURE that NOTHING can separate you from the POWER of My LOVE. Let Me make this UNPRECEDENTED season EASY for you: CALL FORTH AND SUPPORT with intercession My PLANS and PURPOSES, and BLOCK the plans of evil with your AUTHORITY, and REFUSE to partner with FEAR and INTIMIDATION at his threats. LEARN to be VERY SENSITIVE to My Spirit's PROMPTINGS. TRUST Him with your life. His GUIDANCE will keep you SAFE and LEAD you in paths of PROVISION. CULTIVATE a HEARING EAR and a RESPONSIVE HEART. Ask Him to HELP you in this, and He will! My LIGHT in you will SHINE BRIGHTLY against the BACKDROP of FALLING EVIL SYSTEMS and the REVEALING of GROSS DARKNESS. SHINE the LIGHT of My LOVE and your CONFIDENCE in who I AM and what I have PROMISED to all those who are around you. The BEST is yet to come! BEHOLD, I AM HERE!"

ISAIAH 52:5, 6 (TPT) *"And now, what have I here?' says Yahweh? 'Indeed, My people have been taken into bondage without cause while mocking rulers howl; and every day My name is continually despised!' says Yahweh. 'Therefore, My people will know the power of My name, and they will know in that day that I am the one who promised them, saying, Behold, I am here!'"*

MAY 7, 2024: EYE ON THE PRIZE

"I have promised you a GREAT and MIGHTY DELIVERANCE from an enemy that seeks to DESTROY you and any form of FREEDOM. I have promised you that you will RECOVER ALL that has been STOLEN from you, including FINANCES, HEALTH, IDENTITIES, RELATIONSHIPS, and JUSTICE. As wonderful as these promises of DELIVERANCE and RECOMPENSE are, they are not the MOST PRECIOUS thing that you will receive from this season of DARK to LIGHT. The MOST VALUABLE, the MOST ENDURING PRIZE that you will receive, is your DEEPENED FAITH and COMPLETE TRUST in who I AM and in what I can do. You will FOREVER know how POWERFUL, how TRUSTWORTHY, and how LOVING I AM. Our hearts will be so DEEPLY KNIT TOGETHER that NOTHING will be able to SEPARATE you from My LOVE. I have instructed you to CALL IN My RESCUE and My RECOMPENSE, but I don't want you to MISS the MOST ENDURING and MOST PRECIOUS result of this unprecedented season, and that is an INTIMATE and COMPLETELY SATISFYING HEART-TO-HEART RELATIONSHIP with Me. This is the GREATEST PRIZE, and it will go with you into eternity. KEEP YOUR EYE ON THE PRIZE!"

MAY 24, 2024: UNFOLDING

This night I was awakened at 1:23, 2:34, 4:44, and 5:19. I heard the word "Unfolding."

1:23=things are progressing in order like counting 1, 2, 3

164

2:34=further progression

4:44=interaction between God's created earthly order and the Heavenly order of the Angels and Hosts.

5:19=1 Thessalonians 5:19 (NKJV) *"Do not quench the Spirit."*

"Events in your world will LOOK CHAOTIC to the UNDISCERNING, but to you who have asked for the eyes of your spirit to be OPENED, you will see the events as My PLANS that are UNFOLDING. You will RECOGNIZE that I AM SMASHING DARK THRONES and ALTARS to MAKE WAY for My Spirit to FLOOD this Land with the KINGDOM of LIGHT. This Rescue Plan that is UNFOLDING is UNPRECEDENTED. The world has never seen anything like it. I have called you to COME NEAR to My HEART so that I can SHOW YOU what I AM DOING and what the enemy is DOING. That way, you know what to SUPPORT with your POWERFUL PRAYERS, and you know what to OPPOSE with your SPIRITUAL AUTHORITY. The movement of My Spirit as FIRE, WIND, and WATER will also be UNPRECEDENTED. That is why I warn you in 1 Thessalonians 5:19 (NKJV) *'Do not quench the Spirit.'* Do not find yourself OPPOSING what I AM DOING just because you have not PERSONALLY experienced the Spirit in the WAY and FORM He has chosen to come. Don't REACT with SUSPICION, but continually ASK for My DISCERNMENT, and I will FREELY give it. You must be willing to lay aside PRECONCEIVED IDEAS of how I work and the BAD TEACHINGS that you've heard because then My discernment will have a PLACE to RESIDE in you. My plans are UNFOLDING, and you can walk through this transition season from WAR to TRIUMPH in PEACE if you will

DRAW NEAR to Me and SEE things from My PERSPECTIVE. All you have been praying about and longing for is UNFOLDING."

Our wonderful Father gave us powerful promises and precepts as we continued in faith on this unknown and unprecedented journey from Dark to Light.

CHAPTER ELEVEN

Powerful Promises and Precepts

THE PROMISE OF A NEW NATION AND A NEW ERA

Those of us who had been awakened to the peril our nation was facing from dark forces arrayed against it welcomed and celebrated the Father's promises that America would not die—she would live!

AUGUST 29, 2022: A NEAR-DEATH EXPERIENCE

"Let's talk about a NEAR-DEATH EXPERIENCE. The MAIN outcome of a near-death experience is that it DOES NOT END IN DEATH; it ends in LIFE! Your Nation's FREEDOMS and your Nation's LIGHT have been slowly DYING over the years. This has not been an ACCIDENTAL DEATH; it was ORCHESTRATED by hell and carried out by the ARROGANT ELITE, whose purpose was to ENSLAVE you and to STEAL from you. This death of freedom and light has ACCELERATED in the last few years because the darkness began to sense a RISING, RIGHTEOUS OPPOSITION, and PANIC pushed them to RAMP UP their DEATH SCHEMES for your Land. I AM declaring to you that this is a NEAR-DEATH EXPERIENCE for your Nation, and it will end in a REVIVED Nation where LIFE and LIBERTY are once again PRIORITIES and always to be TREASURED. Remember that I AM the God of RESURRECTION POWER and that nothing is too DIFFICULT for Me. I have DETERMINED that America shall LIVE, and she will not DIE! This is My SOLEMN PROMISE to you, and this is the future you should FOCUS on and LEAN INTO. Let your FAITH ARISE as you gaze on My FAITHFULNESS and My POWER. DECLARE and DECREE that America WILL RISE AGAIN as a BEACON of My HOPE and FREEDOM to the world. SHE SHALL NOT DIE—SHE SHALL LIVE!"

Not only did He promise that a new nation would arise from the fires of war but that we were on the brink of a whole new era!

AUGUST 30, 2022: THE DAY THE WORLD STOOD STILL

"The SUDDEN REVEAL of darkness that I bring will be so SHOCKING that it will be remembered as THE DAY THE WORLD STOOD STILL. It will be necessary to PAUSE 'life as usual' so that all realize the MOMENTOUS CHANGES that are necessary to SAVE the world from the darkness that THREATENED to SWALLOW IT UP. ALL eyes must be on the REVEAL that I showcase of DIABOLICAL plans of DEATH and DESTRUCTION and the GREEDY, SELFISH, GRASPING hearts and minds of the arrogant elite and of the fools who served them. THE DAY THE WORLD STOOD STILL will be a day to AWAKEN and to realize how DECEIVED and BLIND they have been. As a new Nation is born out of the FIRES of the wicked and all their corrupted systems, there will be born a VIGILANCE to PRESERVE FREEDOM and to HIGHLY-ESTEEM TRUTH and JUSTICE. A FREE and UN-COMPROMISED media will be demanded by the people, and I have been preparing TRUTH-TELLERS who will fulfill this role with INTEGRITY. A beautiful and strong UNITY will emerge because all the schemes to DIVIDE people will be EXPOSED, and everyone will VALUE being an American. They will join together to REBUILD, to RESTORE, and to make BETTER the foundations of this Nation once again on JUSTICE and RIGHTEOUSNESS. Those who were RADICALIZED will see they were DUPES being used by the darkness. There will be a WIDESPREAD turning to My SON to be CLEANSED and to embrace the beautiful gift of SALVATION. There will be a FRESH START for your Land, and My Army of Light and My Church will JOYFULLY DISCIPLE a Nation. Do not FEAR or be ANXIOUS, but wait for THE DAY THE WORLD STOOD STILL because it will USHER IN A WHOLE NEW ERA."

Amazingly, the Father spoke to me about a "New Day Dawning" way back in my journal from November 11, 2017. This entry was from before I began posting on social media. It was given on "11/11" which was significant to me because He had been showing me that time repeatedly on clocks for years. The positive Biblical meaning of the number eleven: the prophetic, transition, and the eleventh hour.

November 11, 2017: New Day Dawning

"A NEW DAY is close to DAWNING for your nation. It will soon be released; just as the sun moves across your nation in the morning, so My Son will RISE upon and MOVE ACROSS your land bringing RIGHTEOUSNESS, UNITY, LOVE, and APPRECIATION for each other. A SWEEPING CLEANSING process will precede this NEW DAWN. It will EXPOSE ANCIENT CORRUPTION, DECEPTION, and BETRAYAL in this nation's leaders of every mountain of influence. Keep your heart on RESTORATION, RENEWAL, and REFORMATION. Ask for My choice of leader to be INSTALLED on every mountain."

New Era's usually come in on the heels of great changes. The following word was received before President Trump was inaugurated for his second term, and it spoke of tremendous upheavals.

December 13, 2024: Tremendous Upheavals

"TREMENDOUS UPHEAVALS are taking place behind the scenes in your GOVERNMENT, in ENTERTAINMENT, in the FINANCIAL and BUSINESS sector, and in the CHURCH realm.

You are beginning to SEE the SIGNS of these UPHEAVALS, and they will continue to BUILD and become more VISIBLE as the TRANSFER of POWER is brought to COMPLETION and your rightful leader is placed at the HEAD of your NATION. The darkness thinks they can STOP this TREMENDOUS UPHEAVAL of their evil empire by their DARK and DESTRUCTIVE plan, but My TREMENDOUS UPHEAVAL will SHAKE their plans and bring them DOWN in a huge CRASH of DEFEAT. These TREMENDOUS UPHEAVALS are happening because many chose to BACK JUSTICE and RIGHTEOUSNESS in your Land. I have set in MOTION SHAKINGS that have UNCOVERED PROOFS of BRIBERY, CORRUPTION, and TREASON. The GUILTY are being presented with these PROOFS, and that is why you are seeing people FLEE the country, RESIGN from positions of POWER, and HUGE POLICY SWINGS in companies and agencies. As the TRANSFER of POWER is COMPLETED, the TREMENDOUS UPHEAVALS will ACCELERATE and become VISIBLE to all. It will seem a bit CHAOTIC as leader after leader is EXPOSED and REMOVED from power and systems COLLAPSE under the weight of FRAUD and DECEPTION, but know that My TREMENDOUS UPHEAVALS are STRATEGIC and that who and what needs to GO will be REMOVED. I have been behind the DEVELOPMENT of the blueprints for the RECONSTRUCTION and RESTORATION of your REPUBLIC, so do not waste one minute in FEAR because I AM FAITHFUL and POWERFUL to PERFORM My word. My TREMENDOUS UPHEAVALS will bring about the DAWN of a NEW ERA of JUSTICE and RIGHTEOUSNESS."

This word was fulfilled as DOGE (Department of Government Efficiency), headed by Elon Musk, uncovered vast amounts of corruption which caused huge policy swings in companies and agencies, resignations, and the collapse of some of these systems.

SHELTERED FROM THE COMING STORM

A storm of epic proportions was forming over our nation as the clash between the dark and the light intensified. The Father gave us wonderful promises of being kept safe and sheltered from the storm that was intended for the darkness.

MAY 2, 2020: THE SHADOW OF THE STORM

"The shadow of the storm grows ever closer. Can you hear the distant thunder, and can you see faraway flashes of lightning? The storm is approaching, and nothing will stop it. It will be so widespread that NO ONE will be able to ESCAPE being caught in it. There will be NO PLACE TO RUN and NO PLACE TO HIDE for those evil schemers and plotters who wanted to destroy your Nation and your President. Those of you who are walking with Me will find a sure and SAFE SHELTER in the SHADOW OF MY WINGS. You will observe the storm, but you will not be caught up in it. As this GIANT storm cleanses your Land, watch with Me and declare that all My purposes in the storm will be revealed, and that after the storm passes, MY PEACE and MY BEAUTY will rest on your Nation. The atmosphere will be cleansed of evil and idolatry, and new growth and blessings will abound."

OCTOBER 29, 2022: THE POWER OF MY VOICE

"The FREQUENCIES of My VOICE caused the CREATION POWER that formed the earth in great PRECISION and BEAUTY. THE POWER OF MY VOICE can shape mountains and bring great PEACE to the heart of man. You will now be a WITNESS to a GRAND DISPLAY of THE POWER OF MY VOICE being released as a STORM against the wicked. The same FREQUENCIES that cause a glorious creation will ATTACK and BRING DOWN those systems and people who are seeking to establish strongholds of darkness and destruction. My frequencies are in PERFECT HARMONY—a SYMPHONY OF LIFE AND PEACE. If you tune to My frequencies, you will be KEPT in PEACE even in the midst of My frequencies TEARING DOWN darkness. I AM coming as a POWERFUL STORM of LIGHTNING and THUNDER to deal with the attempt of darkness to take CONTROL of your lives and of nations around the world. My SKY-SPLITTING LIGHTNING will REVEAL all the dark SCHEMES and PEOPLE, and who they really are will be seen by all. My DEEP, RUMBLING THUNDER will roll across your Land as a frequency that SMASHES STRONGHOLDS and PLANS of the darkness. It will FLATTEN leaders as I confront them with My HOLY POWER. The landscape of your Nation will be changed. It will be a CLEAN SLATE for My people to BUILD on as they partner with My GLORY. Remember that the STORM is for the WICKED, and that THE POWER OF MY VOICE will destroy them. I AM inviting you to weather the STORM close to My HEART because you will receive My frequencies of PEACE and REST, and you will be ready to step in and help Me REBUILD on the foundation of My

GLORY. THE POWER OF MY VOICE removes darkness and creates beauty and life." PSALM 29

AUGUST 9, 2024: SHELTERED FROM THE STORM

"A STORM is coming to ALL AREAS of your society. Those of the darkness had a STORM of COMPLETE DESTRUCTION planned for you, but your PRAYERS, DECREES, and DECLARATIONS have POSITIONED mighty Host to SURROUND that STORM and to bring it to NOTHING and of NO EFFECT. This is your assignment: continue to CANCEL OUT the enemy's STORM and be BRAVE and CALL IN My STORM. My STORM will be the MOST DEVASTATING STORM the world has ever seen. However, I want your hearts to be at PEACE and COMPLETELY RESTING in My LOVE because I have PROMISED that you will be SHELTERED FROM THE STORM. This STORM is a GREAT DISPLAY of My POWER. To those partnered with darkness, this STORM will EXPOSE them, BLOW AWAY all their LAYERS of PROTECTION, and DESTROY all their EVIL WORKS and SYSTEMS. To those who only know Me in a SUPERFICIAL WAY, they will STRUGGLE with FEAR and ANXIETY, not knowing that the systems they thought were SUSTAINING them were actually STEALING, KILLING, and DESTROYING them. To you, My Army of Light, you have SUNK your FAITH ROOTS DEEP in My HEART, and you have BELIEVED My PROMISES to TEAR DOWN all the DEMONIC STRONGHOLDS in your Land and to REBUILD with Me on GOOD foundations of JUSTICE and RIGHTEOUSNESS. You will EXPERIENCE the STORM in My SHELTER where I will KEEP YOU IN PERFECT PEACE, where you will be SUPERNATURALLY PROVIDED FOR, and you will REST BY MY RIVER OF LIFE and be SATISFIED. The KEY to how you go through this STORM in PEACE is to KEEP CONNECTED to My heart, ASK for My GUIDANCE IN EVERYTHING, TRUST MY DIRECTIONS FOR YOU, and be CAREFUL to LISTEN to voices that BUILD YOUR FAITH and not YOUR ANXIETY LEVEL. I AM YOUR SHELTER IN THE STORM."

PROVERBS 1:33 (TPT) *"But the one who always listens to me will live undisturbed in a heavenly peace. Free from fear, confident and courageous, that one will rest unafraid and sheltered from the storms of life."*

PROMISES TO BE SAVED FROM DEATH AGENDAS INTO A GOOD FUTURE

Who can forget the COVID 19 "Plandemic" that was released on the world by those partnered with darkness? The Father called us to partner with Him in defeating this scheme, and He promised to bring to justice those behind such evil.

MAY 3, 2020: DECLARE A HAPPY ENDING

"DECLARE A HAPPY ENDING to this health crises that was concocted, set in motion, and then released on the world by POWER HUNGRY, DESPERATE PEOPLE under the influence of demonic powers. They have been using this plan against the world for years by engineering and then spreading viruses and bacteria to bring about disease, destruction, and to promote expensive cures and vaccines that enriched them and caused more harm than good. Ask of Me because I am ready and willing to expose these dark plots and to bring down people and organizations that promoted this evil. These people and projects were promoted as humanitarian, but in reality, they sought to KILL, STEAL, AND DESTROY. Partner with Me in calling forth the exposure of evil by those who plotted it and those who promoted them as good. Declare the release of My HAMMER of JUSTICE, and declare a HAPPY ENDING to this real-life story."

Psalm 37:37 (TPT) *"But you can tell who are the blameless and spiritually mature. What a different story with them! The godly ones will have a peaceful, prosperous future with a HAPPY ENDING."* (emphasis mine)

APRIL 6, 2022: AT YOUR PERIL

"I AM speaking to the darkness and to those partnered with darkness. If you keep pursuing your WICKED PLOTS, SCHEMES, and ATTACKS, then you do so AT YOUR OWN PERIL. I have had ENOUGH of your DEATH AGENDAS, ENOUGH of your MESMERIZING DECEPTION, and ENOUGH of your STRATEGIES to obtain COMPLETE CONTROL over people and wealth. To those who continue to RAISE your fist at Me and who MOCK My people—you do so AT YOUR OWN PERIL. Instead of inflicting more FEAR and HORROR on My people, you will REAP that FEAR and HORROR sevenfold as your intricate plots and schemes BLOW UP in your faces and you are inflicted with the LOSS and SICKNESS you intended to sow. My Army of Light,

I AM coming to make things right (JUSTICE), I AM coming to pay you back for your losses (RESTORATION), and I AM coming to bless and prosper your Land (FULFILLMENT). Do not DISTRESS yourself over those who have lost their lives in this battle because they have been HONORED in Heaven and are in complete JOY and PEACE. Also, do not LOSE HEART over children and adults who have been ENSLAVED by traffickers or addiction. I have amazing plans of RESCUE, DEEP HEALING, AND COMPLETE RESTORATION. The enemy and his partners have done these things to THEIR OWN PERIL, but I AM visiting the earth with My weighty and powerful GLORY."

ACTS 3:21 (TPT) *"For He (Jesus) must remain in Heaven until the restoration of all things has taken place, fulfilling everything God said long ago through His holy prophets."*

Greek meaning of restoration: restoration of creation to before the fall, David's covenant restored, restoration of perfect health.

APRIL 3, 2023: IT'S NOT THE END OF THE WORLD!

"I have GOOD NEWS for you! IT'S NOT THE END OF THE WORLD! Rather, it's the END of DARK DEATH AGENDAS and the REBIRTH of greater PEACE, PROSPERITY, and FREEDOM than you've ever known. This is the time for My Church to ARISE and SHINE and to FILL THE EARTH with My Kingdom POWER and GOODNESS. You are about to step into a season of GREAT TRIUMPH from deep DARKNESS and PERVERSION into a life of GLORY and CLEANNESS. Because this will be such a SUDDEN and ENORMOUS change for the world, I have been

PREPARING you, My Remnant, to STEWARD this coming season of PEACE and PLENTY. I have STRENGTHENED you in the INNER man, and I've GROWN your FAITH ROOTS in Me DEEP and STRONG. Your hearts are Mine, and you will not be pulled OFF COURSE from seeking Me by PROSPERITY or PROMINENCE. Yours will be OPEN HANDS that I can pour WEALTH through, and it will BLESS YOU and the WORLD around you. FAVOR and POSITION will not be an IDOL because your life is LAID DOWN in SERVICE to Me. It has been CRUCIAL to gather EVIDENCE and build UNBREAKABLE cases against the arrogant ones partnered with darkness so that they are given UNSHAKEABLE JUDGMENT and JUSTICE. It has been just as CRUCIAL that your hearts have been PURIFIED and made READY to RULE and REIGN in My name. Everything is going to COME TOGETHER in a BEAUTIFUL RESURRECTION for your Nation, and it will FLOW OUT to ALL the world."

In the place of the death agendas, the Father promised justice, restoration, and fulfillment. Judgment and justice were being released because the Father explained to us that we were in a "Harvest" season.

The Promise of Judgment and Justice

November 3, 2019: Confronting of Evil

"The confronting of evil is on the horizon. Those who have foolishly served darkness and thought they would continue to be rewarded with riches and power will find themselves stripped of both. They will reap the consequences of all the darkness and deception they have sown. Their life dreams will lie in ASHES under their feet, burned up by My righteous judgment. They thought they were protected from My justice, but it will hit them headlong like a roaring freight train that totally DERAILS their lives; they will experience the LOSS of all things and some the loss of their lives. The ones who served evil seemed to prosper, but their day of reckoning is here, and they will see that they have chosen foolishly. True riches and reward await those who have chosen to believe Me and to give their lives to Me. They will be given freedom and reward."

PSALM 112:5, 10b (TPT) *"Life is good for the one who is generous and charitable, conducting affairs with honesty and truth ... The wicked slink away speechless in the darkness that falls, where hope dies and all their dreams fade away to nothing, nothing at all!"*

Woven throughout the entries on judgment and justice, the Father reminded us that we needed to know both His kindness and His severity.

SEPTEMBER 17, 2022: UNDERSTAND MY JUDGMENTS

"I want to PREPARE your hearts for this SEASON of JUDGMENT that is coming on the earth. This is not the FINAL judgment that will be released at the end of time, but it is one of My APPOINTED SEASONS of JUDGMENTS and JUSTICE because I have HEARD the cries of My people who have SUFFERED LOSS and GREAT INJUSTICE. My JUDGMENTS tip the SCALES of JUSTICE back into BALANCE so that RIGHTEOUSNESS can once again be ESTABLISHED in a Nation. My JUDGMENTS will SHOCK some of you who have been taught that I only show MERCY and KINDNESS and that I no longer PUNISH the WICKED. You must understand that even My harsh JUDGMENTS are an EXTENSION of My KINDNESS, because for some it will be the ONLY thing that SAVES them from ETERNAL SEPARATION from Me. It is My DESIRE that you ALIGN your HEART with Mine in this season of JUDGMENT and that you TRUST My ways that are above your ways. Do not find yourself actually OPPOSING Me by trying to give UNSANCTIFIED MERCY —that is extending mercy to what, in My wisdom, I AM JUDGING. TRUST Me like you have never trusted Me before, and you will see My judgments bring about great good."

DECEMBER 15, 2021: HOW DOES THE EARTH RESPOND TO JUDGMENT?

"I have laid out for you in My Word both My KINDNESS and My SEVERITY. It is always My desire to show MERCY and KINDNESS, but when men completely partner with the enemy and his plans of DEATH and DESTRUCTION, then I must respond with My JUDGMENT and JUSTICE to rescue My people, to AVENGE them of their cruel adversary, to bring RESTORATION and RECOMPENSE, and to heal the land the wicked desecrated. When I move across your Land with judgment and justice, it will cause VIOLENT REACTIONS in the earth because of the SUDDEN shift in the spiritual realm. The natural things speak of the invisible so that even those who don't know Me have a WITNESS before their eyes that I AM

moving and that I AM real. I AM the TRUTH being brought to light, the complete EXPOSURES of evil and corruption, and RIGHTEOUSNESS and JUSTICE being restored."

NAHUM Chapter 1 (MSG) lays out this word from the Father. (I've added some possible modern-day applications.) *"God is serious business ... He avenges His foes ... He's powerful, but it's a patient power ... Still no one gets by with anything ... Tornadoes and hurricanes are the wake of His passage, storm clouds are the dust He shakes off His feet ... Earth shakes in fear of God. The whole world's in a panic ... His anger spills out like a river of lava, His fury shatters boulders. God is good, a hiding place in tough times. He recognizes and welcomes anyone looking for help ... But cozy islands of escape He wipes right off the map [Epstein's Island] ... Nineveh's [the elite] an anthill of evil plots against God, a think tank for lies that seduce and betray. And God has something to say about all this: even though you're on top of the world, with all the applause and all the votes, you'll be mowed down flat [fraudulent administration] ... It's all over with Nineveh [the corrupt] ... Your gods and goddesses go in the trash. I'm digging your grave. It's an unmarked grave. You're nothing—no, you're less than nothing! ... the latest good news: peace! A holiday, Judah [God's people]! Celebrate! Worship and recommit to God! No more worries about this enemy. This one is history. Close the books."*

ROMANS 11:22 (NASB) *"Behold then the kindness and severity of God; to those who fell, severity, but to you, God's kindness, if you continue in His kindness; otherwise you also will be cut off."*

July 18, 2023: The Weight of Darkness and Rebellion

NUMBERS 16:31-33 (NKJV) *"Now it came to pass, as he (Moses) finished speaking all these words, that the ground split apart under them (those challenging God's choice of Moses), and the earth opened its mouth and swallowed them up, with their households and all the men with Korah, with all their goods. So they and all those with them went down alive into the pit; the earth closed over them, and they perished from among the assembly."* (emphasis mine)

The Father speaks:

"REBELLION against the Most High God has grown among the ARROGANT elite to a SHOWDOWN between their GROSS EVIL and the LIGHT and GOODNESS of My HEART. Their DARKNESS and REBELLION have MULTIPLIED until they are FLAUNTING it before the world and INVITING OPEN REBELLION against Me. The WEIGHT of this GROSS EVIL is BEARING DOWN on My creation, and the earth is GROANING under the GROSS DARKNESS. I have told you this season of RESCUE, JUDGMENT, and JUSTICE will be like the RED SEA DELIVERANCE. The earth will SHAKE as the Children of Light call forth My JUDGMENTS and JUSTICE, and you will see the earth RESPOND by OPENING ITS MOUTH and SWALLOWING UP THE WICKED, and you will see them NO MORE. My FIRE will BREAK OUT and CONSUME the wicked and their platforms. The evil FOOLISHLY called for this SHOWDOWN because they were DECEIVED into believing they could win. I have COMMISSIONED you, Army of Light, to join Me in this SHOWDOWN. Come with your SWORDS of TRUTH, the HIGH PRAISES of your God on your lips, and

DEMAND as My Sons and Daughters that DARKNESS and REBELLION bow their knee and come under My JUDGMENT and JUSTICE. DECLARE LIGHT and LIFE to ARISE over hearts and over your Nation. The earth will RESPOND to your WARFARE, and it will SWALLOW UP the gross darkness at My command and RELEASE the clean and enduring FEAR OF THE LORD and an era of PEACE and PLENTY."

HARVEST SEASON

JULY 8, 2022: A MATURING HARVEST

"The HARVEST of EVIL and the HARVEST of RIGHTEOUSNESS have been MATURING in your Nation. SEEDS of evil and SEEDS of good that people have sown in the soil of their lives are coming to MATURITY. This is a season of EXPOSURE, and the FRUIT of everyone's lives is being brought to MATURITY before the world. There will no longer be a way to HIDE the HARVEST of your life—whether it is a DARK HARVEST or whether it is a HARVEST OF LIGHT. All will be REVEALED. I AM releasing this season of harvest in RESPONSE to your cries for RIGHTEOUSNESS and JUSTICE for your own lives and for your Nation. I AM releasing My SPIRITUAL harvest to align with your NATURAL harvest cycle. You are seeing the FIRST FRUITS of a BUMPER HARVEST SEASON. Monuments and leaders have begun to COME DOWN, and that will INCREASE throughout your summer and reach its PEAK in your Fall HARVEST season. My HARVEST of GLORY is also being released so that people do not DESPAIR and LOSE HEART when they see the

DEPTH of evil and how DECEIVED they have been. My GLORY brings My PRESENCE, My POWER, My HEALING, and My HOPE. My glory RE-CENTERS HEARTS on Me, and UNDERSTANDING will be imparted for the need of My JUDGMENT and JUSTICE. I have revealed the enemy's plans for LACK, DESTRUCTION, and CRASHES. Don't agree with those plans! Send that harvest into the enemy's camp, and you call in My GREATER HARVEST of PLENTY, PEACE, HEALTH, and FINANCIAL BLESSING. I set before you two HARVESTS—choose LIFE and oppose DEATH. All will be revealed in this season of A MATURING HARVEST."

AUGUST 4, 2024: SEEDTIME AND HARVEST

"The world is now approaching the FULLNESS of My HARVEST season. The world will be FORCED to acknowledge My principle of SEEDTIME AND HARVEST as what they have SOWED in their lives will now have to be HARVESTED. The enemy is usually trying to PUSH AHEAD My TIMELINES and SEASONS and INSERT his DARK PLANS of CHAOS and DESTRUCTION. However, in the case of this season of SEEDTIME AND HARVEST where everything in people's lives will be EXPOSED, he is trying to STOP this HARVEST of GOOD and EVIL. Once the GROSS EVIL is brought to the LIGHT in those partnered with him, his hopes of WORLD DOMINATION will come CRASHING DOWN. That is why you see so many DISTRACTIONS, PROTESTS, and THREATS coming through Leviathan's LYING mouth. The enemy knows he must STOP the EXPOSURES of SEEDTIME AND HARVEST because he knows his carefully-laid WEB of LIES and DEATH AGENDAS will be brought CRASHING DOWN and SWEPT into the DUSTBIN of history. Do you see now that we have the enemy on the DEFENSE and that your SPIRITUAL WARFARE has TURNED the TIDE against an ARROGANT EVIL AGENDA that they believed couldn't FAIL? Well, you have partnered with Me and My Host, and we have declared, 'YOU HAVE LOST! WE HAVE WON!' Your WORSHIP and your FERVENT PRAYERS of FAITH are CHANGING the FREQUENCIES in the atmosphere over the nations. These FREQUENCIES are BREAKING UP the DARKNESS and making WAY for My GLORY to FLOOD in. My GLORY brings all My PROMISES of HEALING, RESTORATION, and REWARD. My GLORY also EXPOSES the HARVEST of everyone's lives—either GOOD or EVIL, and both will be REPAID. The good will receive My BLESSING of MORE than you can CONTAIN, and the evil will be required to PAY BACK ALL that has been STOLEN and will be held ACCOUNTABLE for their DARK DEEDS. Keep CALLING IN the season of SEEDTIME AND HARVEST, and you will see the FULLNESS of My PROMISES for your life and your nations."

REWARDS AND THE WEALTH TRANSFER

We received exceedingly wonderful promises of rewards for our perseverance and our overcoming faith. The wealth transfer from the wicked to the righteous was another element of promised blessing for us.

REWARDS

APRIL 22, 2020: PRESS IN, PRESS IN, PRESS IN!

"This is not the time to be DISCOURAGED nor to turn back from the angry, defiling onslaught of the enemy. DO NOT LAY DOWN YOUR WEAPONS nor LEAVE THE BATTLEFIELD at this crucial time in the fight. Come to Me to be ENCOURAGED and to be STRENGTHENED and to be REMINDED that My plans have not changed—there will be VICTORY for those who PRESS IN to Me and who PRESS FORWARD into the fray of battle and who PRESS IN to the victory that they see coming with their spiritual eyes. Don't be left out of the REWARDS that will come to those who remain in the battle and who remain in faith that I Am who I say I Am and that I Am faithful to My promises. I have given you the privilege of partnering with Me in the battle, in the victory, and in the rewards of the spoils of the war. Be strong and courageous—I Am is with you! Press in, press in, press in!"

DECEMBER 31, 2021: THE DIVINE REWARD

"You are still here. You are still by My side and FIGHTING against the darkness and BELIEVING that what I have promised will come true. There may have been moments of doubt or impatience, but you have chosen to REALIGN yourself with Me and to STAND in faith. WHAT YOU HAVE LONGED TO SEE WILL UNFOLD BEFORE YOU. Have you longed for action and movement? Well, here it comes! I AM a REWARDER OF

FAITH and ENDURANCE. Your rewards will come in many forms. You will look with SATISFACTION as you see corrupt people and leaders meet with My JUSTICE. VINDICATION of all you've believed and proclaimed will be a SWEET REWARD. You will begin to receive PAYBACK for all the corrupt stole from you financially—this will continue for several years. I will BLESS everything you put your hand to, and your FRUITFULNESS will expand. I will reward you with My NEARNESS, and your spiritual SIGHT and HEARING will expand. Blessed are those who BELIEVE My promises and CLING tightly to My FAITHFULNESS. You are positioned for a DIVINE REWARD."

HEBREWS 10:32, 33, 35, 39 (TPT) *"Don't you remember those days right after the Light shined in your hearts? You endured a great marathon season of suffering hardships, yet you stood your ground. And at times you were publicly and shamefully mistreated, being persecuted for your faith; then at other times you stood side by side with those who preach the message of hope ... So don't lose your bold, courageous faith, for you are destined for a great reward! ... But we are certainly not those who are held back by fear and perish; we are among those who have faith and experience true life!"*

A year later, the Father spoke a similar word of encouragement about staying in the battle until we saw the victory and to continue to believe His promises.

December 19, 2022: Press In, Press On, Press Through

"Stay with Me, Army of Light, as we PLOW through these FINAL days of FIERCE battle. Stay CONNECTED with My PRESENCE all through your day and night by ACKNOWLEDGING I AM there, that I AM your STRENGTH, and that I have PROMISED you the VICTORY. Together, we are going to PRESS IN, PRESS ON, and PRESS THROUGH until you see the DAWNING of a NEW DAY. Do not BACK OFF or RUN from the battle—PRESS into the fight. I AM by your side, and so are My MIGHTY FIGHTING HOST. Do not be FOOLED by the enemy's INTIMIDATION because we are a POWERFUL marching force that makes the EARTH SHAKE as we go forward and PRESS ON THROUGH the enemy's troops who have been knocked OFF BALANCE by our forceful marching. They are PERPLEXED and SHAKEN because we are PRESSING ON THROUGH their ranks. As we PRESS ON through their SHAKEN and DIVIDED troops, we will secure a major VICTORY and OVERTHROW of the darkness. A SIGN of this victory will be when your rightful leader is RESTORED, but many other victories will be accomplished against their DEEP and DARK AGENDA. As you move into your new year, there will still be BATTLES, but they will not be this INTENSE, and you will have times of deep REST and RESTORATION. When you face battles in this coming year, they will be DIFFERENT because you will be FIGHTING FROM MAJOR VICTORIES and with much GREATER CONFIDENCE in My POWER and in My PROMISES FULFILLED. My beautiful Children, PRESS IN, PRESS ON, and PRESS THROUGH to STUNNING victories and great REWARDS."

DECEMBER 21, 2022: EPIC BATTLES, EPIC SEASON, EPIC REWARDS

"This time that you are living in will be labeled an EPIC TURNING POINT for the world. It will begin in your Nation, but it will flow out into all the world. Believe Me when I say that the EPIC BATTLES you have fought will lead to EPIC REWARDS that are more than you can imagine. You will continually say, 'Faithful, faithful God!' The battles for FREEDOM, LIGHT, and JUSTICE will have been so worth it when you see the PEACE and PROSPERITY that righteousness brings. The LIES, the HATRED, and the DARK SCHEMES will be WIPED AWAY. There will only be enough memory of the days of TYRANNY to make you DILIGENT to GUARD the TRUTH and FREEDOM. My light is ILLUMINATING their darkness, and it will be severely JUDGED, PUNISHED, and SWEPT AWAY. Behold, a NEW DAY, a NEW BEGINNING for the Land of the FREE and the home of My BRAVE-HEARTED Warriors."

JANUARY 30, 2023: SHOCK AND AWE REWARDS

"I AM God—there is no other who can COMPARE to Me in POWER, in MIGHT, or in LOVE. What I have done in the PAST for My people, I will do AGAIN. Every time Israel TURNED to Me in REPENTANCE for wandering AWAY from Me and turning to IDOLS, I RESPONDED with FIRE, WATER, and GREAT POWER to DELIVER them and to RESTORE their Land back to them. When a nation turns from Me, it OPENS THE DOOR for DECEPTION and TYRANNY to enter. My Remnant, My Army of

Light, had EYES TO SEE the CREEPING DARKNESS, and you CRIED OUT to Me in REPENTANCE for your Nation, and you PETITIONED Me for DELIVERANCE and a CLEANSING of your Land. I have heard your righteous cries, and I AM MOVING on your behalf with a mighty RESCUE OPERATION. I AM peeling back the DECEPTIVE COVERING on those partnered with darkness, and I AM EXPOSING their SELFISH GREED, their DEATH AGENDAS, and their DISGUSTING CORRUPTION and PERVERSION. A GREAT AWAKENING will be the result, and many voices will join yours in CRYING OUT in REPENTANCE and asking for DELIVERANCE. You will see the FULFILLMENT of all you have been praying and longing for. Life is about to be UPGRADED all around the world, but My BEST and FINEST REWARDS will come to you, My Remnant, My Army of Light, because you have STOOD IN FAITH with Me, and you have continued to PROCLAIM My PROMISES to an unbelieving world. You have been FAITHFUL to Me, and I AM about to SHOCK AND AWE you with My REWARDS. Well done, Army of Light!"

THE WEALTH TRANSFER

EXODUS 12:36 (NLT) *"The Lord caused the Egyptians to look favorably on the Israelites, and they gave the Israelites whatever they asked for. So they stripped the Egyptians of their wealth!"*

NOVEMBER 23, 2021: THE BLESSING AND THE CURSE

"Am I able to release BLESSING and CURSING at the same time? You will be WITNESSES of this coming to pass before your eyes in this season. It will be such a CONTRAST that the world will take notice. While evil systems are being JUDGED and brought DOWN, I will BLESS, SUSTAIN, and PROSPER those who belong to Me. It will be a SIGN and a WONDER to you and a RUDE WAKE-UP CALL to those who serve darkness. They will watch their fortunes CRUMBLE and their wealth transferred to the people of My Light. It's important that you WALK CLOSELY with Me in this season and look to Me for what to do and what not to do with your finances. Do not REACT to FEAR or evil reports, but RESPOND to My leading and My guidance."

SEPTEMBER 7, 2024: HOW WILL YOU HANDLE WEALTH?

"HOW WILL YOU HANDLE THE WEALTH that FLOWS to you when the TRANSFER happens from the WICKED to the RIGHTEOUS? I want you to ENJOY the WEALTH, and I want you to experience the FREEDOM of being DEBT-FREE—that is owing no man anything. However, I want you to realize that this JOY and FREEDOM will be SHORT-LIVED if you have not learned to be a GOOD STEWARD of what you have now. Are you a GIVER and a SAVER? Or are you always SPENDING BEYOND what you have been entrusted with? Are you JEALOUS and RESENTFUL of others who always seem to have MORE than you do? You may have a SPIRIT of POVERTY over you and your generations that needs to be BROKEN, and you must come OUT of AGREEMENT with CONTINUAL LACK and CHOOSE to BELIEVE I AM a GOOD and GENEROUS PROVIDER. GRUMBLING and RESENTMENT will NOT ATTRACT My PROVISION, but THANKFULNESS and FAITH in My GOODNESS will. You may be going through a SEASON of LACK as a TESTING and TRAINING GROUND for a FUTURE WEALTH TRANSFER. Do you maintain a GRATEFUL HEART and a FAITH EXPECTANCY that I will COME THROUGH for you? If you FIX your EYES on WEALTH instead of on Me, it can become a STUMBLING BLOCK in your life. You will be a STINGY GIVER, and you'll begin to live BEYOND what you have been entrusted with and will find yourself IN DEBT AGAIN. Ask Holy Spirit to SEARCH YOUR HEART for any WRONG MOTIVES regarding WEALTH and to help you become someone I can ENTRUST with WEALTH. Kingdom finances are built on JOY, THANKSGIVING, GIVING, and SHARING. It will CREATE a CYCLE of BLESSING in your family and in your nations. Now is the time to ask yourself, 'HOW WILL I HANDLE WEALTH?'"

The powerful and wonderful fulfillment of these promises was amazing, but the Father had an even more exciting future planned for the earth and for His people.

CHAPTER TWELVE

On Earth as It Is in Heaven

Remember praying this phrase in the Lord's Prayer: "Your Kingdom come, Your will be done, on earth as it is in Heaven?" The Father's plan has always been to establish the Kingdom of Heaven on the earth among mankind who are the crown of His creation. The sin and rebellion of mankind has delayed the fulfillment of this prayer spoken by King Jesus Himself. However, this did not surprise the Father, Son, and Holy Spirit. In fact, the Father and Jesus had made a covenant together before the creation of the earth that the Son would serve as a perfect sin offering in order to reconcile God and man.

HEBREWS 13:20-21a (NLT) *"Now may the God of peace—who brought up from the dead our Lord Jesus, the great Shepherd of the sheep, and ratified an eternal covenant with His blood—may He equip you with all you need for doing His will."*

2 TIMOTHY 1:9 (NLT), *"For God saved us and called us to live a holy life. He did this, not because we deserved it, but because that was His plan from before the beginning of time—to show us His grace through Jesus Christ."*

1 PETER 1:20 (TPT) *"This was part of God's plan, for He was chosen and destined for this before the foundation of the earth was laid, but He has been made manifest in these last days for you."*

THE KINGDOM AGE

The Church has not always recognized that the sacrificial death of Jesus was to accomplish more than the wonderful gift of salvation; it was also to take back the authority over the earth because man's sin had foolishly given that authority to the great deceiver, Satan. Jesus' death and resurrection won back the authority over the earth, and He delegated that authority to us. The infilling of the Holy Spirit into the Believer's life was meant to transform us into His image and to empower us to live as Sons and Daughters of His Kingdom.

ROMANS 8:15, 19, and 21 (NKJV), *"For you did not receive the spirit of bondage again to fear, but you received the Spirit of adoption by whom we cry out, 'Abba, Father' ... For the earnest expectation of the creation eagerly waits for the revealing of the sons of God ... Because the creation itself also will be delivered from the bondage of corruption into the glorious liberty of the children of God."*

What glorious news that we have been called to rule and reign upon the earth as His Sons and Daughters.

REVELATION 5:10 (NKJV) *"And have made us kings and priests to our God; and we shall reign on the earth."*

When King Jesus came to the earth, His supernatural Kingdom came with Him. He came to fulfill Isaiah 61:1-2a (AMP) *"The Spirit of the Lord God is upon Me, because the Lord has anointed and commissioned Me to bring good news to the humble and afflicted; He has sent Me to bind up (the wounds of) the brokenhearted, to proclaim release (from confinement and condemnation) to the (physical and spiritual) captives and freedom to prisoners, to proclaim the favorable year of the Lord..."* Jesus quoted these verses from Isaiah in Luke 4:18-19 at the beginning of His earthly ministry. During His time on the earth, He opened blind eyes, unstopped deaf ears, healed sickness and disease, comforted broken hearts, and brought the dead back to life. As the perfect Lamb sacrifice, He became salvation, healing, and deliverance for us.

When Jesus quoted these words from the book of Isaiah in the Temple that Sabbath day, He stopped mid-sentence, closed the scroll, and declared to the listeners that He had come to fulfill these verses. What an astonishing and life-giving announcement went out into the atmosphere that day! But why did He stop mid-sentence with, *"To proclaim the favorable year of the Lord?"* The verse continues in ISAIAH 61:2b (AMP) *"And the day of vengeance and retribution of our God ..."* Some have believed this speaks of a final day of judgment on the earth, but if you keep reading the following verses, you will realize they are speaking of a day when the Lord would deal decisively with His enemies (PSALM 2) to make way for His Kingdom to flourish.

The rest of the verses (ISAIAH 61:2b-11) go on to list a job description of those who embrace the good news Jesus brought, do the things Jesus did, and take part in establishing the Kingdom on the earth. We are called to comfort those who mourn with the Good News and to give them a garment of praise.

ISAIAH 3b (AMP) *"So they will be called the trees of righteousness (strong and magnificent, distinguished for integrity, justice, and right standing with God), the planting of the Lord, that He may be glorified."*

We are called to rebuild, restore, and renew what has been ruined and devastated by the evil empire and selfish men and women partnered with the enemy. As the verses continue, they speak of the wealth of the nations coming to the righteous (wealth transfer), receiving a double portion for the shame and humiliation we have suffered, and coming into His joy and His rewards. His power will cause all of these things to spring up as a witness to the nations. Righteousness and justice, the foundation of His Kingdom Throne, will once again fill the land.

Everything that God does and blesses expands, and so the Kingdom has continued to expand up to our day. In ages past, the Kingdom was often hindered and almost hidden by the darkness, but the Father has shared with us that this is the time that He has chosen to remove enthroned evil and those who partner with it in our nations. The Father clearly laid this out long ago, and the Book of Daniel carries this message.

DANIEL 2:44-45 (TPT) *"In the days of those kings of iron and clay, the God of heaven will set up an eternal kingdom that will never be destroyed nor ruled by other people. It will shatter and bring all other kingdoms to an end, and it will stand forever! This is the meaning of what you saw in your vision: a rock cut out of a mountain—but not by human hands."* (Jesus) *The rock that shattered the iron, the bronze, the clay, the silver, and the gold (representing man's kingdoms) to pieces is His eternal kingdom. The Great God has revealed to you, the king, what will take place after this. The dream is true, and its interpretation trustworthy."* (Emphasis mine.)

The Father's goal is to further expand the reach, the power, and the blessing of this Kairos moment of time called the Kingdom Age.

Here is a sampling of the many wonderful journal entries where the Father spoke to us concerning His Kingdom Age. During this war season, many of us would repeatedly be shown repeating numbers. One of those sequences that was seen by multitudes of the Army of Light was 2:22. The following entry was received on 2/22/2020—that's a lot of "2's!" The Father showed us a Scripture promise tied to these numbers.

FEBRUARY 22, 2020: THE OPENER

ISAIAH 22:22 The Key of David

"I have declared My Body to be the OPENER of My Kingdom rule and ways in this important hour. I have laid the authority of My Word and My ways upon you so that we partner together to bring about My Kingdom authority and rule at this time on the earth. You bear My name, and you carry out My commands as My sons and daughters. This day you will help ESTABLISH a new day of authority over sickness, war, and poverty—all the areas the enemy has sought to bring down the crown of My creation. What you BIND and close off

will be shut and locked, and what you LOOSEN and free will be opened and no one will be able to shut. The key of David has now been given to those who look to Me with eyes of faith and who are not distracted by what the enemy is stirring up and flinging in their face to cause fear and anxiety. Keep focused on My face, My eyes, My voice, and you will TRIUMPH with Me."

July 14, 2020: A Season of Restoration and Recompense (repay, reward)

"This day marks the beginning of a season of RESTORATION and RECOMPENSE to your family and for your Nation. This season will spread throughout the world bringing great joy and freedom. The grip that a small group of people have who are given over to evil, greed, and a hunger for power is coming to an end. Little by little, their strong grip on the world's finances is being loosened. Little by little, their control over such areas like disease prevention and cures is being pried off. Little by little, their control over governments, lawmakers, and judges is being swept clean. Keep pressing forward, Army of God, and partner with Me to push back the darkness and to bring in the light of the KINGDOM. While the darkness is being crushed, I am releasing payback to those stolen from in the form of debt cancellation, prosperity, new ideas and innovations, restored health, and cures for diseases that have plagued the world. Beloved, this is why the battle has been so fierce and the attacks so rampant. The enemy is in desperation-mode to maintain his ancient strongholds, but I am arising in this season to help My people take back their nations and to establish My KINGDOM RULE and REIGN in the earth. Rejoice! RESTORATION and RECOMPENSE are here!"

It was important that we knew what had allowed the darkness to infiltrate every area of society. For the most part, the Church had remained silent and uninvolved, and that created a vacuum in society that evil quickly filled.

JANUARY 28, 2023: A DAY IS COMING ...

"A DAY IS COMING, My faithful Army of Light, when you will no longer be FORCED to live under evil leaders who seek to DESTROY you or to CONTROL you. Their plan was EXTENSIVE, very DARK, and covered over with DECEPTION and DELUSION. My Beloved Church was not waging an EFFECTIVE spiritual war against this RISING DARKNESS because they bought into an ESCAPIST MENTALITY—TARES SOWN among the WHEAT. Their focus was on ESCAPING all areas of culture because they saw darkness in them; thus, they ABANDONED society to the darkness and allowed it to RULE in their place. They HUNKERED down behind their stacks of freeze-dried food and waited to be TRANSPORTED to Heaven out of the darkness they FEARED. Let Me assure you that when My Son brings His Bride home to meet Me, she will be a STRONG, BEAUTIFUL, VICTORIOUS BRIDE who helped ADVANCE My Kingdom of Light and who FOUGHT BY MY SIDE to DEFEAT darkness and to RULE and REIGN with Me. It's time the Church FACED HER FEARS and came out of HIDING. You are not called to ESCAPE; you are called to REIGN with Me. You are not called to HIDE from the darkness; you are meant to SHINE My BEAUTIFUL LIGHT into the darkness and to bring My Kingdom RULE and WAYS across all areas of your society. Don't MISS the TIME of your VISITATION! I AM coming to RESCUE you from the dark death agenda and to bring in My LIFE and LIGHT. It will be those who BELIEVED My PROMISE and FOUGHT by My side in FAITH who will receive GREAT REWARDS. The world is getting ready to FREAK OUT at My coming shakings, but to you, they will not be OVERWHELMING because you see with My eyes and know that A DAY IS COMING when we will TRAMPLE evil into the dust and a NEW DAY will dawn for JUSTICE, RIGHTEOUSNESS, and FREEDOM."

The Father let us know that He was performing the Rescue of the Ages, but He was also establishing His Kingdom on the earth.

MARCH 15, 2024: IT WILL BE DONE!

This word began with a brief visit to the Throne Room. I was sitting by the Father's knee, and I heard the voice of many waters booming out, "It will be done!" At this command, the Hosts and Angels shot out of the Throne Room in all directions to fulfill His word.

MATTHEW 6:10 (TPT) *"Manifest Your Kingdom realm (or come and begin Your Kingdom reign) and cause Your every purpose to be fulfilled on earth, just as it is in heaven."*

The Father speaks: "This is the ESSENCE of what I AM doing in your day. When Heaven and earth AGREE, IT WILL BE DONE! My GROWING REMNANT are CRYING OUT for the POWER of the DARKNESS to be SMASHED and for My RESCUE to come and SET THEM FREE from the SLAVERY and BONDAGE they have been HELD CAPTIVE by. Whenever darkness is TAKEN DOWN and My FREEDOM and LIGHT FLOOD IN, there you will find My KINGDOM BEING ESTABLISHED. My Kingdom is established where My WILL IS DONE. That includes INDIVIDUAL LIVES and NATIONS. I AM not just coming to RESCUE you from TYRANNY and DARKNESS; I AM coming to ESTABLISH My KINGDOM in its place. My Kingdom is full of LIGHT, FREEDOM, PEACE, and PLENTY. Its foundations are RIGHTEOUSNESS and JUSTICE. I don't have to remind you how TWISTED these have become in your day. The enemy will tell you that My Kingdom is RESTRICTIVE, but I tell you that the FREEDOM TO DO what is RIGHT and JUST will fill your life with FAVOR, PEACE, and FULFILLMENT. My BEAUTIFUL REMNANT, your CRIES for My Kingdom TO COME and My WILL TO BE DONE on EARTH as it is in HEAVEN have been HEARD. My voice has THUNDERED in the Throne Room, 'IT WILL BE DONE!" And so it shall be."

DECEMBER 9, 2024: THE EXPANSION OF MY KINGDOM AGE

"THE KINGDOM AGE that you and your world are ENTERING INTO is an age of EXPANSION, SHALOM, and INCREASED ANOINTING. We have partnered together to DEFEAT the LIFE-STEALING, TYRANNICAL DARKNESS and as this evil empire COLLAPSES and is put UNDER your feet, you will see THE EXPANSION OF MY KINGDOM AGE. DANIEL 2:45 (TPT)'*Then, all at once, the entire statue collapsed into a heap of rubble. The iron and clay, bronze, silver, and gold were all pulverized as fine as chaff on the summer threshing floor. The wind blew the shattered pieces away, leaving not a trace behind. But the Boulder that hit the statue grew into a massive mountain that covered the whole earth.'* You will SEE this Scripture FULFILLED in your day. My Heavenly atmosphere of SHALOM will FLOOD the earth in the place of FEAR, HATRED, and DEATH AGENDAS. My SHALOM will bring GREAT PEACE, BEAUTIFUL REST, and NOTHING MISSING, NOTHING BROKEN. As Light DISPLACES darkness in all areas of society, an INCREASED ANOINTING will be RELEASED. You will have the POWER and the AUTHORITY to REVERSE THE CURSE of DEATH AGENDAS that have been sent against you from TAINTED MEDICATIONS, harmful IMMUNIZATIONS, unhealthy MODIFIED FOODS, IMPURE WATER AND AIR. You will be given the authority to STOP the DEATH and to RELEASE FULLNESS of LIFE—My LIFE, KINGDOM LIFE. This INCREASED ANOINTING will also affect the governmental mountain. You are to take AUTHORITY over all the TYRANNICAL and EVIL LAWS put in place by the darkness. You are to CALL THEM DOWN and WIPE THEM OUT and WELCOME the CLEAN SWEEP of My Spirit as JUSTICE and RIGHTEOUSNESS ROLL IN to WIPE OUT all evil agendas and foundations. Breathe in the SWEET and CLEAN AIR of FREEDOM, as we move into THE EXPANSION OF MY KINGDOM AGE."

Jesus told the Church to occupy until He returns. LUKE 19:13 (KJV) *"And he called his ten servants, and delivered them ten pounds, and said unto them, 'Occupy till I come.'"* The Father began to call us "Sons and Daughters" of the Kingdom who were learning to rule and reign with Him.

SONS AND DAUGHTERS OF THE KINGDOM

The Father's message has been consistent since November 12, 2017, when He began speaking to me about the Kingdom Age and raising up Sons and Daughters who would learn to rule and reign with Him. This entry from 2017 was before I began to post on social media, so this is the first time this journal entry has been made public.

NOVEMBER 12, 2017: SEASON TO CO-REIGN

"Your heart is in SYNC with My heart that this is NOT the time for the catching away of the Church, but it is time for My Bride, My Army, My City to ARISE to My side and learn to CO-REIGN with Me in bringing and establishing My Kingdom on this earth. This is not a time to FOCUS ON ESCAPE. It is a time to STAND and give NO further GROUND to the enemy. After you have learned to STAND, it is time to learn to ADVANCE into every area of culture and government, advancing in My LOVE, POWER, and AUTHORITY. This is the DESTINY and CALL on My Church, My Bride, My Friend. My DEEPEST DESIRE is to have you PARTNERING with Me in bringing LIGHT into the darkness, ORDER into the chaos, BEAUTY into the ugliness, GRACE and MERCY into STRIVING and CONDEMNATION. AWAKEN, RISE UP, GIRD YOURSELF in My STRENGTH and

BEAUTY, and STAND by My side as we move together to bring My KINGDOM TO THIS EARTH.'"

MARCH 8, 2023: YOU ARE ROYALTY

"Grasp this fact: as BLOOD-BOUGHT Sons and Daughters of the Most High God, you have become CO-HEIRS with Jesus. You have been saved, healed, and delivered, and you have become ROYALTY because ROYAL BLOOD now flows in you. This is the basis of your AUTHORITY over darkness. The enemy works hard to CONVINCE Believers that they are HELPLESS against the darkness and that they must HIDE from the darkness. But I tell you that you are MORE THAN CONQUERORS: Romans 8:37 *'Yet in all these things we are more than conquerors and gain an overwhelming victory through Him who loved us (so much that He died for us).'* The darkness TREMBLES with FEAR when a Believer realizes their AUTHORITY over the enemy and all his plans. The darkness will PUFF itself up and GROWL INTIMIDATING THREATS trying to scare you away from EXERCISING your AUTHORITY. Do what I do and LAUGH at the enemy! As My AWAKENED Sons and Daughters raise their voices in LAUGHTER, in DECREES, in PRAYERS, the FREQUENCIES of these sounds of AUTHORITY will COLLAPSE the enemy's house of cards. You are dressed in the ARMOR OF LIGHT (Romans 13:12), you have the FLAMING SWORD OF TRUTH—not to use against your brothers, but to CUT OFF the heads of LIES and GIANTS. Raise your BATTLECRY, Army of Light. MARCH FORTH to take back your INHERITANCE that was stolen by the darkness. YOU ARE ROYALTY!"

This would be a season of great contrasts between the darkness and the light. What you believed about end times teaching would either set you up to fight or to be defeated before the battle even began.

NOVEMBER 25, 2022: A TIME OF GREAT DREAD

"The ARROGANT ones who tried to DESTROY your Nation and to CONTROL the world will soon be facing A TIME OF GREAT DREAD. (Dread=to be in terror, fear intensely, anticipate with alarm.) These who thought they were UNTOUCHABLE will be FULLY EXPOSED for the world to see. Their CORRUPTION, PERVERSION, and EVIL PLANS will be PARADED before the world. Their WEALTH, their PROTECTION, and their POSITIONS will all be WIPED AWAY. Those who lorded it over you will find themselves at the BOTTOM of the heap, and JUDGMENT and JUSTICE will make the DECISIONS for their lives. This will, indeed, be A TIME OF GREAT DREAD for the darkness. However, this is NOT a time of dread for My people, those called by My name. This is a season of HARVEST and RECOMPENSE for all that has been STOLEN from you. Some in My Body have been taught to HYPER-FOCUS on what they have been taught will happen at the end of time. This causes them to VIEW LIFE from this LENS of LACK and TERRIBLE TROUBLES instead of viewing My WHOLE COUNSEL revealed in My Word and in My heart. I have called you to ARISE and SHINE, to be the LIGHT of the world and the SALT of the earth, to OCCUPY until I return, and to BELIEVE My promise that I will ALWAYS LEAD YOU IN TRIUMPH IN CHRIST. Those who embrace My WHOLE COUNSEL will lead FRUITFUL and

ABUNDANT lives. Those who HYPER-FOCUS on the end being years of suffering and loss will live with NO HOPE for the future, and they will not INVEST their lives in bringing My KINGDOM to earth as it is in Heaven. Their lives will be spiritually STUNTED with LITTLE FRUIT produced for My Kingdom. Yes, there is A DAY OF DREAD for the wicked, but this is to make way for a SHINING ERA of My GOODNESS being displayed on the earth and in My people. It is a season of a HARVEST of PLENTY in both the natural and spiritual realms as many come FLOODING into My Kingdom. GOOD TIMES are just ahead."

Don't you love a mystery revealed? The Father promised exposure of both darkness that was holding us back and the uncovering of wonderful mysteries that would ignite passion and purpose.

JUNE 27, 2023: MYSTERIES REVEALED

"The NEW ERA you are entering will be a time of MYSTERIES REVEALED. Darkness will be UNCOVERED like never before. Its SCHEMES, its WEB OF LIES, and the WAYS it uses to ENSNARE people into its SHADOWS and BONDAGE will be LAID BARE. Wherever there are people who are PARTNERING with darkness—especially those who PRESENT themselves as people of LIGHT but who are COMPROMISED by WILLFULLY CHOOSING DARKNESS and keeping it HIDDEN under a FAÇADE —these will all be EXPOSED. This EXPOSURE will be across ALL seven mountains of society, including My CHURCH. I need a HOLY (set apart) people who REFUSE to partner with the darkness so that the **LIGHT** of My **GLORY** will **SHINE** through them **FULLY**. My **SPIRITUAL MYSTERIES** will also be **UNCOVERED** and **REVEALED** like at no other time in history. These **TREASURES** have been in My Word all along but have been kept **HIDDEN** until this time when they will come into **FULFILLMENT** in this **KINGDOM ERA**. Pray that those teachers in My Body who are caught up in teaching **DOCTRINES OF DEMONS** would receive a **RELEASE** of My **REVELATION LIGHT** that would **CORRECT** their course. If they do not **STOP DISEMPOWERING** My people and **STEALING** the **GLORIOUS FUTURE** of My **KINGDOM ERA** here on the earth, then I will **REMOVE** them. **WAKE UP, CHURCH!** I **AM** not coming to take you **OUT** of this world; I **AM** coming to take you **INTO** a **GLORIOUS ERA** of **RULING** and **REIGNING** as Sons and Daughters of **LIGHT**. **POSITION** your hearts in **HUMILITY** to receive My **MYSTERIES REVEALED**, and be **READY** to **LET GO** of any areas where you have been believing doctrines of men and demons. My **MYSTERIES REVEALED** carry My **FIRE** to **BURN AWAY DARKNESS** and to **IGNITE PASSION** and **PURPOSE**. Enter into My **MYSTERIES REVEALED**."

The Father began to instruct us as His Sons and Daughters how to deal with the rising darkness and the storms the darkness was bringing. We had to learn to take authority over the darkness in the power of Jesus' Blood and to bring in the peace of Heaven to change the atmosphere.

MAY 6, 2022: STORM WARNINGS

"The enemy and those partnered with him are FRANTICALLY and ANGRILY stirring up STORMS. They want to make My Army of Light PAY for daring to STAND FOR LIFE AND TRUTH and for attempting to REVERSE THE CURSE they so carefully constructed for your Nation. Should you be AFRAID of these storms? ABSOLUTELY NOT!!! My Son SPOKE PEACE to the storm, and He CALMED the wind and the waves. You are My blood-bought sons and daughters, and I have given you My Son's AUTHORITY to exercise on earth. You have the AUTHORITY to speak to these STORMS generated by the darkness. Hold up your EDICT for your Nation written in My Son's BLOOD, and COMMAND the WINDS (enemy-generated backlash) and the WAVES (the agitation of the people by dark powers of FEAR and HATRED) to be STILL, and RELEASE the PEACE OF HEAVEN into the atmosphere. Take the WIND of ANGRY, MISGUIDED PROTEST, and DEFLATE its source like a balloon leaking air. SPEAK to the WAVES of DESTRUCTIVE BEHAVIOR, and DISCONNECT them from their dark power source. Tell the anger and destruction to CEASE and for people to be brought into their RIGHT MINDS—suddenly AWAKENED to the truth. I AM giving you STORM WARNINGS so that you can NULLIFY the works of darkness and bring in My PEACE. Army of Light—you were made for this day!"

Based on His eternal Word, He laid out a blueprint for His Sons and Daughter's to follow to bring in the victory.

JUNE 20, 2022: THE CUTTING EDGE (A BLUEPRINT)

"In the coming months, you will see the enemy empty out his arsenal of evil plans in order to cause great DESTRUCTION and FEAR and to gain CONTROL over the people of your Land. You are not to respond as HELPLESS BYSTANDERS, nor are you to stand by CLUCKING your tongue because you think I AM judging your whole Nation. This is the very day you were made for! This is the time to ARISE wearing the SHINING ARMOR of My GLORY (Ephesians 5:14)! You have been given the MOST POWERFUL WEAPONS known to man: My NAME (John 14:14), My AUTHORITY (Mathew 16:19), My WORD (which is a HAMMER-Jeremiah 23:29, and a SWORD-Ephesians 6:17), the HIGH PRAISES OF GOD (Psalm 149:6-9), and your Heavenly PRAYER LANGUAGE (Acts 2:4, 1 Corinthians 14:2, 1 Corinthians 14:15). These weapons equip you to be the CUTTING EDGE in the battle ahead—not defending your territory but MOVING OFFENSIVELY to TAKE BACK what has been STOLEN in the past and to PREVENT further attacks that seek to take by FORCE and by FEAR all your FREEDOMS AND LIBERTIES. I have DEPLOYED the Host of Heaven to go BEFORE you, to be IN your ranks, and to come BEHIND you providing forward MOMENTUM and STRENGTH to all who have SWORN ALLEGIANCE to Me. Because you are My CUTTING EDGE, do not allow anything the enemy tries— protests, media lies, lab-created sickness, destructive weather, threats of war, financial breakdown—to go UNCHALLENGED. Take AUTHORITY over all these dark plans and bring them CRASHING DOWN; RELEASE My good plans and My glory into your Land; COUNTER lies with My truth; DECLARE an outbreak of healing to triumph over any outbreak of sickness;

209

in the face of financial loss, AFFIRM that I AM your source and generous PROVIDER; NULLIFY threats of war with My peace; remember you have authority over destructive weather stirred up by the enemy. My STRENGTH (Psalm 31:4) and My SWORD are always available to you—be MY CUTTING EDGE!"

Even though we were faced with giants who were carrying out death agendas against us, it was revealed to us that our eternal covenant released resurrection power that overcame death. We were to arise and take back our nation, our families, and the Church for the Kingdom. As co-heirs with Christ Jesus, we need to see ourselves wearing crowns and learn to rule and reign in partnership with the Father.

NOVEMBER 5, 2023: PUT YOUR CROWN ON!

"You have seen the DEVASTATING effects that DARKNESS has had on your Nation and on your own family. You have seen the POWER of MEDIA to MESMERIZE and CAPTIVATE people with LIES. You have seen a COMPROMISED medical system contribute to DECLINING HEALTH and even to UNNECESSARY DEATHS. You can now clearly see the GIANTS in the land, but how do you DEFEAT these GIANTS and BRING DOWN their DEATH AGENDAS? They seem so POWERFUL and so HUGE. What DIFFERENCE can you make? Remember that My Sons and Daughters who have been washed in the BLOOD of My Son and whose lives have been SURRENDERED back to Me have become part of the ETERNAL COVENANT established before time began and SEALED by My Son's SACRIFICE and BLOOD. His TRIUMPH over SIN and DEATH released RESURRECTION

POWER into the world, and it WON BACK AUTHORITY over the earth that mankind had given away. When you are JOINED into the BLOOD COVENANT, you are CO-HEIRS of RESURRECTION POWER and ALL the AUTHORITY of the KINGDOM. It is now time for you to ARISE in your COVENANT POWER and TAKE BACK the LAND, TAKE BACK your FAMILIES, and TAKE BACK the CHURCH for My KINGDOM. Jesus paid the ULTIMATE price for your CROWN OF AUTHORITY. Now, PUT YOUR CROWN ON, and RULE and REIGN with Me. David believed in My COVENANT with Israel, and he BROUGHT DOWN the GIANT with one stone and DELIVERED a whole nation. You have a SUPERIOR COVENANT, and it contains GREAT POWER and AUTHORITY. Time to PUT YOUR CROWN ON and use your VOICE, your PRAYERS, your DECREES, your DECLARATIONS to BRING DOWN the GIANTS and to RELEASE the KINGDOM of LIGHT into each area where darkness has STOLEN the GROUND. Realize that your VOICE and your FAITH have GREAT POWER. Declare to the darkness, 'You may not have my nation!' 'You may not have my family!' 'You may not have the Church!' 'I decree these are Kingdom territories, and I take them back in the name of My Victorious King Jesus!' 'Darkness, be exposed and come down!' 'Lies and brainwashing be exposed and destroyed!' 'I speak over my nation and my family that we will serve the Lord and bear good fruit for the beautiful Kingdom of God!" My people, PUT YOUR CROWNS ON!"

The wonderful news that we received from the Father for this warfare season is that He did not expect us to gut this out on our own. He was more than willing to lend us His strength, His comfort, and His warrior strength.

JANUARY 16, 2025: WARRIOR STRENGTH

"WARRIOR STRENGTH is needed in this hour to SEE YOU THROUGH to the VICTORIOUS ending of this war from DARK to LIGHT. Remember that I AM READY and WILLING to MEET your every NEED, and I will GLADLY SUPPLY you with WARRIOR STRENGTH. This is a SUPERNATURAL STRENGTH that only comes from RELATIONSHIP with Me. I don't expect you to gut out this intense season in your OWN STRENGTH. You are Sons and Daughters of the Most High King and HEIRS to the Kingdom of SUPERNATURAL LIFE and LIGHT. You are to live from that Kingdom RIGHT NOW. Don't allow the enemy to CONVINCE you that you have been ABANDONED or IGNORED and that you have to make it through on your own. The TRUTH is, I will NEVER leave you or fail you, and I will SUPPLY ALL your needs from My rich storehouse of grace and from My heart of endless love for you. The enemy is TERRIFIED of your WARRIOR STRENGTH, and he is doing everything he can to DISTRACT and DISCOURAGE you and get you to SLACK OFF your WARFARE or to LEAVE the battlefield just before your biggest BREAKTHROUGH. Don't let the enemy STEAL your WARRIOR STRENGTH and ROB you of SWEET VINDICATION and GREAT REWARDS. I welcome you to come to Me in your WEARINESS, TRAUMA, and HOPE DEFERRED. I will ENFOLD you in My arms, KISS you tenderly, COMFORT your heart, and REFILL you with WARRIOR STRENGTH and SHINING EYES. I will RENEW your vision to see BEYOND the smoke and noise of the battlefield. I will give you WARRIOR STRENGTH and eyes to see a future of TRIUMPH, LIGHT, and JOY."

Another key component of the Kingdom Age was the return across the earth of the fear of the Lord.

THE FEAR OF THE LORD

The fear of the Lord is clean and enduring, and it promotes righteous living and true freedom. It is rightly discerning His character—both His kindness towards those who come to Him through the Blood of His Son and His severity towards unrepentant evil. The Father first spoke to me about the fear of the Lord sweeping our nation even before I began to post on social media. His message has not changed or altered over these years of battle.

NOVEMBER 14, 2017 : YOU WILL LOOK TO ME

"When I MOVE on behalf of your Nation, there will be NO DOUBT that I AM behind it. You will see SECRETS UNCOVERED SUPERNATURALLY with DOCUMENTS and CONVERSATIONS, supposedly destroyed, brought to LIGHT. This will cause the FEAR OF THE LORD to SWEEP across this Nation—there will be PANIC and CHAOS in the camp of the enemy, and great JOY and FULFILLMENT released among the righteous. A NEW DAY is coming, so HANG ON, continue to PRAY that My will be done and My Kingdom come, and LOOK TO ME to fulfill My word and promises for your Nation. The enemy has OVERPLAYED his hand and has become so BLATANT that all can see the LYING, DISTORTION, and VICIOUS ATTACKS he has orchestrated through CORRUPT vessels. My light will TRIUMPH over darkness every time. I AM FAITHFUL to My promises, and I AM well able to PERFORM My will among men. REST in My goodness, and PARTNER with Me in bringing in My Kingdom."

DECEMBER 18, 2019: REASON TO LAUGH AND REJOICE

"I will be giving the world a reason to laugh and a reason to rejoice as CORRUPTION is exposed and JUSTICE takes place in your Nation because it will flow out from your Land into all the world. Those with eyes to see will recognize the POWER of My strong right arm, and it will give them HOPE. When they see My light uncover darkness, they will welcome My light into their own nations. The fear of the Lord will sweep the nations, causing many to REEVALUATE what they thought of Me, and they will search for Me and find Me as a TRUSTWORTHY ANCHOR and a willing defense of their lives. This is a season of GREAT HOPE AND DREAMS COME TRUE for all who have looked to Me for help. Their cries and their trust will be VINDICATED."

DECEMBER 19, 2019: PRAY!

"Pray for your Nation to become one again ... the UNITED States of America. Release My truth and My exposures of evil and corruption into the atmosphere. Declare that nothing of darkness will remain hidden from My Light. Declare that strongholds of DECEPTION and the TWISTING OF TRUTH and the calling of light as darkness and darkness as light would be DEMOLISHED by My hammer of justice smashing them and that FORTRESSES of TRUTH AND CLARITY AND PURITY would be built in place of these structures of evil. Release the clean and enduring fear of the Lord as the disclosures of pure evil, lying, and hatred come to the light. The fear of the Lord will bring WISDOM and VISION, and this will result in a complete change of the atmosphere from DIVISION and CONFUSION to an atmosphere of UNITY, CLARITY, and WISE THINKING. Partner with Me in bringing about this shift from division to unity. This will release even more prosperity, peace, and well-being into your Land."

JULY 29, 2022: AWE AND WONDER

"After I have FURIOUSLY driven My chariot of FIERY EXPOSURE and JUDGMENT across your Land, the ground and the people will TREMBLE in SHOCK as the DEEP DARKNESS and HATRED towards them is LAID BARE before the world. As those who were thought to be UNTOUCHABLE (including former presidents and those in high positions of control over power and wealth), are brought CRASHING DOWN, and who they really are and what they had planned for your DESTRUCTION is revealed, the FEAR OF THE LORD will sweep over the world. The fear of the Lord is CLEAN and ENDURING, and it REMOVES fear and the fear of man. When the many FEARS that the enemy sows are DISEMPOWERED, people will be able to see CLEARLY, and they will see My Son for who He is, and they will want to be part of My Kingdom of Light. DECEPTIONS and LIES will FALL AWAY as the fear of the Lord CLEANSES peoples' vision. They will CLEARLY see that it is My hand that has RESCUED them from their dark enemy, and they will know My POWER and My LOVE. Army of Light, you have fought VALIANTLY by My side to WIN this war of light over darkness. Now, you will become an Army of Harvesters who help bring in the nations to My Throne of GRACE through the BLOOD of My Son. Just as JUDGMENT and JUSTICE swept across your Land, so what follows will be an era of AWE and WONDER. AWE and WONDER of who I AM and of what I will RESTORE to you—more than you can think or imagine! Look ahead to when the war is won, and call in My AWE and WONDER."

OCTOBER 31, 2023: TREMBLE

"TREMBLE before Me, O nations of the earth. TREMBLE before Me, all those who have chosen darkness. TREMBLE before Me, all you who have been made clean by the BLOOD of the Lamb. The whole earth will TREMBLE when My FOOT touches the earth and My HAMMER BLOW of JUSTICE strikes the ground. When My VANQUISHING TRIUMPH is displayed before the heavens and the earth, ALL WILL TREMBLE and ALL will know that I AM GOD. This inner TREMBLING that you feel is THE FEAR OF THE LORD. It is RIGHTLY DISCERNING MY CHARACTER—both My KINDNESS and My SEVERITY. It is knowing My SOVEREIGNTY and My AWESOME POWER but realizing that I have DELEGATED DOMINION of the earth to man. Most of My Church LOST SIGHT of this fact that part of your MANDATE was to RULE and REIGN as SONS and DAUGHTERS of LIGHT, and DARKNESS OVERTOOK the areas you were meant to be the SALT that PRESERVES and the LIGHT that EXPOSES the darkness. Now your eyes have OPENED, you have REPENTED for HIDING your LIGHT, and you have CALLED on Me to come and DELIVER you from the enemy you allowed to grow so strong that it THREATENS to OVERPOWER and CONTROL you. I have asked you to PARTNER with Me as My Army of Light, and you have learned to be a VALIANT WARRIOR. We will have a RESOUNDING VICTORY that will cause the nations to TREMBLE. Welcome this TREMBLING; it is the HOLY, CLEAN, and ENDURING FEAR OF THE LORD. As it SWEEPS the earth, IDOLS will FALL, hearts will REPENT and be CLEANSED by the BLOOD, and RIGHTEOUSNESS and JUSTICE will PREVAIL. TREMBLE before Me."

The fear of the Lord is connected with the restoration of all things.

NOVEMBER 26, 2024: THE RESTORATION OF ALL THINGS

"What do I mean when I say in My Word (Acts 3:21) the PROMISE of a season of THE RESTORATION OF ALL THINGS? Does ALL THINGS really mean ALL THINGS? I say what I mean, and I mean what I say. You can EXPECT and join Me in CALLING FORTH THE RESTORATION OF ALL THINGS. ALL THINGS!!! This means RESTORATION in your HEALTH. I AM REVERSING the CURSE of every DEATH AGENDA of Big Pharma. I AM RELEASING your bodies and your minds from the EFFECTS of drugs that were PURPOSEFULLY mixed with DEADLY SIDE

EFFECTS. I AM RESTORING your AIR, your WATER, and your LAND so that they SUPPORT HEALTH and LONG LIFE instead of SHORTENING LIFESPANS. I AM RESTORING the CHURCH that has been COMPROMISED with FALSE doctrines regarding the SUPERNATURAL and the END TIMES teachings. These false doctrines have STRIPPED My Body of its POWER, its PURPOSE, and My PRESENCE. I will have a GLORIOUS Church that RULES and REIGNS with Me. I will RESTORE PROSPERITY, CREATIVITY, and INVENTIONS and CURES that have been withheld. I will RESTORE FAMILIES, RELATIONSHIPS, and those caught in the LIES and CONFUSION of gender identity and orientation. I will RESTORE the PURITY and POWER of the GOOD NEWS, the Gospel of My Son, and many will come RUNNING into the Kingdom. I will RESTORE TRUE JUSTICE and RIGHTEOUSNESS as the FOUNDATION of your Nation. Say goodbye to LAW-FARE, BRIBES, CORRUPTION, and BLACKMAIL. Schools will be CLEANSED of FALSE IDEOLOGIES and FAKE HISTORY. I will RESTORE your true history, and learning will be based in the FEAR of the LORD because that is the source of true WISDOM. This is what you have been FIGHTING for, and this will be your GREAT REWARD—THE RESTORATION OF ALL THINGS."

JANUARY 2, 2025: RECOVERY MODE

"In 2025, both your nation and the Church will be in RECOVERY MODE. In your nation, you will be RECOVERING FREEDOMS that have been lost, RECOVERING JUSTICE and RIGHTEOUSNESS in government, and RECOVERING the VOICE of the people to INFLUENCE policies and laws. In My Church, you will be RECOVERING the FEAR of the LORD as I CLEANSE the Body of PERVERSION, GREED, IDOLATRY, and CORRUPTION. The Church will RECOVER the FIRE and PASSION of REAL RELATIONSHIP with Me as the RELIGIOUS SPIRIT is EXPOSED for its PRIDE and HYPOCRISY. The Church will RECOVER a TRUE REVELATION of the KINGDOM AGE as FALSE DOCTRINES introduced by man are EXPOSED and DISCARDED. The enemy and the religious spirit will FIGHT these RECOVERIES in your nation and My Church. PARTNER with Me in CALLING IN this year of the RECOVERY MODE, and quickly CUT OFF enemy INTERFERENCE with your sword of TRUTH. LOVE people who are still DECEIVED, but FORCEFULLY EVICT the enemy's plans to STEAL RECOVERY. There will also be RECOVERIES of FINANCES, HEALTH, and RELATIONSHIPS. I will do MIRACULOUS things. I just ask you to be THANKFUL and to WATCH OVER and PRESERVE what I RECOVER for you and your nation. RECOVERY is part of My Rescue Operation, so CONFIDENTLY DECLARE that 2025 is a year of the RECOVERY MODE."

God's Kingdom is being established on the earth through the faith and obedience of His Sons and Daughters. The fear of the Lord and the release of His amazing glory opened a pathway for the dawn of the Golden Age.

CHAPTER THIRTEEN

The Dawn of the Golden Age

GOD'S GLORY

God's glory is the very essence of who He is. The glory is His light, His love, His power, His strength, His supernatural nature, and His wisdom. Here are a few entries where the Father spoke of His glory coming to the earth.

DECEMBER 28, 2021: FULL OF GLORY

"**Are you ready to be FULL OF MY GLORY? I have been PREPARING you as My VESSEL to be able to carry a FULL measure of MY GLORY. This preparation process can be uncomfortable and even painful as I remove what would**

HINDER you or keep you back from being able to RECEIVE all MY GLORY that I desire to fill you with. MY GLORY is My VERY PRESENCE, and it will FLOW forth from you releasing HEALING, COMFORT, LOVE, and JOY. It will meet the needs of those I bring across your path, and they will receive a SLICE of My presence that will cause them to HUNGER for more. MY GLORY being released will be a HUGE part of bringing HEALING, UNITY, and RESTORATION to your Land. Even as MY GLORY goes out to touch and heal, it will also serve to EXPOSE the darkness and corruption so that it can come under My JUDGMENT and JUSTICE. I AM bringing MY GLORY across your Nation, but it will only reach its FULLNESS if you WELCOME it into your own heart and RELEASE its power all around you. Say, 'Yes!', to MY GLORY."

COLOSSIANS 1:27 (TPT) *"Living within you is the Christ who floods you with the expectation of glory! This mystery of Christ, embedded within us, becomes a heavenly treasure chest of hope filled with the riches of glory for His people, and God wants everyone to know it!"*

JANUARY 10, 2023: BREATHE IN HEAVEN

"You have been great soldiers of Light, and now I want to PREPARE you to be CARRIERS OF MY GLORY. After this war is WON, there will be a need for HEALING of bodies and minds, a RESTORATION of all that has been stolen, and a CLEANSING of sin and its negative effects on peoples' lives. This kind of healing, restoration, and cleansing are found in MY GLORY, which is the VERY ESSENCE of WHO I AM. One of My promises to you in this WARFARE season has been the promise of the RELEASE of My glory to come FLOOD the earth. I can release a CLOUD of My GLORY upon a place or a gathering of people, and it will bring the Kingdom of Heaven to earth in that place. I will also RELEASE My GLORY through My SONS and DAUGHTERS who have POSITIONED themselves to be CARRIERS of My GLORY. You become carriers of My LIGHT, My PRESENCE, My HEALING, and My RESTORATION. Would you like to be a CARRIER of My GLORY? I AM waiting for you to ASK for it, and I will JOYFULLY release it to you. Imagine yourself in My Throne Room ... it's full of LIGHT, SOUNDS, COLORS, and RAW POWER. The four Living Creatures are present in great power moving around My Throne. I AM on My Throne, and from My being FLOWS My GLORY, and it is full of LIFE, RADIANT LIGHT, and LOVING POWER. Let it FLOW into you, and watch it begin to MANIFEST to those around you and those who you pray for—near or far. When My GLORY rests on a place, amazing things take place there; but when My GLORY rests on My Sons and Daughters, it can MANIFEST wherever they are, and it will go WHEREVER they RELEASE it in prayer. Stand before Me and BREATHE IN HEAVEN."

MARCH 17, 2023: MY GLORY: INCREASING REVELATION OR INCREASING BLINDNESS?

"My GLORY is HERE and will continue to INCREASE across your Land. It is your CHOICE—your free will—that will DETERMINE how My GLORY AFFECTS YOU. If you are partnered with DARKNESS, My GLORY will cause you INCREASING BLINDNESS.

You will be kept IN THE DARK about My PLANS and PURPOSES, and you won't be able to ACCESS the GUIDANCE of the darkness. CONFUSION and PANIC will overtake your ARROGANT confidence and your COMPLEX DARK SCHEMES. If you continue to pursue darkness, My GLORY will eventually CRUSH you, and you will LOSE EVERYTHING. Sadly, there is another group who will not be blessed by My GLORY, and that group are those in My Church who LISTEN to the VOICE of the RELIGIOUS SPIRIT. My GLORY is causing them INCREASING BLINDNESS because they REFUSE to acknowledge that I AM a SUPERNATURAL God. They BLINDLY continue to CRITICIZE how I AM moving in this season to REVITALIZE My Body. Their HARDNESS of heart will INCREASE their BLINDNESS and will cause them to be INCREASINGLY IRRELEVANT. Pray that they would be AWAKENED to the POWER of My Spirit and My GLORY. For those whose HEARTS and EYES are turned TOWARDS Me and who are LONGING for My GLORY to fall on their LIVES and on their NATION, My GLORY will bring INCREASING REVELATION of My POWER and My WISDOM WAYS. You will BATHE in the LIGHT of My GLORY, and it will bring SALVATION, DELIVERANCE, HEALING, RESCUE, and WISDOM for the choices you need to make. My GLORY is here and will be INCREASING. Choose to EMBRACE My GLORY, and you will receive INCREASING REVELATION of My GOODNESS and My POWER."

From these entries, you can see how powerful and needed the Glory of God is for our world to supply all that is needed to restore the foundations of society to justice, righteousness, peace, and love. It again highlights the contrast between dark and light. His Glory will bring judgment to the darkness and great blessing to the light. As His Glory covers the earth and His Kingdom reign is established, the Golden Age will arise. The Father first spoke of it as "A Rising Dawn" or "A New Dawn."

A RISING DAWN

AUGUST 14, 2022: A SETTING SUN, A RISING DAWN

"The SUN IS SETTING on an EVIL EMPIRE that tried to rule in My place. Oh FOOLISH ONES who believed the LIES of the Deceiver. He told you that you would be GREAT, that you would have WEALTH, and many POSSESSIONS. You did receive these things, but he attached to them DARK SPIRITS of GREED, LUST, and PERVERSIONS. You who think you have great power CANNOT EVEN CONTROL your own desires—they RULE OVER YOU. If only you had chosen to believe in My GOODNESS, My POWER, and My SON. When I BLESS and PROSPER, I ADD NO SORROW TO IT. Your SELFISHNESS grew to such bounds that you thought you DESERVED it all, but My people cried out to Me for a RESCUE, and a MIGHTY RESCUE they will have. Everything you thought you had GAINED, you will LOSE. Some of you will lose your lives in the RESCUE OPERATION, and the rest of you will be FORCED to watch as the SUN SETS on your DARK AMBITIONS, and a NEW RISING DAWN blesses My people. This RISING DAWN will be filled with My GLORY, My HEALING, and My ABUNDANCE. Instead of your PERVERSIONS and ATTEMPTED CONTROL, there will be WHOLENESS and GREAT FREEDOM. My people, you have chosen LIFE and FREEDOM when you receive My Son's SACRIFICE, and you will

WITNESS the SUN SETTING on the evil empire and A NEW DAWN RISING for you and your Nation."

DECEMBER 15, 2022: THE DARKNESS WILL GIVE WAY TO A NEW DAWN

I was awakened at 5:25 a.m. by someone speaking to me in a dream: "Luke 1:37." I got up & looked up that verse: *"For with God nothing (is or ever) shall be impossible."* Wow and amen! Gabriel said this statement about Elizabeth's barren womb and Mary's virgin womb.

"No matter how DARK it may look for the LIFE of your Nation, I AM assuring you that a NEW DAWN is coming. I AM LIFE, and I can bring forth LIFE from a DEAD womb, and I can CREATE LIFE outside of man's ability and power. I have been FORMING a NEW Nation in the HEARTS of My people. You are each CARRYING an IMPORTANT PART of this new Nation that I AM creating. Will I bring it to fullness and then not allow it to be BIRTHED? Will I allow the enemy to take its life or PREVENT it from being BORN? I tell you NOTHING IS IMPOSSIBLE WITH ME! The Nation I have been growing deep inside of you is the TREASURE OF DARKNESS, and it will be brought forth with great JOY and GLADNESS of heart. A nation can be born in a day, but realize I have been preparing it in HIDDENNESS, out of the SIGHT of the enemy, and he will be DUMBFOUNDED when I bring this new Nation to BIRTH. What I have done in HIDDENNESS will be REVEALED before the world, and WONDER and AWE will fill hearts as THE DARKNESS GIVES WAY TO A NEW DAWN."

OCTOBER 24, 2023: TOO GOOD TO BE TRUE

"I want you to look ahead to a future that you will say is TOO GOOD TO BE TRUE. Gaze with your spiritual eyes and SEE BEYOND the THREATS, the DARKNESS, and the DESTRUCTION to a world that is being RESTORED and REBUILT beyond your WILDEST IMAGINATION. 'Oh,' you will say, 'This is TOO GOOD TO BE TRUE!' Even as it grows dark for a short time, HOLD FAST to the vision of the DAWN of a NEW DAY of PEACE, PURITY, and PLENTY. These are not just words LIGHTLY spoken. I have DECLARED them from My mouth, and they will COME TO PASS as surely as My command of 'Light be!', brought your world into BEING. I have also told you that I have PASSED JUDGMENT on your enemies in the courts of Heaven, and those SPOKEN JUDGMENTS will come to earth and be FULFILLED. This is why I tell you NOT TO FEAR! If you will QUIET your heart before Me, I will show you the JUDGMENTS coming for the wicked, and I will show you My PROMISES to you being fulfilled. As you PARTNER with My heart and CALL IN My JUDGMENTS of those who sought to DESTROY you, also CALL FORTH My PROMISES of a future of PEACE, PURITY, and PLENTY. You will exclaim, 'IT'S TOO GOOD TO BE TRUE!'"

MAY 27, 2024: THE NINTH HOUR

"Your Nation has reached the NINTH HOUR in its history. The day My Son was crucified, it grew DARK until the NINTH HOUR, and the enemy thought he had WON. THREE DAYS later, the enemy was SURPRISED with his most CRUSHING DEFEAT. I used the enemy's DARKEST PLANS to BLOW BACK on him, and the VICTORY and POWER of SALVATION was released to the world. The GREATEST DARKNESS RELEASED THE GREATEST LIGHT. This pattern will play out in your Nation. The NINTH HOUR will bring about a SHORT TIME of DARKNESS, and the evil empire will think they have WON, and they will COMPLETELY EXPOSE themselves—ALL OF THEM. The LIGHT of My RESCUE will SUDDENLY PIERCE their darkness and SPOIL their victory party. You will see some of their SHOCKED and STUNNED faces as they are TAKEN AWAY HANDCUFFED and under heavy guard. Once again, a CRUSHING DEFEAT will be the enemy's PORTION. Those who partnered with darkness will SLAM FACE-FIRST into the ROCK of ALL AGES, and they will receive My JUDGMENT and JUSTICE. Many around you will be FEARFUL and MOURN because they think ALL IS LOST, but you will know when the SHORT DARKNESS FALLS that a GREAT VICTORY is VERY NEAR. You will look for the LIGHT of My Rescue, and you will ANTICIPATE a Nation being SAVED IN A DAY. You will be the LIGHTS in the darkness to spread HOPE among the HOPELESS and to INSPIRE WORSHIP and PRAYER that will TURN HEARTS and EYES BACK TO ME. Quite SUDDENLY, it will be the DAWN of a New Era, and you will walk into it with My VINDICATION and My rewards."

DECEMBER 3, 2024: A NEW DAY OF DESTINY DAWNS

ROMANS 13:12 (TPT) *"Night's darkness is dissolving away as a new day of destiny dawns. So we must once and for all strip away what is done in the shadows of darkness, removing it like filthy clothes. And once and for all we clothe ourselves with the radiance of light as our weapon."*

"As I bring the darkness DOWN and put it UNDER YOUR FEET, A NEW DAY OF DESTINY WILL DAWN. It will be a season of LIGHT, LOVE, PEACE, JOY, CREATIVITY, and TRUE JUSTICE. It will be filled with ABUNDANCE and the FULFILLMENT of your LIFE'S PURPOSE. The DOWNFALL of the darkness is happening, and NOTHING WILL STOP ITS COMPLETE COLLAPSE. A NEW DAY OF DESTINY for My Royal Priesthood will DAWN. How do you PREPARE your HEART for this COMPLETE CHANGE from dark to LIGHT? Allow My Spirit to SHOW you any areas of DARK SHADOWS in your own life so that you can bring them to the Light by CONFESSION and REPENTANCE, and WELCOME the Light of HOLINESS to CONSUME any areas of DARK SHADOWS in your heart. Be FREE! It was for FREEDOM that Christ set you FREE. A LIGHT-FILLED LIFE is very POWERFUL in My Kingdom, and it REFLECTS My HEART to the world. Your light-filled life PIERCES the darkness, and it is a WEAPON that DEFEATS darkness. It DRAWS men to its brightness—like a LIGHTHOUSE or a CITY on a hill. Behold, A NEW DAY OF DESTINY DAWNS."

Our light-filled lives of freedom have helped birth the dawn of a new day of destiny. The dawn of a new day opened up the Father's promise of the "Golden Age." On January 20, 2025, Donald John Trump was sworn in as our nation's forty-seventh President. During his inaugural address to the nation, he declared that we were entering into the "Golden Age." I was sure I had heard that phrase before, and as I checked my journal entries, I found the

Father had spoken to me about the "Golden Age" six months before the President's declaration.

THE GOLDEN AGE

JULY 13, 2024: A VEIN OF GOLD

I was taken to the Council Chamber of Heaven and stood gratefully behind my Elder. (See page 339 for more information on the 24 Elders.) I told him how good it was to be with him again, and he reached back and patted my hand affectionately. I became aware of something new in the usual blue/green/turquoise background of this Chamber. It was a vein of gold that ran around the whole room —like veins you would see in marble. It was spreading around the room like a river. I heard an Elder say, "The Kingdom Age coming to earth will be known as the Golden Age."

The Father shared:

"I AM releasing A VEIN OF GOLD into the NATURAL and SUPERNATURAL REALMS, and it will run through the whole Kingdom Age. It will SUPPLY both MATERIAL and SUPERNATURAL RICHES. Like never before, you will see a NEVER-ENDING SUPPLY of BOUNTY fill your lives. It will BLESS you with ABUNDANCE, and it will FLOW THROUGH your hands to BLESS others. Any GREED or GRASPING for the VEIN OF GOLD will cause it to go DEEP UNDERGROUND so that darkness cannot have ACCESS to it. In the supernatural, the VEIN OF GOLD will supply the TRUE RICHES of the Kingdom. Great REVELATION and UNDERSTANDING of My Word will be found. You will be able to TAP INTO the DEPTHS of My HEART and all of the TREASURES of LOVE waiting to be MINED by you. Gold must be taken out of the rock to be useful. I AM your ROCK of SALVATION, PROTECTION, and PRESERVATION. I AM inviting you to SEARCH for the VEIN OF GOLD that is in Me and to MINE the DEPTHS of the RICHES I have for you there. As you find the supernatural TREASURES of My VEIN OF GOLD, you will find that it MANIFESTS in your NATURAL life as well. Be in WONDER of the GOLDEN AGE that is planned for you."

AUGUST 2, 2024: THE GOLDEN REIGN OF A GOOD KING

"The battle sounds, the scare tactics, the false narratives will one day be SILENCED and REMOVED by My STRONG RIGHT ARM and My powerful FORCES OF LIGHT. The darkness had set up a chessboard game that had NO OPTION of you WINNING. You were meant to all be turned into their PAWNS who would SERVE their CRAVEN DESIRES. Because My Remnant have CRIED OUT for DELIVERANCE and because they have ALIGNED their HEARTS with Mine, I AM ARISING to make a SECRET MOVE that will put the enemy in CHECKMATE. I will then CLEAR the BOARD with My POWERFUL RIGHT ARM, and the darkness will be CLEANED off the CHESSBOARD, and their CRASH will be EPIC. SUDDENLY what seemed like a SURE VICTORY will become a CRUSHING DEFEAT for the darkness. They were set on IMPRISONING and CONTROLLING you, but that will become their PORTION. This CRUSHING DEFEAT of the darkness will MAKE A WAY for the KING of GLORY to bring in THE GOLDEN REIGN OF A GOOD KING. I AM that GOOD KING that will ESTABLISH the Kingdom Age of GLORY, GOLD, and

GOODNESS. Does that seem TOO GOOD to be TRUE? Remember that I AM the God of MORE THAN YOU CAN THINK OR IMAGINE. See beyond the SMOKE-FILLED BATTLEFIELD, and I will give you a vision of THE GOLDEN REIGN OF A GOOD KING."

These were such powerful promises given to us by a good, good Father! Imagine our delight and surprise when the Father told us we would begin to receive, as first fruits, the rewards stored up for the Golden Age before it was established in the earth.

NOVEMBER 10, 2024: THRIVE!

Thrive: grow, flourish, progress, prosper, increase.

"There are many who look at this season of great warfare and upheaval as a time to JUST SURVIVE, but I tell you it is a season for My Sons and Daughters to THRIVE. 'What? You might ask? When everything is in such turmoil, how can I thrive?' The answer to that is you have BELIEVED Me when I told you this is the LAUNCH of the KINGDOM AGE, and your FAITH has CONNECTED you to the UNLIMITED RESOURCES of Heaven. I AM coming to SHOW OFF and SHOW FORTH My POWER, My HOLINESS, and My GLORY to the world as I RESCUE your world from CERTAIN DEATH by a CORRUPT and DESPERATE enemy. I AM giving My faithful Army of Light a FORETASTE of the GOLDEN AGE that is coming. Watch Me supply you with ABUNDANCE in your FINANCES and MIRACULOUS HEALING for your bodies. I AM POURING OUT these things BEFORE the war is WON as the FIRST FRUITS of your REWARDS stored up for

My faithful Army of Light. DO NOT look at this season as a time when you will SUFFER LACK. Set your eyes and your faith on My Heavenly RESOURCES because this is your time to THRIVE! When I cause you to THRIVE, you will have an OVERFLOW to share with others. Declare: 'This is not a season to SURVIVE. It is a season to THRIVE in my Father's Kingdom resources.'"

Our faithful Father began to unfold for us what the Golden Age would look like and what it would entail.

JANUARY 29, 2025: WHAT IS THE GOLDEN AGE?

"The ADVANCING and EXPANDING Kingdom Era will be known as THE GOLDEN AGE. My GLORY is GOLDEN, and My GLORY will INHABIT the Kingdom Era. My GOLDEN GLORY will INVADE every dark scheme that has come to KILL, STEAL, or DESTROY. My GLORY is filled with My GOODNESS, a greater GRACE, My JUSTICE, and My RIGHTEOUSNESS. As My GOLDEN GLORY DISPLACES the darkness, the atmosphere will become CLEANER, PURER, and the skies will be BLUER. My GOLDEN GLORY will OVERTAKE CORRUPT, CONTROLLING, and THIEVING financial systems. The result of purified systems will be FREEDOM and UNHINDERED WEALTH. My GOLDEN GLORY will BURN through the PERVERSIONS and ADDICTIONS that were purposely sown into your societies. What took the darkness DECADES to introduce and what was meant to CONSUME your life with SHADOWS and SHAME will be SWEPT AWAY by the PURIFYING FIRE of My GOLDEN GLORY. I AM not just coming to RESCUE your nations from TYRANNY and DESTRUCTION; I AM coming to ESTABLISH My Kingdom among you: 'Let Your Kingdom come, let Your will be done, on earth as it is in Heaven.' Everywhere I RULE, My GLORY is present. Because it is the very ESSENCE of who I AM, it contains EVERYTHING you will need to live a FULL and ABUNDANT LIFE: HEALTH, WEALTH, FREEDOM, RIGHTEOUSNESS, JUSTICE, PEACE, and a DESIRE to be in UNION with Me. Great CREATIVITY will FLOW from the GOLDEN AGE because I AM the Master Creator, and the FREEDOM to DREAM, PLAN, and CREATE will fill the air where GREED, CORRUPTION, and IMPURITY once reigned. Partner with Me in CALLING FORTH My GLORY to fill the earth and to bring in the GOLDEN AGE."

JANUARY 31, 2025: PROSPERING

3 John 1:2 (TPT) *"Beloved friend, I pray that you are prospering in every way and that you continually enjoy good health, just as your soul is prospering."*

"Do you understand that My desire and My plan for your life is that you would be PROSPERING in every way: body, soul, and spirit? The mind of man CUTS MY GENEROSITY SHORT and thinks that you can only PROSPER in one area of your life instead of EXPECTING ABUNDANCE and PROSPERING in EVERY part of you because that is My DESIGN and PLAN for you. I gave your body an IMMUNE system so that it could fight off disease, and I created your body to be able to HEAL itself at a cellular level. One of the evil empire's death agendas has been to CRIPPLE mankind at a cellular level so that it SHORT CIRCUITS My ORIGINAL DESIGN of HEALING. That is why I have instructed you to **REVERSE THE CURSE** of this evil agenda and to **SPEAK** to your body—**LIFE, PEACE, HEALING,** and **WHOLENESS.** It is also My desire that you **PROSPER FINANCIALLY** and that you have an **ABUNDANCE** to share. How can you help supply others' needs if you are not **PROSPERING**? **PROSPERITY** and **ABUNDANCE** will be hallmarks of the **GOLDEN AGE.** It is My **GREATEST DESIRE** that you **DRAW NEAR** to Me and that you ask that our hearts would be **JOINED TOGETHER** in a **GLORIOUS UNION.** It is from this union that **FRUITFULNESS** is born. **PROSPERING** in your spirit is the **WEALTH** of an **INTIMATE** and **RICH** relationship with Me. It will result in **MULTIPLIED BLESSINGS** flowing to you and through you to **BLESS** all those whose lives you touch. **WELCOME** My ways of **PROSPERING** you body, soul, and spirit."

MARCH 10, 2025: THE GOLDEN AGE

"I want to give you a **VISION** and a **HOPE** for the unfolding of the **GOLDEN AGE.** The **GOLDEN AGE** will be marked by increasing **FREEDOM** in every area of life. The enemy's dark plans of **SLAVERY** and **BONDAGE** will be **SWEPT AWAY** by the light and the glory of the **GOLDEN AGE.** So many **SHACKLES** will be removed from your life. The **SLAVERY** to the **DEBT SYSTEM** established by the evil empire will be **BROKEN** as the wealth of the wicked is given back to the righteous. Getting rid of the **SHACKLE** of debt will **FREE** people's time and **RELIEVE** the pressure and anxiety off their emotions. There will be **NO NEED** for **FALSE COMFORTERS** to try and **NUMB** the weight of debt and the way it **STEALS** all your focus. You will have **FREE**

TIME to PURSUE good and satisfying relationships with spouses, families, and friends. Healthy relationships CLOSE the DOOR to being SHACKLED into perverted desires and secretive lusts. As healthy AIR, FOOD, WATER, and MEDICINES are RESTORED from the destruction of all the DEATH AGENDAS, the SHACKLES of DISEASE and IMPAIRED HEALTH will FALL OFF. There will be TIME and ENERGY for a naturally healthy lifestyle that will create active and full lives. More and more people will be drawn by My GLORY into a TRUE BORN AGAIN entrance into My Kingdom rather than a POWERLESS form of religion that is all mind-based instead of Spirit-based. This will TRANSFORM entertainment and media because people who have truly entered relationship with Me will DESIRE what is GOOD, HOLY, and UPLIFTING. When the pressure of GREED and DEBT are removed from businesses, they will operate with INTEGRITY towards people and the environment. The GOLDEN AGE will be an era of SHACKLES FALLING OFF and the EMBRACING of My GLORY and the FULLNESS of life that I always meant for My creation to experience. Life in the GOLDEN AGE becomes a CIRCLE OF BLESSING with no more shackles."

MARCH 27, 2025: THINK BIGGER!

"Let Me EXPAND your thinking and your capacity to DREAM about the Kingdom Era, the Golden Age that you are entering. I AM telling you that you need to THINK BIGGER because it is going to be the FULFILLMENT of HOPES and DREAMS that you have carried in the WOMB of FAITH and that you will SEE

BIRTHED in a season of FULFILLMENT and FRUITFULNESS. It's going to be BIGGER than you can IMAGINE, more MEANINGFUL than you have ever known, so THINK BIGGER! Will it happen all at ONCE? In My WISDOM, I know exactly WHEN and HOW to release the Kingdom Age of Golden Glory. I AM making sure that your CHARACTER can HANDLE the awesome blessings coming your way. I don't want you to FALL into PRIDE, GREED, or CORRUPTION because you were not ready to receive in HUMILITY and THANKFULNESS and in turn BLESSING others out of what you have been given. In this season of establishing My Kingdom Age, there will be SUDDENLIES, and there will be things that UNFOLD PROGRESSIVELY according to My WISDOM WAYS. This will help you MANAGE your EXPECTATIONS of WHEN and HOW LONG it may take to see all the seven mountains be brought into My LIGHT and RADICALLY TRANSFORMED. I will tell you that NOW is the TIME to DEMAND that TRUTH be spoken on the airwaves, that CORRUPTION be EXPOSED, and that the OBSTRUCTIONS to JUSTICE be BLOWN AWAY and BURNED UP by My fiery ARROWS of TRUTH and RIGHTEOUSNESS. Call forth a HUGE WAVE of TRUTH, JUSTICE, and RIGHTEOUSNESS to ROLL across your land, clearing the way for My Kingdom RULE in the Golden Age. Now is the time to realize you have the POWER and AUTHORITY in Me. THINK BIGGER!"

With growing confidence, we face the future knowing the Father will fulfill all His promises to us—in fact, we were told to "think bigger!" What He has for us is beyond our imagination and bigger than our hopes and dreams.

CHAPTER FOURTEEN

Dreams, Visions, and Encounters

W e must understand that the Father of Lights dwells in the supernatural realm, outside of time and outside of our five natural senses. He delights in drawing us into His supernatural realm where He can speak to us through dreams, visions, and encounters.

DREAMS

Here is what the Father said to me regarding dreams:

OCTOBER 16, 2020: DREAMS

"I often speak to My people in dreams. When you are asleep, I have your UNDIVIDED attention, and I can speak to you in

VISIONS and NIGHT PARABLES. Dreams are MYSTERIES for you to unlock and discover. As you learn to unlock the mystery of your dreams, you will find you have come to KNOW ME on a deeper level. In dreams I can show you future events that will take place, I can show you areas of your heart that are hidden from you and where My Spirit needs to bring His transformation. I can show you people, churches, governments that need change and deliverance so you can pray for them to awaken to their need for Me. Be faithful to RECORD your dreams and seek My Spirit to help you interpret your dreams. He is your faithful COUNSELOR and INTERPRETER of dreams."

JANUARY 6, 2020: DREAM: SUDDEN ACCELERATION!

This dream involved me in a pickup truck. In the last scene of the dream, I am parked, and suddenly the truck starts moving on its own and rockets up into a steep climb into the sky. I woke myself up calling, "Jesus!" I can still feel that steep climb, the surge of adrenaline, and my absolute powerlessness to do anything to stop this ACCELERATION!

What the Father said to me about this dream:

ACCELERATION

"Put on your seatbelt, because acceleration is about to begin in your life and in the life of your Nation! This will happen suddenly and with such force that you will catch your breath in surprise. The waiting is over, and now you must adjust to this new reality of swiftly moving beyond your ability to control or to stop. **You have trusted Me in the waiting and the stillness; can you now trust Me as events happen rapid-fire, one on top of another? THIS WILL BE THE RIDE OF YOUR LIFE! I've saved the best for last, so enjoy!"**

Dreams helped prepare us for what was coming in the future. It canceled out fear and helped us look to the future with faith and hope.

July 9, 2020: Dream/Vision and Word Concerning the Corona Virus

---

Dream/Vision

I saw a scary, worm-like creature with long, spiky, black hairs all over it. It was sitting up in a comfy bed. It wasn't large, but its bobbing head continually looking around was unnerving and intimidating.

Interpretation:

The Holy Spirit revealed to me that this was the demonic entity behind the virus currently plaguing us. It's very comfortable where it's lodged and is constantly looking for ways to cause fear and intimidation. Head bobbing in a creature can mean: aggression, declaring its territory, dominance. The important part of this dream/vision is that this demonic entity is being exposed.

Word: Swoop in for the Kill!

"I have exposed the demonic force behind the Corona virus. In its arrogance it has found a place to rest in PEOPLE'S FEAR,

but I am showing you that its pride has placed it in a VULNERABLE place. NOW is the time to strike a DEATH BLOW to this ugly scheme of the enemy that has been perpetuated through those who partnered with him in order to destroy and bring down President Trump. Take your SWORD of TRUTH and plunge it into this demonic entity, and call for the FIRE of GOD to burn it up until it is ashes. Those who relied on it to protect and fulfill their dark agendas will also CRUMBLE as TRUTH AND FIRE expose this ugly scheme. I am by your side—GO IN FOR THE KILL!"

JULY 22, 2020: DREAM: CHRISTMAS IN JULY

I had a vivid dream just before waking up on this morning. I dreamed I woke up, looked out my windows (vision), and much to my surprise, it was SNOWING in July! The ground and every tree and plant were covered with a blanket of pure, white snow. I tried to text family and friends but was having difficulty texting due to a new feature that had been added to my messages.

INTERPRETATION:

God is showing me there is a SUDDEN change in the season that will be marked by His BLESSING, COVERING, and PURITY (snow). My voice is hampered right now from declaring it (censorship), but the obvious fact of the snow will be undeniable that God's BLESSING, CONTROL, and POWER are on display.

I HAVE COMMANDED A BLESSING

"I have commanded a blessing to fall on the righteous, and NOTHING the enemy tries will take that blessing away. He may try to silence your voice, but this will not take away the very APPARENT blessing I have given to My people. Just like you can't HIDE snow in the summer, so you won't be able to deny the GREAT and PURE BLESSINGS that I am laying on My people as a covering. Receive this blessing by FAITH, and PRAISE ME for it, and watch blessings SUDDENLY appear in your life like a surprise snowfall in July. As you praise Me, I will DEFEAT your enemies, bring them to justice, and release your voice. This is My declaration to you that there is a SUDDEN change of season to BLESSING and PURITY."

OCTOBER 16, 2020: DREAM: MESSAGE—TRIALS FOR TREASON AND LYING

The night before hearing this word, I dreamed I heard voices of men and angels telling me to LISTEN to the words being spoken. These were the words: "Without warning of any kind, TRIALS will begin for TREASON and LYING."

INTERPRETATION:

This dream was an assurance that prophetic words from Heaven given through men and angels would be fulfilled. SUDDENLY, with no warning given the ungodly, trials would begin for traitors and liars.

OCTOBER 15, 2021: DREAM: THE TROUBLED YOUNG WOMAN

DREAM:

A young woman is wandering around town, troubled about the business she and her husband run and unsettled about their relationship. She realizes she doesn't really know who she is or what she wants from life. A store owner asks her if she knows about "Cecile." She realizes her husband is having an affair. The young woman is devastated and starts aimlessly walking. Hope arises in the midst of her losses that now she'll find out who she really is, and there is great freedom in that.

INTERPRETATION:

The young woman represents the USA who is experiencing anxiety about its financial health and who finds out they have been betrayed by man who turned out to be untrustworthy and lying. Cecille means: blind, sixth. Six is the number of man, out for themselves and not depending on God or serving Him. These godless men want to keep us blind to what they are doing to our Nation—betraying her. This is a difficult situation for the young Nation, but she receives a revelation from the Spirit of Life that she will find freedom and who she really is.

From the Father: "I AM communicating to you in this dream for your Nation that you are going to receive some hard blows in the hidden things that are uncovered, but I will see you through to a NEW DAY of FREEDOM, and you will discover your true PURPOSE and DESTINY in being partnered with Me. There is great HOPE even in loss because what you will be

losing was built on untrustworthy men whose goal was to BLIND you from the truth. I AM visiting your Land with the Spirit of TRUTH and the Spirit of LIFE. Walk with Me into FREEDOM and FULFILLMENT."

ISAIAH 62:2, 4b (AMP) *"The nations will see your righteousness and vindication (by God), and all kings (will see) your glory; and you will be called by a new name which the mouth of the Lord will designate ... and to Him your land will be married (owned and protected by the Lord)."*

DECEMBER 12, 2022: THE CONVERGENCE OF ALL THINGS

I had a DREAM/VISION last night. I heard a voice say, "THE CONVERGENCE OF ALL THINGS." I saw sections like "Seeing," "Knowing," "Covert Actions," "Military," "Courts," and listed under each section were TRUTH TELLERS. I saw that all these voices of truth were coming together in a CONVERGENCE that would completely expose the truth and all those who were doing evil. As all these truths CONVERGE, they will cause an ERUPTION of truth.

This morning, I heard the Father say this:

"It is time for THE CONVERGENCE OF ALL THINGS. All the STREAMS OF TRUTH that I have inspired will now come together to bring about a FLOOD OF EXPOSURE. This is also the time where HEAVEN and EARTH CONVERGE in one FOCUSED purpose: to BRING DOWN an evil empire and to RESTORE justice and righteousness to the earth. This joining together of Heaven's armies and strategies are becoming one with My Army of Light as they make My BATTLE STRATEGIES their battle strategies. This will be the most COMPLETE PICTURE so far in earth's history of My Sons and Daughters of the DAWN rising into their DESTINY TO RULE AND REIGN WITH ME. Not only will evil be crushed beneath your feet, but you will have come into the realization of who you were made to be in My Kingdom. This will be a SUPER FAIL for the darkness. Not only will they LOSE their evil empire, but a whole Army of ENLIGHTENED ones have now arisen to take their places and to OCCUPY until I return. When I WIN, I WIN BIG! Nothing will stop THE CONVERGENCE OF ALL THINGS."

ISAIAH 58:8 *"Then your light will break out like the dawn, and your healing (restoration, new life) will spring forth; your righteousness will go before you (leading you to peace and prosperity), the glory of the Lord will be your rear guard."*

AUGUST 29, 2024: IT WILL OVERTAKE YOU

This word began with a dream I had on August 28, 2024. I was in the upper story of an older hotel-type building. I stuck my head out of the window and turned my head to see a lovely rainbow arching over the huge mountain in back of the hotel. The main color I remember seeing was lavender.

INTERPRETATION: "A RAINBOW OVERTAKING ME"

I have "stuck my neck out" spiritually in believing God's promises for this season, and He is assuring me that His promises and His covenant blessings will overtake me. Usually, things behind you in a dream would represent the past, but in this case, they speak of being overtaken by His goodness. Meaning of color lavender: it's a combination of purple (royalty, covenant) and white (purity); it is Holy Spirit breathing into the earth new beginnings in the steadfast love of holiness; it is loving removal of impurities, and blessings of impartation.

"You have been WATCHING and WAITING for My PROMISES to come to you, but I tell you that SUDDENLY, they WILL OVERTAKE YOU. All the HARDSHIPS, LOSSES, and WARFARE will all be WORTH IT when My BLESSINGS OVERTAKE YOU. My promises will CROWN your life with My GOODNESS, My PURITY, and My COVENANT PROMISES. You will LACK NOTHING, and you will have PLENTY to SHARE with those who DID NOT BELIEVE My prophets but CLUNG to the TRADITIONS and DOCTRINES of men. When they see the WONDER of what WILL OVERTAKE YOU, they will be AWAKENED to FAITH in a LIVING, SUPERNATURAL God. I will SURPRISE them with My LOVE and My GOODNESS, and they will JOYFULLY PURSUE My HEART and My WAYS. Because you have STAYED on the BATTLEFRONT with Me and have not turned back and because you BELIEVED My promises of a RESCUE and the DAWNING of the KINGDOM AGE, your REWARDS will be GREAT. My blessings will be FULL and AMAZING but with My PURITY on them so that they do not cause GREED or HOARDING. As you are FREELY BLESSED, you will FREELY GIVE, and the CYCLE of BLESSING will be established. The Kingdom Age will be ushered in as My BLESSINGS OVERTAKE YOU."

Sometimes dreams will contain specific spiritual intelligence and direct action items that we can use in our prayers, decrees, and declarations.

June 13, 2024: This Is America's Day!

I had a long dream last night, but I only remember the last scene where I was declaring three statements or headlines that had been given to me. I only remember the last statement, and I was reading it aloud to Barrack Obama. It said: "THIS IS AMERICA'S DAY!"

The Father speaks:

"This is My NEWS HEADLINE to the darkness and to My America. I AM assigning My Army of Light to DECLARE this PROMISE to the heavenly and earthly realms—'THIS IS AMERICA'S DAY!' I want you to declare it UNTIL you SEE it COME to FULFILLMENT. Those partnered with darkness and those who don't BELIEVE that I still act SUPERNATURALLY anymore will SCOFF at your declaration. The darkness believes (except for moments of PANICKY DOUBT) that their DEATH AGENDAS will bring the world into SUBJECTION to their CONTROL. Sadly, many in the Church have been taught I AM words on a page and that I NO LONGER ACT in SUPERNATURAL WAYS. This gives them an EXCUSE NOT TO FIGHT the darkness, and they HIDE BEHIND a FALSE SHIELD that says I AM JUDGING AMERICA, and so I will be taking the Church off the earth. Quite the OPPOSITE is the TRUTH. I AM RAISING UP, TRAINING, and STRENGTHENING a WARRIOR BRIDE who will FIGHT BY MY SIDE to MAKE WAY for the KINGDOM AGE. To My MISLED and still ASLEEP Church I say, I AM NOT building up a WIMPY Church that cannot CUT IT in the day of BATTLE and who has to be SNATCHED out of the way because they had LITTLE POWER over the enemy and his dark schemes. I AM calling you to AWAKEN, BELIEVE that I AM still the GREAT I AM, and JOIN the ranks of My Forces of Light. Help us bring in the VICTORY, and you will share in the SPOILS of war. As My people keep declaring, 'THIS IS AMERICA'S DAY!' it will make INROADS into the DEATH SCHEMES, and it will WEAKEN the CONFIDENCE of the darkness. They will be OVERCOME by My Army's FAITH and LIGHT, and you will see with your eyes that THIS IS AMERICA'S DAY!"

The coded messages in dreams often come with the numbers that appear in the dream. Each number has a Biblical meaning related to the Hebrew letter it represents and how the number is used in Scripture. Sometimes the numbers will refer to a Bible verse with that address.

JULY 20, 2024: GIVE US A FRESH START!

I had a quick dream last night at 1:23 a.m. (a sequence of coming events). In the dream, there were numbers floating in the air all around me, and I grabbed the number 85 and pulled it to me. (8=new beginnings, resurrection; 5=grace, empowerment.) This led me to Psalm 85.

The Father shared:

"Let the words of this Psalm be on your lips, and cry out to Me, 'GIVE US A FRESH START!' PSALM 85:6, 7 (TPT) *'Revive us again, O God! I know You will! Give us a fresh start! Then all Your people will taste Your joy and gladness. Pour out even more of Your love on us! Reveal more of Your kindness and restore us back to You!'* You have seen the BROKENNESS, DIVISION, and HATRED that the enemy and his PAWNS of darkness have SOWN into the world. They have foolishly sown to the WINDS of DESTRUCTION, and they will now REAP the WHIRLWIND as I DELIVER the nations from their DARK TYRANNY. My WHIRLWIND of JUDGMENT and JUSTICE will come SUDDENLY, and it will RIP AWAY the FACADES and OPEN UP every DARK DEED and HIDING PLACE. All their riches will be SUCKED UP and FLUNG OUT to all of you. They will be left EXPOSED, STRIPPED of EVERYTHING, and the DESTRUCTION they planned for you will fall on them ... HARD. Then, it is time to cry out, 'GIVE US A FRESH START!' This will be My response: PSALM 85: 12, 13 (TPT) *'Yes, the Lord keeps raining down blessing after blessing, and prosperity will drench the land with a bountiful harvest. For deliverance and peace are His forerunners, preparing a path for His steps.'* This is My PROMISE, and I WILL DO IT!"

VISIONS

Visions are similar to dreams except they can happen either when you are asleep or awake. Dreams are mostly symbolic and metaphorical, while visions can contain symbolism but are often more literal in their interpretation. Here are some of the visions I experienced during this season of the Rescue of the Ages.

MAY 14, 2020: GOING AGAINST THE FLOW

VISION:

I saw a quick vision of a large bear trying to move upstream in a rapidly flowing river and trying at great peril to jump up a pouring waterfall.

The Father responded:

"The enemy (the bear in your vision) is now forced to go against the flood of exposures of evil that are coming out. This evil scheme of the enemy to unseat President Trump is being revealed as a FLOOD of evidence that uncovers the evil plans. The enemy is now forced to try and keep moving against that flow, and the whole scheme and those who participated in it are in danger of DROWNING. The bear is angry and growling, but don't allow that to intimidate you—he cannot withstand the flood of truth that is coming. Use your AUTHORITY to declare that any obstructions to the flood of truth would be removed and smashed in My name, and you will see the river of truth grow more powerful until nothing can stand in its path. See with My eyes that the dark, powerful, scary bear is in a place of great peril. DECLARE My light over the darkness and My truth over the lies."

Isaiah 59:19 (MSG) *"In the west they'll fear the name of God, in the east they'll fear the glory of God, for He'll arrive like a RIVER IN FLOOD STAGE whipped to a torrent by the wind of God."* **(Emphasis mine.)**

Visions often contain spiritual intelligence and point us to prayer strategies for stopping the enemy's plans or furthering the Father's Kingdom plans.

DECEMBER 1, 2021: THE GEARS ARE TURNING

I had a brief vision of a complex set of gears and parts all in a line ready to be put together.

The Father spoke these words:

"I have been meticulously building a MECHANISM to bring about JUDGMENT and JUSTICE to your Nation. It is like a COMPLEX system of GEARS and PARTS that must all be assembled in order so that the gears will turn the wheels of DISCOVERY, JUDGMENT, and JUSTICE. Your prayers for righteous leaders and judges have helped assemble this complex system that will BRING DOWN corruption and evil. This gear system is now assembled and beginning SLOWLY TO TURN—have you seen evidences that the TIDE IS TURNING TO JUSTICE? Keep watching, because My GEAR system is slowly beginning to bring about a TURNAROUND in your Nation where good is no longer called evil and evil will no longer be able to DRESS UP as good. As gears begin to turn, the start-up is slow, but it will pick up SPEED and MOMENTUM and an AVALANCHE of exposures and trials will take place. It has taken time, but I have built this GEAR SYSTEM so that it cannot FAIL—the fact that you waited for Me to act will be rewarded with VINDICATION as you see My promises for JUDGMENT and JUSTICE come to pass. Listen ... the GEARS are turning!"

MARCH 10, 2022: A VISION AND A WORD:

I saw a brief vision this morning. I saw God's GREAT HAMMER of EXPOSURE strike full-force on the United States. SHOCK WAVES went out from the blow and uncovered every dark and hidden EVIL and CORRUPTION. Then a tsunami of JUDGMENT and JUSTICE rolled across the Land and SWEPT all the corruption away. Then a BROAD RIVER of His RIGHTEOUSNESS began to flow from the center of the Nation, and it flowed both east and west. It went westward across the Land and also covered Alaska and Hawaii and then flowed out westward to the world. The eastward flow went across the Atlantic towards Europe and all other nations until it met the westward flow. At the same time, the river of RIGHTEOUSNESS flowed north to Canada and south to those nations below the USA. This beautiful river of His RIGHTEOUSNESS was covering the world!

The Father speaks: "Use this vision as a PRAYER PATTERN. I have shown you what I have PROMISED to do, and I want you by My side to CALL IT FORTH so that you SEE COME TO PASS what your heart has BELIEVED. CALL FORTH My hammer of exposure, SEND a tsunami of judgment and justice across your Land, and RELEASE My river of righteousness out into your Nation and FLOWING OUT into all the world. This is the day; this is the hour for ANSWERED PRAYER. I will HEAL your Land, and I will HEAL your bodies. I will JUDGE evil and CLEANSE your Nation. This is an EXTENDED HARVEST SEASON for you and your Land of LIGHT and BLESSING; for the CORRUPT who mocked Me and refused to humble themselves before Me, it will be a DARK harvest. Begin every day by asking that your

heart would be JOINED TO MY HEART. Then you will be in UNION with Me. You will SEE what I see, KNOW what I know, LOVE what I love, HATE what I hate, SAY what I say, and DO what I would do. Your FAITH will be STEADIED, your HEART will be at PEACE, and your LIFE will be FRUITFUL and FULFILLING. I love you deeply and completely, and I welcome you into My heart!"

NOVEMBER 12, 2022: A VISION: THE EAGLE LANDED

This morning as I waited in God's presence, I saw in the Spirit an ENORMOUS EAGLE that landed outside my sunroom. It was imposing, captivating, and terrifying. Its eyes burned with HOLY FIRE that inspired awe. I asked the Father what the eagle represented, and He responded:

"It is the RETURN of your RIGHTFUL LEADER, DJT, and the HUGENESS of the call on his life to RESTORE HONOR, RIGHTEOUSNESS, and JUSTICE to your Nation. The PIERCING, FIERY EYES of the eagle SEARCH OUT the enemies of your Nation, and they call you to SHOULDER and CARRY your part in the REBIRTH and REBUILDING of your Land. In the coming days, you will see with your natural eyes that THE EAGLE LANDED, and that My CALL on his life has been FULLY ACTIVATED. He cannot carry this ENORMOUS CALL alone. You must COMMIT to join him in RE-ESTABLISHING and PRESERVING FREEDOM in My covenant Nation. Let this cry be on your lips, "GOD BLESS AMERICA and GOD KEEP HER STRONG.'"

May 11, 2023: When I Arise from My Throne

I received a short but powerful vision this morning. I saw the Throne Room of Heaven with the Father seated on His Throne. As I watched, He arose from His Throne, and I saw and heard tremendous power thundering out from Him as He did the simple act of arising. The power kept rolling out until it began to shake the earth.

"I AM ARISING FROM MY THRONE with GREAT PURPOSE. As My TREMENDOUS POWER ROLLS OUT FROM MY ARISING, you will see Me FULFILL all My PROMISES to you. The POWER from MY ARISING will bring DREAD and SHOCK to My enemies as My RIGHTEOUS JUDGMENTS hit them like a FREIGHT TRAIN. All the BRIBED JUDGES and JURIES will be hit with a FORCE that UNCOVERS the TRUTH, and all the money they have received for giving UNJUST JUDGMENTS will be TAKEN from them. They will face SHAME, LOSS, and TRUE JUDGEMENT and JUSTICE will SLAM into them. The RIPPLE of POWER FROM MY ARISING will hit the LYING MEDIA and LEADERS in their MOUTHS. My SUDDEN PRESENCE in their midst will cause their ARROGANT CONFIDENCE to be SHAKEN. They will find themselves STUTTERING, STAMMERING, and in their PANIC, WRONG WORDS will come out of their mouths that will EXPOSE the TRUTH and will BRING DOWN the HOUSE of CARDS stacked against you. WAVES of POWER FROM MY ARISING will SLAM into the HIDDEN places in the earth, BREAKING OPEN the hiding places of GREAT RICHES and the BEAUTIFUL CHILDREN they have EXPLOITED. BOOM! Those who EXPLOITED your WEALTH and your CHILDREN will be

SHAMED and EXPOSED before the world. The peoples will CRY OUT for JUDGMENT and JUSTICE, and these dark ones will receive it in FULL MEASURE. My Army of Light, continue to CALL on Me to ARISE FROM MY THRONE and to RELEASE My GREAT POWER into the earth, and you will witness what happens as I ARISE FROM MY THRONE."

OCTOBER 9, 2023: GLORY FIRE MISSILES

VISION:

This morning as I sat with the Father, Son, and Holy Spirit, I was shown a map of the USA. It was night, and I was high above overlooking our Land. Thick dark clouds were above the Nation, but I could see PINPOINTS OF BRIGHT LIGHT all over the States. Some areas had a greater concentration of lights, but all States had some lights. These lights were the PRAYERS of the Army of Light. You may feel all alone in some of the darker areas of this Nation, but you have been STRATEGICALLY placed there as a needed light in the darkness. I saw as we prayed and launched decrees and declarations that our pinpoint of light shot through the dark clouds above us as a GLORY FIRE MISSILE. These missiles BROKE through the dark schemes over our Land, and then GLORY LIGHT would STREAM from Heaven and light up that area. Some of the GLORY FIRE MISSILES went to other nations, and I saw a BARRAGE of our prayers RAINING DOWN on Israel and encountering the missiles the enemy is sending their way and EXPLODING them in the air before they could land and do damage. Keep praying; our prayers are powerful!

The Father speaks:

"My Army of Light, you are growing in STRENGTH and FAITH, and the GLORY FIRE MISSILES of PRAYER that you are LAUNCHING are STRIKING the MARK and DESTROYING and DISABLING the enemy's schemes all over your world. These GLORY FIRE MISSILES you release are EMPOWERED and DIRECTED by My Host, as it says in My Word: 'Who makes His angels winds, and His ministering servants flames of fire (to do His bidding)' HEBREWS 1:7, AMP. As you release GLORY FIRE MISSILES of prayer through the GATHERING DARKNESS, I will release back to you My GLORY LIGHT, and it will REST on you, and it will bring SUPERNATURAL PROVISION, HEALING, and PROTECTION from the darkness. It is your FAITH in My GOODNESS, My POWER, and My PROMISES that INFLAME your GLORY FIRE MISSILES of prayer. Just as SWORDS are formed in the forge of extreme HEAT and FLAME, so your FAITH has been TRIED in the constant onslaught from the darkness. You have not GIVEN UP or GIVEN IN, but you have allowed Me to STRENGTHEN and FORM you into GLORY FIRE MISSILES that will DESTROY the enemy's schemes of darkness."

FEBRUARY 14, 2025: A SECRET WEAPON: THE TRAIN OF HIS ROBE

As I was resting in the Father's love this morning, I began to see His garments made out of shimmering light. The train of His robe flowed around me as a renewing light and a fragrance of love.

"I AM deploying a SECRET WEAPON into the earth at this STRATEGIC time in history in order to BREAK the POWER of ADDICTIONS, LIES, and HATRED. These DARK WEAPONS have been sown into the atmosphere of the nations by the evil empire. Their plan was to WEAKEN, DISTRACT, CONFUSE, and cause CRIPPLING SHAME so that they could easily CONQUER a WEAKENED people and a DISARMED Church. Here is My SECRET WEAPON that I AM releasing into the earth that will OVERCOME the dark agendas and that is the FRAGRANCE of My LOVE and the POWER of My LIGHT. The TRAIN OF MY ROBE is moving and touching the earth. As you wait in My presence and receive the TOUCH of My TRAIN and allow My LIGHT to RENEW you and BREATHE in the FRAGRANCE of My LOVE, you will be SET FREE of LIES, GRIEF, and SHAME. After you have received My LIGHT and My LOVE, then I want you to SEND IT OUT into the atmosphere. Declare that you are sending My LIGHT and LOVE into the AIRWAVES, and then do a prophetic act of WAVING the LIGHT and the FRAGRANCE of My LOVE into the air. LIGHT WAVES will MOVE OUT from you to IMPACT lives, and the FRAGRANCE of My LOVE will WAFT into the atmosphere. My LIGHT and My LOVE are the REAL DEAL—nothing can compare to their POWER to OVERCOME ADDICTIONS, GANGS, DISAPPOINTMENTS, HATRED, and DIVISIONS. Join Me in using this SECRET WEAPON to OVERCOME DARKNESS and HATRED using the LIGHT and LOVE that come from THE TRAIN OF MY ROBE."

ENCOUNTERS

Another way that the spiritual realm of Heaven interacts with us living in the natural realm is through encounters. The Holy Spirit initiates these encounters, and they often involve our spirits visiting places in Heaven in order to receive messages, assurances, and assignments. One of the first places that Holy Spirit took me was to the War Room of Heaven. I didn't even know there was a War Room in Heaven before I was taken there! I was taken to the War Room of Heaven over a period of two years. I will share some of those visits with you.

HEAVEN'S WAR ROOM

The War Room of Heaven was filled with a large, oval conference table. At the head of the table was the Father's chair, and the other seats were filled with the twenty-four Elders. The twenty-four Elders are mentioned throughout the Bible but most often in the book of Revelation where we see them seated around God's holy Throne.

In the New Testament, they are called the "Twenty-four Elders." The Biblical meaning of the number 24=Heavenly government and worship. In the Bible we see these Elders functioning as part of Heaven's government and as extravagant worshipers before the Father's Throne.

In the Old Testament, they are spoken of as the "Council of the holy ones."

PSALM 89:7a (TPT) *"You are a God who is greatly to be feared as You preside over the council of the holy ones."*

PSALM 89:7 (NASB) *"A God greatly feared in the council of the holy ones, and awesome above all those who are around Him?"*

PSALM 111:1 (TPT) *"May every one of His lovers hear my passionate praise to Him, even among the council of the holy ones."*

In these verses, the word "council" is *sode* in the Hebrew. It means: assembly, circle of familiar friends, a secret council, intimacy with God. I always see them in a circle around a table or the Throne. The word "holy" is the Hebrew word *Kodosh*, which means: sacred, holy, Holy One, saint, set apart. The twenty-four Elders are spoken of often in the New Testament Book of Revelation.

REVELATION 7:11 (NKJV) *"All the angels stood around the throne and the 24 elders and the four living creatures, and fell on their faces before the throne and worshiped God ...."*

REVELATION 7:13 An Elder asks John a question, and then answers it for John.

REVELATION 4:4,10; 5:6, 8, 9; 7:10, 11, 12, 13, 16, 17; 11:16, 17; 14:3;19:4

These verses speak of worshiping, falling before Him, throwing down their crowns, holding the harp and golden bowls of the prayers of the Saints, they see the Lamb, they sang a new song when it is announced that Jesus is worthy to open the seals.

The Bible does not reveal to us (at least I have never discovered a place in the Bible) where these twenty-four Elders came from. Some theologians believe they are the heads of the twelve tribes of Israel plus the twelve Apostles from the New Testament. However, John spoke to the twenty-four Elders in Heaven on his visitations when he was caught up into Heaven. John is one of the twelve

Apostles, so was he talking to himself in the future? Could be, but my feeling (this is just a feeling, I can't give you chapter and verse from the Bible) is that they are very ancient beings that might have been one of God's original creations. They are so wise, and they have such an honored place in Heaven.

When I was taken to the War Room of Heaven, I saw the Father meeting with the twenty-four Elders, and they were strategizing plans for the Rescue Operation. I was always assigned to stand behind one particular Elder and to place my hand on his shoulders. Having my hands on his shoulders gave me strength to stay in the encounter. That is why I call him "my Elder." I have grown to love and respect him very much. In my first encounter in the War Room, I heard a series of statements the Elders made as they conversed with the Father around the table. This is what I heard on that first visit.

JULY 19, 2020: STRATEGIES OVERHEARD FROM THE WAR ROOM OF HEAVEN

1. **"The enemy is trying to wear down the saints with his multitude of evil schemes."**

2. **"They must be RESOLUTE against DISCOURAGEMENT."**

3. **"They must know that the multitude of schemes are flying off a dying crocodile who has been caught in his own trap and is now in a death spiral of defeat."**

4. **"This is their strategy for defeating bad reports: Bring them to NOTHING in Jesus' name, declare they are DEFEATED. Declare that His KINGDOM will be RAISED UP in the place of the bad report."**

The Father then spoke to me:

IT'S ALL COMING DOWN

"What you are witnessing is the IMPLOSION of an ancient scheme of the enemy to DEFILE and DESTROY the world and to plunge it into the deepest DARKNESS under the control of perverse and arrogant people. The implosion is in slow motion right now, but as more and more facts are brought to the light and more and more offer testimony against the wicked, the SPEED of the implosion will pick up until the whole scheme lies in the dust. There will be no place to HIDE and no DEFENSE available and no more corrupted people in place to protect their evil ways. TRUTH and JUSTICE WILL PREVAIL. I have spoken, and it will come to pass. I am OVERPOWERING the darkness with My Army of Light. Continue to stand by My side sharing My HEART and My battle STRATEGIES."

In this encounter the Army of Light was given strategies to combat the dark schemes of the enemy and a promise that truth and justice would prevail in the end.

OCTOBER 2, 2021: UPDATE FROM THE WAR ROOM

I am standing behind one of the twenty-four Elders again with my hands on his shoulders as he's seated around the conference table in the War Room. The room is filled with a buzz of excitement. The Father gives a low laugh, and I hear Him say:

"The time is very near for the release of all that I have promised My faithful ones who have stood in faith believing My promises of healing and restoration. It gives Me great joy to fulfill all their hopes and dreams for their Nation, and it gives Me great pleasure to release abundance and great miracles of healing that will bless them and be multiplied to others. Their faith will soon be vindicated, and great will be their peace and celebration. This delights My heart! "

He looks directly at me and says:

"Tell My people not to flinch or give up at the coming implosions in the ranks of the wicked, because these implosions will send out shock waves that will shake and topple many things you have depended on. Haven't I proved My faithfulness and power to you? Throw the weight of your life, and place all your dependency on Me, and I will display supernatural provision and healing to you. It's very important that they remain focused on Me, worshiping Me, declaring My light is coming to overpower the darkness. Call forth the rebuilding that I want to do, and stay very close to Me."

OCTOBER 10, 2021: FROM THE WAR ROOM OF HEAVEN

I was unexpectedly taken again to the War Room of Heaven. I am ushered in and take my place behind one of the twenty-four Elders. The Elder reaches back to pat my hand, and it melts my heart. Quiet, serious conversation is heard but undergirded by confidence in the Father's plan that is unfolding.

The Father speaks:

"The SHAKINGS in the natural and in the spiritual realm will increase from this day forward. When My people see shakings in the natural, they will know that a shaking is also taking place in the spiritual realm. The whole demonic structure hell has built has already been shaken and damaged, but even GREATER DESTRUCTION is being unleashed against them that will bring the whole structure DOWN INTO RUINS. What they have sowed into your Nation—FEAR, TRAUMA, TERROR, SICKNESS, LOSS— will now be REAPED by them in full."

A murmur of agreement and support rises from the Elders. The Elder I am standing behind speaks:

"This is the perfect time for a Harvest Season, and the Reaper Angels have been dispatched to harvest your Land, and they will gather the evil to receive JUDGMENT and JUSTICE, and they will gather those whose hearts are ready to be brought into the Kingdom."

The Father adds: "Tell My people to WELCOME the Reaper Angels and to support My plans by WORSHIPING Me and DECLARING My power and goodness and STAND FIRM in My promises to you and your Nation. I AM arising to perform My word."

OCTOBER 17, 2021: REPORT FROM THE WAR ROOM

I'm in the War Room in Heaven, and I hear a buzz of excited conversation. I hear parts of phrases as the Elders talk amongst themselves.

"Launch OPERATION RESCUE!" "Counter measures are now in place to PROTECT the Saints from the coming UPHEAVALS and SHAKINGS." "We have planned well for this day; we just need the Saints to STAY CLOSE to the Father and not PANIC and make foolish moves or decisions." "This will be a season of RECONNECTING HEARTS who have been MISLEAD by the corrupt media back to the Father and back to TRUSTING Him and His prophets. It will also be a season of reconnecting ESTRANGED family and friends who didn't understand the SPIRITUAL significance of this time and whose hearts have been VEILED by believing SECULAR voices over SACRED voices." "Good things are coming after the CRASH and BURN."

The Father adds:

"We are launching OPERATION RESCUE. Unprecedented SHAKINGS and OCCURRENCES will happen, but remember I've already told you there will be a HAPPY ENDING. GOOD will triumph over EVIL, LIGHT will outshine the DARKNESS, and JUSTICE will be dealt to the CORRUPT and EVIL. I AM your REFUGE and your STRONG TOWER, and you can bring others who are panicking and troubled into this place of safety. Live in My LOVE and in My PRESENCE. BREATHE Me in and EXHALE any fear or anxiety. I AM your faithful and true Father who has ARISEN to come and fight for His children and for your Land.

Let your heart be LIFTED UP knowing that you and your Land's REDEMPTION is very near."

O, what a faithful and loving Father to tell His children what was coming so that we were prepared and we would not be afraid! In the next encounter in the War Room of Heaven, I am shown how important it is for us to pray often in our prayer languages. I was also given an assignment from the Father that has become the guide for everything I do in ministry.

JANUARY 22, 2022: INVITED TO THE WAR ROOM OF HEAVEN

My lookout Angel invited me to come to the War Room of Heaven. There is great activity and movement in the hallway outside the War Room, and inside there are more Angels and Hosts then I've ever seen. There is excited talk and pointing to screens on the "walls." I have to slip through the crowd to stand behind my Elder, and he smiles at me and pats my hand, and I bend to kiss the top of his head—I feel such love for him.

The Father speaks:

"I'm calling this meeting to order; let's begin."

A deep silence and reverence fills the room, and awe of His great power seeps into all of us as we wait. I feel prompted to speak out a message in tongues. I am listened to intently—like I'm giving them directions that they need to remember. I'm humbled and stunned as I realize the Father is having the Holy Spirit give the Angels and Host battle plans and directions through my yielding to speaking in my prayer language.

The Father speaks:

"You have your marching orders and your assignments. Go forth, My Angels, go forth, My Host, go forth, My Sons and Daughters, and let's WIN THIS WAR against the darkness. I AM releasing more SIGNS and WONDERS to let people know that I AM on the MOVE. Angels, Hosts, you have your orders to PROTECT the Children of Light as I shake the world AWAKE." He turns to me and says, "Daughter, it is your assignment to keep My people ENCOURAGED and FOCUSED on My heart and My promises. After the war is won, there will be GREAT PEACE, JOY, and PLENTY in every area of their lives. I AM coming with My strong right arm of POWER to make things RIGHT, and you will see both My SEVERITY and My KINDNESS displayed. Each of My Sons and Daughters has an important part to play in this RESCUE OPERATION. Be FAITHFUL to respond to Holy Spirit's leading, and you will fulfill your assignment. A BRIGHT FUTURE awaits those who TRUST in Me."

The War Room fades away, and I'm back in my sunroom again, totally in awe of our God's power and of the part He's entrusted for all of us to carry out.

JANUARY 31, 2022: REPORT FROM THE WAR ROOM OF HEAVEN

I'm invited once again to the War Room of Heaven. My Lookout Guardian Angel escorts me there and stays at the door while I go and stand behind my Elder. It's such a place of complete strength, love, and sound wisdom—ancient wisdom from before time ever began. Now, I'm hearing the conversation in the room.

"The Angels and Hosts have been deployed to the frontlines all over the earth."

"The Army of Light (that's us!) has been rapidly trained and seasoned over this last earth year, and they are now ready to fight the major battles coming with the strength of enduring faith. The Lion's roar has filled them with fire, and they are ready to torch the enemy and burn up his plots and schemes."

"The Army of Light will notice a major change in the battles in this new season. Instead of long, drawn-out conflicts with only small victories, they will fight hard, with great power, with wise strategies, and the victories will come quickly, and they will be huge."

The Father speaks to me: "Tell My people that there are FIERCE BATTLES ahead, but they are STRONGER than they've realized. Encourage them that I, My Host, and My Angels are going before them and fighting alongside them. Speak COURAGE to their hearts that these hard-fought battles will be SHORT and the VICTORIES RESOUNDING. I want them to know My BEST for them is very near. My Valiant Warriors, fight with us and receive the CROWN of VICTORY."

The visit ends, and I'm trembling inside at the power of the Father's words and His awesome plans.

Because Heaven is outside our time and because the spiritual precedes the natural, my last visit to the War Room of Heaven was in 2022. At that time, they saw the victory as already being won and their part in the strategic war planning as being complete. Now, we will watch it unfold in our natural realm.

MAY 28, 2022: TAKEN TO THE WAR ROOM OF HEAVEN

My lookout guardian Angel invites me to visit the War Room of Heaven, and I take his hand, and we're off flying through the sky above earth's atmosphere where dark skies and shining stars streak by. A little breathless, I arrive at the door of the War Room. I'm so aware of the intense battle we are waging for our Nation right now that the mood in the War Room catches me off-guard. It is an atmosphere of relaxed conversation, smiling faces, and in front of each Elder is a piece of cake! No one is eating yet; they are patiently waiting for a signal to begin the celebration in earnest.

The Father speaks:

"You may be surprised to see Heaven's Council so relaxed and smiling when all on earth seems CHAOS and threatened DESTRUCTION. I wanted to bring you up here to give you HEAVEN'S VIEW of this war in order to STRENGTHEN your FAITH and HOPE in My POWER and My PROMISES. The enemy is well-known for his WEBS of DECEPTION and LIES that he entraps people in to defeat their faith and obscure My voice. While the enemy and those partnered with him were planning your DEFEAT, I was quietly, behind the scenes, setting up an INTRICATE TRAP for every SCHEME and every PERSON involved in darkness. This INCREDIBLE TRAP will SPRING all at once and will EXPOSE their DARKENED HEARTS and their EVIL SCHEMES. There will be a LOUD TRUMPET in the heavens when My TRAP springs SHUT, and heavenly and earthly THRONES will come CRASHING DOWN. Heaven can REST because they know all that is left is for the TRAP to be SPRUNG, and My finger is POISED to do that. This is as sure as

pushing the first domino in the set-up will cause ALL the dominoes to fall."

I'm standing behind My Elder in the War Room, soaking in the atmosphere of joy and celebration. He reaches back and lays his hand on mine, and I feel strength and joy and expectation fill my heart. I'm back in my sunroom filled with joy and expectancy.

In 2024, the Father began to take me to a new place in Heaven called "the Council Chambers of Heaven." In this room, the twenty-four Elders were functioning as a governing body over the affairs of nations on the earth.

COUNCIL CHAMBERS OF HEAVEN

JANUARY 5, 2024: THE SHIFT OF THE AGES

On the 3rd of January and again this morning, I was taken briefly to the Council Chambers of Heaven where the twenty-four Elders are meeting with the Father to determine the future of the nations. This is a larger, more open room than the War Room. The atmosphere in the room is bluish-green. There is a large, oval table with the twenty-four Elders around it. Nations are being weighed in the balances—large golden scales are in the room floating above the ground a bit above eye level. I see a nation being weighed, and a voice announces, "You have been weighed and found wanting." The Elders then discuss what will be coming to that nation. All I heard this morning was an announcement, "THE SHIFT OF THE AGES HAS COME."

The Father speaks:

"This is not just a season of CHANGE for your world—it is THE SHIFT OF THE AGES. The DOOR of the past history of the world is RAPIDLY CLOSING, and a DOOR is FLINGING OPEN to a NEW DAWN and a NEW ERA. This SHIFT OF THE AGES is a TRANSITION from the world before Jesus, after Jesus and the birth of the Church, and now comes the SHIFT into My KINGDOM AGE where My Sons and Daughters take their RIGHTFUL PLACE in TAKING BACK the world from the GRIP of LIES and DARKNESS as they RULE and REIGN with Me and have ACCESS to ALL of Heaven's RESOURCES. Because this is THE SHIFT OF THE AGES, you will need to WALK CLOSELY with Me as these are NEW PATHS. I will COUNSEL you through My VOICE, My written WORD, and through My PROPHETS. ISAIAH 30:18b-21 (TPT) *'He waits to be gracious to you. He sits on His throne ready to show mercy to you. For Yahweh is the Lord of justice, faithful to keep His promises. Overwhelmed with bliss are all who will entwine their hearts in Him, waiting for Him to help them ... How compassionate He will be when He hears your cries for help! He will answer you when He hears your voice! Even though the Lord may allow you to go through a season of hardship and difficulty, He Himself will be there with you. He will not hide Himself from you, for your eyes will constantly see Him as your teacher. When you turn to the right or turn to the left, you will hear His voice behind you to guide you, saying, "This is the right path; follow it.'* Put your CONFIDENCE in My DESIRE and My ABILITY to speak directly to you. THE SHIFT OF THE AGES will bring SHAKINGS and GREAT CHANGES, but I AM your Rock of REFUGE and your sure FOUNDATION."

JANUARY 14, 2024: THE FRAGRANCE OF OUR PRAYERS

As I set my heart to be lifted up into His presence this morning, I began to dimly see the Council Chambers in Heaven with the twenty-four Elders seated around the oval table. I saw the blue-green atmosphere of the room. Then, I began to smell a very sweet incense aroma. It just kept wafting over me, and My Elder told me it was the PRAYERS OF THE SAINTS. There were so many faith-filled prayers and decrees from the saints that the room was filled with a pink cloud of incense and prayers. I realized I wasn't dressed in regular clothes like I have been every time before on my visits to the twenty-four Elders. This time I was in a royal pink gown with a pink sparkly crown. The Elders were nodding in approval, and my Elder reached back, patted my hand, and said firmly, "You are royalty." The Father was breathing in and enjoying the fragrance of our prayers, and He spoke:

"My children's cries for FREEDOM have been heard, and they will be ANSWERED. There is a BEAUTY of WORSHIP that has joined to the INCENSE of the PRAYERS of FAITH. This worship has come forth from My people in their BROKENNESS, in their LOSS, and even in their CONFUSION or DOUBT. They have pressed in and TRUSTED Me as their ONLY TRUE SOURCE of LIFE and DELIVERANCE. I will ARISE (I saw Him stand up, and a hush filled the room), and I will RESPOND to this beautiful SACRIFICE of PRAYER and WORSHIP by My mighty right arm of JUDGMENT and JUSTICE. My children will be RESCUED, and they will be brought into FREEDOM and WHOLENESS. They will see with their own eyes My VINDICATION and My REWARD."

JANUARY 22, 2024: A VISIT TO THE COUNCIL CHAMBERS OF HEAVEN—STEADY AND FOCUSED

I smelled the sweet incense of the prayers of the Saints and saw its pink mist, dotted with small particles, and it carried me to the Council Chambers of Heaven. I stood behind my Elder and received his strength and tuned myself to the atmosphere of Heaven. I began boldly declaring: "This is the season for the exposure of all that is dark and corrupt and that has been hidden or disguised. Let it be exposed, exposed, exposed!" The Elders nodded in agreement, and I heard a few "here, here's" by them. I reversed the curse of all the agendas launched against our physical health. I then spoke words of worship and lifted my hand towards the Father seated at the head of the table. I was aware of His white hair and saw a few flashes of blue fire from His eyes. I thanked the Elders for being faithful and true to the Father for so long a time and told them I wanted to be like them—faithful, wise, and trusted counselors to the Father. The Elders impressed on me that my assignment for this year was to keep the people steady in the Father as His judgments hit the earth. I boldly declared, "Let His judgments begin now at this minute of time and go forth to their completion!" I immediately looked at my phone, and it was 9:09! (Twice is a witness that judgment and completion of its cycle have begun.)

The Father spoke: "MARK THIS DAY as the BEGINNING of a SERIES of CRUSHING JUDGMENTS that have been released against those partnered with darkness. Their THRONES will COLLAPSE under the WEIGHT of the DARK EXPOSURES that will be UNCOVERED of who they really are and what their death agendas are. Keep CALLING FORTH the EXPOSURES and MOW DOWN any RESISTANCE against FULL DISCLOSURES

coming into the LIGHT. RELEASE COVERING ANGELS over whistleblowers and pray for My COURAGE and LIGHT to fill them. Their TESTIMONY will help the DECEIVED and DELUDED to AWAKEN to the TRUTH. Keep My Army of Light STEADY in their TRUST and HOPE in Me, and REMIND them to keep their eyes FOCUSED on Me. Then they will BRAVELY follow Me into the dawn of a NEW ERA."

OCTOBER 6, 2024: AN IMPARTATION OF STRENGTH

I was taken to the Council Chambers of Heaven where the Elders and the Father were seated around the conference table. I placed my hands on my Elder's shoulders, and he placed his hand over mine and said, "Everything is going to be all right."

The Father said:

"This day I AM releasing AN IMPARTATION OF MY STRENGTH to My people to SUSTAIN them through the HEAT of the BATTLE. (He then breathed out, and I breathed in and received a wave of strength and stability.) My faithful Warriors, you are GOING TO MAKE IT THROUGH to the end of this war, and you will see a GREAT VICTORY over the TYRANNY and the HATRED of the darkness. What seems like a MOUNTAIN of TROUBLE and DESTRUCTION will SUDDENLY COLLAPSE under the weight of your WARFARE and My GLORY. As FIERCE and HARD as this battle is, the JOY, VICTORY, and FREEDOM will be SO MUCH GREATER. You will be ACKNOWLEDGED in Heaven as one who DID NOT SHRINK BACK because you CONTINUALLY BREATHED in My STRENGTH and kept yourself ENCOURAGED in My PROMISES. The WEEPING of those who have suffered GREAT LOSSES will endure for a night, but WONDERFUL JOY and RECOMPENSE will come in the DAWN of the VICTORY over the darkness. I will FLOOD the land with My GOODNESS while the darkness is EXPOSED and BROUGHT DOWN by their own evil. I will answer your cries for JUSTICE. It will come, and those partnered with darkness will be CRUSHED under the weight of My righteous right arm of JUDGMENT. They IGNORED the cries for MERCY from their victims, so their cries for MERCY will NOT BE HEARD. Be STIRRED in your spirit to FIGHT ON to the end. It is coming SOON, and you will be GLAD you did not leave the battlefield before My MIGHTY TRUMP of VICTORY is sounded. The CRASH of EVIL SYSTEMS will be heard worldwide, and the clean and enduring FEAR of the LORD will sweep over the world. This will release a GREAT HARVEST for the Kingdom, and the REBUILDING will be based on WISDOM, RIGHTEOUSNESS, and JUSTICE FOR ALL. BREATHE in My STRENGTH and FIGHT by My side. The VICTORY IS ALREADY YOURS."

PSALM 19:9 (NASB 1995) *"The fear of the Lord is clean, enduring forever; The judgments of the Lord are true; they are righteous altogether."*

NOVEMBER 16, 2024: A REORDERING OF YOUR WORLD

I was drawn into the Council Chambers of Heaven and found myself behind my Elder with my hands on his shoulders. I listened in on the conversation between the Elders and the Father as they discussed how our world should be reordered after the Rescue Operation. They spoke of less focus on technology and more focus on relationships. My Elder turned to me, and I saw his eyes for the first time—blazing blue with Heavenly fire, and he earnestly said to me: "Do not limit the limitless Father."

The Father speaks:

"Heaven has a plan for REORDERING YOUR WORLD after the Rescue Operation. I want you to have this CONFIDENCE that no matter how much OVERTURNING and how CHAOTIC your world looks as the PRECIPICE comes, Heaven has a SOLID and WELL-PLANNED REORDERING OF YOUR WORLD. This REORDERING will use technology from the past and BRILLIANT technology in your NEAR FUTURE, but TECHNOLOGY will NOT be your FOCUS. It will merely be a TOOL that ENHANCES your life but doesn't RULE it. RELATIONSHIPS will be KEY to REORDERING YOUR WORLD. Deep and satisfying relationships will be your FOCUS, and they will be of GREAT BENEFIT and DEEP JOY. As the world WAKES UP from almost being taken over by the darkness and sees My Rescue Operation, the Light of My NEW DAWN will bring grateful hearts and tear-stained faces that will TURN TO Me and DESIRE to KNOW and WALK with Me. What will a nation LOOK LIKE where people have learned to be RELATIONAL with each other and with Me? My GLORY will REST over these nations, and darkness will FLEE. IMAGINE AWAY about how BEAUTIFUL, PEACEFUL, and SATISFYING life will be when we REORDER YOUR WORLD. DO NOT LIMIT YOUR LIMITLESS GOD! I will accomplish ALL I have promised you. Watch, as the REORDERING OF YOUR WORLD unfolds."

I CORINTHIANS 2:9 (TPT) *"Things never discovered or heard of before, things beyond our ability to imagine—these are the many things God has in store for all His lovers."*

FEBRUARY 20, 2025: YOUR LIGHTNING SWORD OF JUDGMENT

PSALM 45:3 (TPT) *"Now strap Your lightning sword of judgment upon Your side, O Mighty Warrior so majestic! You are full of beauty and splendor as You go out to war!"*

I found myself in the Council Chambers of Heaven, standing behind my Elder. All the Elders arose as one, and they took off their crowns and laid them on the table. They looked beyond the Father, who had also arisen, with anticipation. Suddenly, Jesus appeared on a huge, white war horse. Jesus and the horse were about eight feet off the ground, and He had a lightning sword strapped to His thigh. Even though it was sheathed, the sword gave off flashes of lightning power. The Father nodded His head to His Son, and the war horse took off with great power towards the earth. Awe, wonder, and anticipation filled the room.

The Father speaks:

"I have released My Son with His LIGHTNING SWORD OF JUDGMENT to visit the earth with TRUTH and JUSTICE. DO NOT FEAR any dark scheme of the enemy—no matter how POWERFUL it looks—because when My Son draws His LIGHTNING SWORD OF JUDGMENT, TRUTH and JUSTICE will SHATTER and EXPOSE ALL the LIES and DECEPTIONS, and ALL those partnered with darkness will be BROUGHT TO JUSTICE before the world. Let **NOTHING MOVE** you or **SHAKE** you from this vision of the Son of God as your Majestic, Mighty Warrior come to **RESCUE** your nation with His **LIGHTNING SWORD OF JUDGMENT.**"

Psalm 45: Biblical meaning of 45=PRESERVATION

My visits to the Council Chambers of Heaven filled me with great assurance that Heaven was overseeing the nations and that a stable and good future was before us.

Another place I was taken multiple times was the Throne Room in Heaven. The Throne Room is full of power, lights, colors, sounds, angelic beings, and the twenty-four Elders. I caught a glimpse of His awesome power and beautiful love.

THE THRONE ROOM OF HEAVEN

OCTOBER 10, 2023: RELEASE!

I was briefly taken to a Throne Room in Heaven, and I heard the THUNDEROUS voice of the Lord declare, "RELEASE!" I felt like it was a directive like, "release the Kraken." In response to the word "RELEASE," I saw Host suddenly shoot towards earth as a supersonic missile of light and fire. I trembled inside at the power of His command.

The Father then spoke this:

"As I THUNDERED out 'RELEASE' on this day of 10/10, I set in motion the next phase of My RESCUE OPERATION for Israel and America. I will EXPOSE and BRING DOWN the ARROGANT

TRAITORS within these nations who have PLOTTED DESTRUCTION and CHAOS in order to DEFEAT and SUBJUGATE these lands. The enemy has SPECIFICALLY TARGETED these two COVENANT nations because he hates Me and he hates those I love. The number ten marks My LAW, My PERFECT ORDER, and My JUDGMENTS (10 plagues of Egypt) against those who OPPOSE My Kingdom RULE and REIGN. The schemes the darkness launches will be met with Heaven's OVERWHELMING and SUPERIOR FORCES. These plans the darkness has launched will have a MEASURE of success because I AM drawing the darkness FULLY OUT into the OPEN so that ALL the EVIL PLAYERS are EXPOSED before the world. Then the people of the world will ARISE with ONE VOICE calling for My JUDGMENT and JUSTICE to be RELEASED in FULL MEASURE against those partnered with darkness. My Army of Light will LEAD the way with My Host onto the battlefield echoing My cry of, 'RELEASE!'"

MARCH 15, 2024: IT WILL BE DONE!

This word began with a brief visit to the Throne Room. I was sitting by the Father's knee, and I heard the voice of many waters boom out, "It will be done!" At this command, the Hosts and Angels shot out of the Throne Room in all directions to fulfill His word.

MATTHEW 6:10 (TPT) *"Manifest Your Kingdom realm (or come and begin Your Kingdom reign) and cause Your every purpose to be fulfilled on earth, just as it is in heaven."*

The Father speaks: "This is the ESSENCE of what I AM doing in your day. When Heaven and earth AGREE, IT WILL BE DONE! My GROWING REMNANT are CRYING OUT for the POWER of the DARKNESS to be SMASHED and for My RESCUE to come and SET THEM FREE from the SLAVERY and BONDAGE they have been HELD CAPTIVE by. Whenever darkness is TAKEN DOWN and My FREEDOM and LIGHT FLOOD IN, there you will find My KINGDOM BEING ESTABLISHED. My Kingdom is established where My WILL IS DONE. That includes INDIVIDUAL LIVES and NATIONS. I AM not just coming to RESCUE you from TYRANNY and DARKNESS; I AM coming to ESTABLISH My KINGDOM in its place. My Kingdom is full of LIGHT, FREEDOM, PEACE, and PLENTY. Its foundations are RIGHTEOUSNESS and JUSTICE. I don't have to remind you how TWISTED these have become in your day. The enemy will tell you that My Kingdom is RESTRICTIVE, but I tell you that the FREEDOM TO DO what is RIGHT and JUST will fill your life with FAVOR, PEACE, and FULFILLMENT. My BEAUTIFUL REMNANT, your CRIES for My Kingdom TO COME and My WILL TO BE DONE on EARTH as it is in HEAVEN have been HEARD. My voice has THUNDERED in the Throne Room, 'IT WILL BE DONE!" And so it shall be."

APRIL 21, 2024: FIRE STARTERS

This morning as I was approaching the Father on the path to my garden in Heaven, I saw a golden stairway going up, and I realized the Father wanted me to go with Him to the Throne Room. We entered the Throne Room, and it was hushed as we proceeded to

His Throne. As I sat beside Him, I saw Hosts as far as my eye could see, and they were all holding a fire in their hands. I heard the words, "Fire Starters." After I received the fire into my heart, the Father asked me to join Him in releasing the Fire Starters to the world. In unison we declared, "Fire Starters, go!"

"I AM releasing My FIRE STARTERS all over the world to those who bear My name. This FIRE that I AM sending out will PURIFY HEARTS of FALSE MOTIVES, IDOLS, and COMPROMISE. This HOLY FIRE will BURN UP where the lines have been BLURRED between the HOLY and the PROFANE. This is NOT a matter of adopting OUTWARD RIGHTEOUS BEHAVIOR. Haven't you seen enough examples of this lately in the Church where lives of DISCIPLINE and RELIGIOUS BEHAVIOR were only a COVERUP for INWARD CORRUPTION and the DEFILING of many? My FIRE STARTERS will IGNITE TRUE HOLINESS and the FEAR OF THE LORD, and it will bring RADICAL REFORMATION to My Church. My HOLINESS WITHIN is a LIGHT in the DARKNESS. It makes you a SAFE LIGHTHOUSE for the BROKEN and those CAPTIVE to DEGRADING SINS. You become a place to ANCHOR their lives as I CLEANSE and PURIFY their hearts and they enter the TRUE FREEDOM of My HOLINESS. Will you welcome the FIRE STARTERS to IGNITE your heart? If you say, 'yes!' and allow the FIRE to do its CLEANSING and EMPOWERING work, then you become a FIRE STARTER, and you will IGNITE those in your sphere of influence. SPONTANEOUS COMBUSTION will take place as you touch people's lives. Goodbye, LUKEWARM, COMPROMISED CHURCH. Hello, FIRE STARTER, PASSIONATE CHRIST-FOLLOWERS!"

There were a few times when the Father allowed me to be an unseen visitor to a secret meeting of the evil empire. We were given effective prayer strategies to counter their dark plans.

BEHIND ENEMY LINES

APRIL 23, 2022: AN EVIL MEETING

I'm seeing a meeting room with a large, oval table and maybe as many as forty people around it. At the head is Obama who is obviously running this meeting of evil minds. I hear him say with urgency, "We've got to speed up the release of the pandemic planned for this Fall. It's got to be released early—as early as June."

A scientist looks at him with fear and apprehension, and replies, "But it's not ready to be released that soon!"

Obama cuts him off and storms back, "Make it ready!" The scientist looks cornered and terrified of making a mistake.

PRAYER STRATEGY: Cut off and bind the release of this evil plan. Command it to blow up in the faces of those concocting it and for the sickness to fall on those in this evil meeting. Call in the Host of Heaven to carry out the Father's will in preventing this diabolical scheme.

Obama continues, "At the same time we release the sickness, we need to further cripple the supply chain and crash the market. In the middle of this chaos, we'll arise as the saviors, and people will do anything we say. We'll censor all dissenting voices for the 'good' of the people, and we'll control the narrative again." I sense restlessness and fear around the table, an uneasiness none of them can explain.

PRAYER STRATEGY: Tear down these carefully-built dark schemes against supplies, financial systems, and methods of control. Use the light of God's truth to blow up and dismantle all these schemes. Speak His life and reordering on righteous foundations for all these systems.

The Father shares: "I AM uncovering specific plots and schemes to you so that you can pray FOCUSED and POWERFUL prayers against them. You have been given My POWER and AUTHORITY to tear down every DARK SCHEME of the enemy and the power to CALL FORTH REFORMATION and REBUILDING in these areas. I AM allowing you to hear their plans so that you can bring them to NOTHING in My name. Partner with Me, Army of Light!" (My observation in seeing this meeting is that there is no longer confidence among the band of thieves, and the fact that they are fearful is a weakness, so we counter that with faith and confidence in our great God.)

NOVEMBER 25, 2023: LAUNCH THE SMOKESCREEN

---

*Overheard from the camp of the wicked ... I see a dark room with a conference table with men and women wearing hooded black robes. Angry voices are demanding to know why their evil plans are not working. Loud demands are being given to launch the plan that will devastate the earth and bring it under their control. There is dark power in this room, but I sense an undercurrent of great fear and even rising panic. The dark leader rises and demands silence. He barks out, "We've got to stay focused and united in order to take back control." He points to a man that I know by the

Spirit is someone high up in the Church realm. "You need to ramp up the end times talk and convince people the worst is about to happen. We will step in (a wicked smile fills his face) and supply that worst outcome with our plan of great destruction. We will have them cowering at our feet." A look of scorn crosses his face. "Who can stop us? Certainly not a bunch of sheep who don't know our secret plans."

The meeting fades away, and the Father speaks: "The ARROGANCE of the evil ones will be their DOWNFALL. Even as they schemed destruction in their SUPER SECRET MEETINGS, I have given My Watchmen ACCESS to those meetings, and I AM REVEALING to My FAITHFUL and FAITH-FILLED Remnant where they need to target their prayers to STOP these plans from succeeding, and I AM showing you their areas of WEAKNESS so that you can partner with Me in SOWING MORE FEAR, DIVISION, and FOOLISH DECISIONS into their camp. Ask for My Spirit to CREATE A SMOKESCREEN around that evil camp. They will think they have COVER from EXPOSURE, but I will use the SMOKESCREEN to HIDE from them the POWERFUL OFFENSIVE from My Host and My Army of Light. They will BLINDLY launch their scheme of destruction, but it will BACKFIRE on them as My BREATH BLOWS AWAY the SMOKESCREEN, and they are caught RED-HANDED and FULLY EXPOSED. Imagine their HORROR, as they realize those sheep they thought were so DUMB and BRAINWASHED knew what their plans were, and they ROSE AS ONE to DEFEAT them and to take back their nation for the Kingdom of Light. I told you that those who DECEIVED the world would, in the end, be the MOST DECEIVED. CALL FORTH MY SPIRIT SMOKESCREEN, and PRESS IN for the FINAL BLOW to bring DOWN the evil empire."

Some of my favorite places in Heaven are visits to its gardens. I'm not sure how many gardens there are in Heaven, but I will share visits to two very significant ones.

THE GARDEN OF EDEN AND THE GARDEN OF LIFE

MAY 13, 2024: THREE KEYS TO GOING THROUGH THE BATTLE, THE STORM, THE SHAKINGS

This morning, I saw myself in Heavenly places with a ring of ancient-looking keys. I was suddenly at the gate of the Garden of Eden; it was opened wide, and I walked in. I saw shady groves of trees of every shape and size, fruit-bearing trees, and sunny fields to grow produce. To my great delight and honor, I met Enoch walking in the trees. He was gentle, kind, but very focused. He looked like John Paul Jackson, but Enoch's face was youthful, glowing, even though he had completely white hair. I asked him if he had any wisdom for me, and he gave me three keys for navigating this season on the earth. The Father spoke to me about these three keys:

"**Enoch has shared My WISDOM with you for going through this INTENSE season of the BATTLE, the STORM, and the SHAKINGS. If you will use these THREE KEYS, you will STAY STRONG in the BATTLE, WEATHER the STORM, and be ANCHORED in the SHAKINGS. These THREE KEYS are: LEARNING TO LIVE IN THE FEAR OF THE LORD, A DEEPER FAITH IN MY GOODNESS AND MY POWER, and WALKING CLOSELY WITH ME EVERY DAY. Living in the FEAR of the LORD is RIGHTLY DISCERNING My CHARACTER—it is acknowledging** both My KINDNESS towards righteousness and My SEVERITY towards evil. It is BELIEVING that My ways are ABOVE your ways and that My TIMING is perfect. Your FAITH will DEEPEN in My GOODNESS and My POWER as you remember My FAITHFULNESS to you, the FULFILLMENT of prophetic words from My written Word and from My prophets of this day, and REHEARSE My promises for a RESCUE and a NEW DAY. WALKING CLOSELY with Me every day means you INTENTIONALLY include Me in your JOYS, your SORROWS, your SCHEDULE, your ACTIVITIES, and your DREAMS. WAITING in My presence and HEARING My voice to you will be your LIFELINE and your ANCHOR. PRACTICE these THREE KEYS, and you will go through the BATTLE, the STORM, and the SHAKINGS with STRENGTH, ENDURANCE, and JOY."

SEPTEMBER 14, 2024: A GLORY BATH

The Father has been taking me to a different garden in Heaven. I wonder how many different gardens there are in Heaven? This garden is HUGE in scope. The trees are about 100 feet tall, and the sky seems very high up. The trees and undergrowth are thick and crowded—it's full of life. As the Father and I walked down the path, I asked Him if there was anything He wanted to tell me or say to me, and He replied, "I just want to be with you." Tears well up in my eyes, and I spot a bench where we can sit together. We're joined by Jesus and Holy Spirit, and I lean into the Father. A shaft of misty light appears over me and comes into me, and I hear the words "A Glory Bath." I let it fill me, and I pictured it bringing healing, restoration, and freedom to me.

The Father shared this with us:

"If you will DRAW AWAY with Me, I will POSITION you for A GLORY BATH. This GLORY BATH will bring WHOLENESS, HEALING, STRENGTH, and FREEDOM to you. As you SOAK in this GLORY BATH and BREATHE it in, it will become PART OF YOU. You will become a GLORY CARRIER, and you will be able to IMPART it to others. You will RELEASE it into the atmosphere everywhere you go. It will TRANSFER to anyone you PRAY for. It will GO FORTH and PROPEL your DECREES and DECLARATIONS. Heaven is INTERACTING with the earth in GREAT POWER and LIGHT. Take the time to TURN ASIDE with Me and receive A GLORY BATH."

NOVEMBER 20, 2024: THE CALL TO TRUE SONSHIP

As I sat on a bench with the Father in the Garden of Life, Enoch came and joined us, and the thought came to me that the Father's presence draws like a magnet, and we love to be in the circle of His love. The Father put an arm around Enoch and I. I heard the Father say, "Ah, My ancient Enoch and My modern-day Enoch." I understood that I represented an Enoch generation raised up to walk with the Father in true sonship power and authority. It was communicated to me that Enoch grew into operating as a Kingdom son and that he eventually judged fallen angels and acted as an ambassador of the King declaring the King's pronouncements, decisions, and judgments.

The Father spoke:

"Even as you fight VALIANTLY in these last battles before the GREAT VICTORY, keep in mind that you are in TRAINING to ANSWER THE CALL TO TRUE SONSHIP. The AMOUNT of INFLUENCE that you carry will be determined by HOW MUCH you have allowed Me to INFLUENCE YOUR LIFE. I AM not speaking of the kind of INFLUENCE that the world values. Many the world sees as INFLUENCERS are actually leading people to COMPROMISE or to follow a FORM of RELIGION and not RELATIONSHIP. KINGDOM INFLUENCERS may never be known to the world, but their DECREES, DECLARATIONS, FAITH, and INTIMACY with Me TEAR DOWN the darkness and ESTABLISH Kingdom LIGHT and LIFE. These are TRUE SONS of the Kingdom, and their names and their INFLUENCE are KNOWN in Heaven. There is NO SUBSTITUTE for the PATH to carrying My Kingdom INFLUENCE. That path is making me the SOURCE of your LIFE and STRENGTH, and KNOWING Me DEEPLY and INTIMATELY is your GOAL in life. Your GOAL must be KNOWING My HEART and being YIELDED to My call on your life and NOT SEEKING INFLUENCE. INFLUENCE is a by-product of a life SURRENDERED to Me. If you seek INFLUENCE instead of Me, your gifts will be CORRUPTED by COMPROMISE and SELFISH AMBITION. Look around you at all the CORRUPTION on the seven mountains of society that has resulted from seeking INFLUENCE instead of a SURRENDERED LIFE to Me. The GREAT REWARD of an intimate relationship with Me is DEEP and ABIDING PEACE, complete SATISFACTION, and STRENGTH for every day. As you carry the FRAGRANCE of My PRESENCE, you will carry GREAT INFLUENCE as Sons and

Daughters of the Kingdom. Answer THE CALL TO TRUE SONSHIP."

MARCH 3, 2025: THE BLESSING

I was suddenly in the Garden of Life, and Enoch was speaking to me. He understood and spoke to questions I was having about the future of our nation and the world. He told me that the glorious future that I have seen may take years to reach its fullness, but my union with the Father is my true source of joy. As the good future unfolds, it will be icing on the cake. He reminded me that the day he lived on the earth was very wicked (right before the flood), but he still found great joy and satisfaction from his union with the Father. Enoch then raised his right hand and placed it near my heart. He said these precious words, "I bless you to go deeper into the Father's heart than I did. I bless you to find complete joy and satisfaction in walking with Him." My heart was warm and full, and I know I'm supposed to release this blessing to all of you.

The Father speaks:

"I saw in Enoch a heart that DESIRED a DEEP and INTIMATE relationship with Me. I see that same LONGING in your heart and in the hearts of the Army of Light. I BLESSED Enoch's desire to KNOW Me and to WALK with Me, and our UNION became BEAUTIFUL, POWERFUL, and it brought forth the FRUIT of the Kingdom—even in the midst of GROSS DARKNESS in the world. The SEEDS of LIGHT that he sowed from his UNION with Me are STILL BEARING GOOD FRUIT to this day. Your life can have this LIFE-GIVING POWER as well. This is

LIGHT that SHATTERS the darkness and ESTABLISHES My Kingdom. I BLESSED Enoch's UNION and DEEP WALK with Me, and he has now RELEASED that BLESSING to you. What you have been BLESSED with you can now RELEASE to others. RECEIVE the BLESSING, and RELEASE it to all who HEAR your voice or READ these words. Declare: 'I BLESS you to go DEEPER in your walk with the Father, and I RELEASE DEEP JOY and SATISFACTION from your UNION with Him.' RECEIVE THE BLESSING!"

The dreams, visions, and encounters given to me served to confirm the Father's many promises to us in this season of the Rescue of the Ages.

CHAPTER FIFTEEN

Keeping our Hard-Won Freedom

What a journey this has been walking with the Father and linking arms with the Army of Light all around the world as we witnessed darkness fall and the Kingdom Age dawn. As we near the end of these chronicles of the Rescue of the Ages, not everything the Father promised us has come to fulfillment. I believe in the future I will be adding an epilogue to this book that includes all His promises coming to pass before our eyes.

Before we close out this epic drama that we have lived through, I want to share words the Father spoke that encourage us to be vigilant in keeping our hard-won freedom. He is faithful to give us directions so that we do not ever find our world in such a dire place again.

This first entry addresses keeping our own personal freedom.

FEBRUARY 23, 2020: STRENGTH AND RENEWAL

"As the fierceness of the battle gives way to victory after victory, I will send you much needed strength and renewal. When the battle lessens, don't make the mistake of relying on Me less and less, because this will place you in a very vulnerable position where the enemy can take advantage of your weaknesses and cause you to fall. Keep pressing fully into Me, and I will release My River of Life into you to strengthen and renew you. This will keep you from turning to false comforters that will mess up your life. Keep pursuing Me, trusting Me, and leaning on Me as much as you did in the heat of the battle. This will enable you to recover from war and also to be able to enjoy the spoils of war as a blessing and not a stumbling block. Eyes on Me first, and you will be strengthened and renewed."

The following journal entry addresses being diligent to preserve both personal and national freedom.

APRIL 27, 2022: THE SMOKE WILL BE RISING

"The SMOKE WILL BE RISING for several years as I EXPOSE the wicked and their schemes and I set their lives and their deeds ON FIRE. There are so many in places of leadership who have joined to DARKNESS by GREED and ARROGANCE that it will take MANY FIRES to PURGE their deeds and agendas from your Land. There are also many who were ENSNARED by temptation and became BLACKMAILED and CONTROLLED

PAWNS of the enemy. Their lack of courage to admit their participation in sin will be their DOWNFALL. Darkness is never satisfied with just a little; it DEMANDS to CONSUME you. As My FIRE OF JUDGMENT burns, some will find Me in the ASHES of their lives and find TRUE TREASURE and PEACE. As your Land is PURGED by these fires of judgment and justice, My SPIRIT WINDS will blow away the smoke, and your air will be filled with FREEDOM, CREATIVITY, and REJOICING in My goodness. Do not ever forget the STENCH of the SMOKE RISING from these fires of judgment, and GUARD your heart and your Land from it CREEPING BACK IN AGAIN. Keep your LIFE and your HEART CENTERED in My GOODNESS and My LOVE, and evil will have NO PLACE to gain a foothold."

It will be important to remember what is really important in our lives in order to maintain our freedom. We need to settle in our hearts what really matters.

DECEMBER 11, 2023: WHAT REALLY MATTERS

"When the darkness ATTEMPTS to launch their UGLY SCHEMES of mass destruction and I COUNTERMOVE with a RED SEA moment of RESCUE for your Nation, everything in your FAST-PACED world will be brought to a SUDDEN STOP. In the SHOCK of what has happened and in the JOY of so great a RESCUE, it will be time to RE-EVALUATE your lives. It will be a time for the people of your Nation to ask themselves, 'WHAT REALLY MATTERS?' This season of EXPOSURE of darkness and the TRIUMPH of the Light will bring each person to the VALLEY OF DECISION. Who and what am I LIVING FOR? REAL

RELATIONSHIPS will again become a FOCUS of your lives. Relationship with ME, relationship with your FAMILY, relationship with FRIENDS, and relationship with My BODY of Believers will become the PRIMARY FOCUS of your life again. The things you have FILLED your life with will NEVER SATISFY like DEEP and TRUE RELATIONSHIP with Me and with others. This is because I CREATED you with a NEED for RELATIONSHIP —first with Me and then with others. REAL JOY and SATISFACTION come from CONNECTING HEARTS and MINDS with Me and with family and friends. This will be a HUGE SHIFT for your Nation back into PRIORITIZING RELATIONSHIPS, but it will be a season when you discover WHAT REALLY MATTERS."

We need to keep our fighting skills sharp and ready to meet any new threat to our freedom.

JUNE 23, 2023: THE WHOLE ENCHILADA

"There has never been a time on the earth like these days when I have REVEALED so much of your FUTURE to My Prophets, My Watchmen, and My Prophetic Voices. My Spirit is MOVING ALL OVER THE EARTH, AWAKENING My Sons and Daughters to LEARN and to EMBRACE their KINGDOM CALLINGS. The darkness is ALL-OUT trying to STOP this awakening because as My LIGHT GROWS in you, you are EXPOSING the DEEP DARKNESS and the LIES and DECEPTION that have CAPTURED many. I have given you a BROAD OVERVIEW of a GOOD FUTURE where much of the world will live ACCORDING to KINGDOM WAYS. I have also supplied

DETAILS of the darkness' planned ATTACKS and DIRTY DEEDS so you know where to FOCUS your AUTHORITY to STOP dark schemes and to UNCOVER gross darkness. However, I will never give My people THE WHOLE ENCHILADA of future events, because that would TAKE AWAY your sense of WONDER and AWE as you live each day in My presence. Your FIGHTING SKILLS have been developed at GREAT COST, and I want them to REMAIN SHARP and READY to meet any enemy scheme, now or in future days that you live on the earth. Darkness will be UNDER your feet, but it will still TRY to KILL, STEAL, and DESTROY, so I need My Army of Light to REMAIN VIGILANT and POWERFUL to STOMP on the darkness and to keep it from ARISING again to bring such WIDESPREAD PERVERSION and SLAVERY. I will continue to REVEAL the FUTURE to My chosen voices, but I will never give you THE WHOLE ENCHILADA because I want life to hold MYSTERIES for you to SEARCH OUT and WONDERS for you to see as I UNFOLD a GOOD FUTURE before you."

We will close out this book of records of the Rescue of the Ages with three beautiful journal entries with amazing promises for the future from our faithful Father of Lights.

AUGUST 13, 2022: THE GREENING OF AMERICA

"Eye has not seen, and ear has not heard, nor can your mind imagine all the GOOD THINGS that are in store for a Nation that turns its HEART to Me. This season of My SHAKING JUDGMENT and My FIERY JUSTICE will cause many to seek Me and to SURRENDER their lives to Me through My Son.

AWAKENED HEARTS and MINDS will realize what I have saved them from, and great THANKFULNESS will arise as a BEAUTIFUL SACRIFICE of PRAISE that ascends to My Throne. Things are CHAOTIC and UNCERTAIN right now, so let Me share My PLANS and My FUTURE for your Land. You will see unfold before you THE GREENING OF AMERICA. She will be filled with NEW LIFE, ABUNDANT CROPS, FRESH INVENTIONS, PROSPERITY, GENUINE STEWARDSHIP of your RESOURCES, and a HEALTHY and THRIVING population. Keep the color GREEN around you to remind you of My PROMISES and to STEADY you through the CHANGING OF THE GUARD and the BRINGING DOWN of the ENEMY'S HIGH PLACES. You will see THE GREENING OF AMERICA."

JULY 2, 2024: BY THE DAWN'S EARLY LIGHT

"There will be a night of DEEP DARKNESS for your Nation, but know that it is My HAND COMING DOWN and COVERING YOUR LAND. The deep darkness will be SAFETY and PROTECTION for My people as I TAKE DOWN the EVIL EMPIRE, ROUND THEM UP, and REMOVE THEM from your Land. MASSIVE AMOUNTS of Hosts and Angels will be spread across your Land DRIVING those partnered with darkness out of their HIDING PLACES. Your Military in this Operation Clean-Up will not sleep that night as they ROUND UP those who wanted to COMPLETELY ENSLAVE you, but the darkness will be the ones who LOSE THEIR FREEDOM. My Army of Light will be SUPPORTING this TAKE DOWN of darkness with their POWERFUL PRAYERS and FAITH. You will be FULLY ASSURED that BY THE DAWN'S EARLY LIGHT FREEDOM will be WON for your Nation. Those of the darkness will be SHOCKED and TERRIFIED at how EASILY they were CAPTURED. They thought their HIDEOUTS were completely SECURE and HIDDEN, but NOTHING ESCAPES MY PIERCING LIGHT OF EXPOSURE. As My watchmen and My Army of Light look for the FIRST RAYS OF LIGHT, a Nation FREED from DARKNESS and TYRANNY will EMERGE. Once again, BY THE DAWN'S EARLY LIGHT, your Nation will be SAVED and brought into My Kingdom Era of FREEDOM, PEACE, and PLENTY. HOLD FAST, HOLD STRONG, HOLD TRUE, as the deep darkness GIVES WAY to the DAWNING of My GREAT LIGHT over your Land."

This final entry casts a vision of how this season has also prepared us for an eternity of ruling and reigning as His Sons and Daughters.

JANUARY 16, 2024: A FUTURE OF WONDER

"What you learn in this season of INTENSE BATTLE will carry you through to the SHINING VICTORY. You are learning the importance of DAILY seeking My face, LISTENING for My voice, SOAKING in My presence, and WORSHIPING Me with all your heart and your life. When you HONOR Me with this kind of DEDICATION and CONSECRATION, I will IMPART FAITH, STRENGTH, and COURAGE into your innermost being, and these become the FOUNDATION and the STABILITY of your life. Not only will FAITH, STRENGTH, and COURAGE carry you through this war, it will go with you into ETERNITY where you will FULLY become My Sons and Daughters in My KINGDOM of

LIGHT. My Kingdom of Light is now TOUCHING THE EARTH, and you are AWAKENING to your roles as My Sons and Daughters. Everything you learn here on earth about RULING and REIGNING will be TRANSFERRED to ETERNITY, and you will sit with Me on thrones of power to help Me OVERSEE the EXPANDING Universe. This is My HEART'S DESIRE to have a FAMILY who KNOWS Me, TRUSTS Me, and RULES in LOVE and POWER with Me. I AM inviting you into A FUTURE OF WONDER —will you join Me?"

Thank you for taking this journey of remembrance of the Holy war that we fought to secure our freedom from the evil empire. May future generations be reminded of this fierce battle and join in the determination to keep the freedom that was won in the Rescue of the Ages. May you be blessed with His peace, His glory, and His joy.

ACKNOWLEDGMENTS

My unending love and thanksgiving to the Father for sharing His powerful, gentle, and awesome voice with words that sparked faith, hope, and endurance that carried us through to the happy ending.

My heartfelt thanks to Patty Teichroew and Janet Huxley for proofreading and editing this manuscript and offering inspired suggestions to make it better.

Working with Missy Maxwell Worton of Light Warrior Publishing has been a joy. She fully understands the publishing business, and she is a great encourager and cheerleader along the way. Her attention to detail and helpful suggestions brought a professionalism to my book design and cover. I am forever grateful to Missy for making my book a reality!

Ashley Hagan provided great expertise in formatting and editing my manuscript into a highly-readable and eye-catching presentation. I love how she differentiated the formatting so that you can clearly see what my thoughts and comments are as contrasted with the Father's voice to me. Thank you, Ashley!

Tammy Largin was such fun to work with as we designed a cover that would represent my book well and powerfully. She patiently listened and worked with her original design until Missy and I were totally happy with the outcome. Great work, Tammy! Thank you!

RECOMMENDED
BOOKS AND VIDEOS

Kingdom Come: Understanding the Reign of God on Earth by Johnny Enlow

Awakened: Embracing Freedom in Times of Peril by Dr. Ralph Edward Plumb

The Q Chronicles, Books 1-4 by Dave Hayes (Praying Medic)

YouTube: A Watchman's Journal Channel – Five Video Series "Hearing God's Voice" (Found under the Playlist Tab)
https://youtu.be/EVRDGb3oWbY?si=BxoUYk4k3_jUuvjx

ABOUT THE AUTHOR

Diana Larkin has been journaling the Father's voice to her for decades. Her favorite part of the day is the morning, when she draws away to sit at His feet and to hear what is on His heart. In the beginning, the journal entries were mostly personal and family-related, but over the years, they became about the Church and the nations. The last eight years, the focus became the peril the nations of our world faced from very dark forces who were seeking to facilitate their dark agenda and the Father's promise to come with the Rescue of the Ages and to restore freedom, peace, and plenty.

Diana is an author, speaker, blogger, and vlogger. Her blog, "A Watchman's Journal," can be found on awatchmansjournal.com. She regularly posts videos about what she is hearing from the Father on her YouTube Channel, "A Watchman's Journal," and on her Rumble Channel, "Diana Larkin." Diana posts interview videos with other prophetic voices, dreamers, visionaries, and A Watchman's Journal Team. She also posts her journal entries to six social media sites: X Platform, Facebook, Instagram, Truth Social, Telegram, and Gab. In addition, she has a weekly podcast that is broadcast on 93.3 AM Realtalk Radio.

In her spare time, Diana loves gardening, decorating, sewing, and baking. She and her husband, Don, live in North Carolina and have three grown daughters, their spouses, and ten beautiful grandchildren who light up their lives!

VISIT THE WEBSITE

Awatchmansjournal.com

Welcome to A Watchman's Journal Ministry! A good Father speaks to His children—words of comfort, direction, warning, love, assurance, promises, and shared laughter. This website is about hearing, cherishing, and responding to the Father's voice through the journal entries I have posted in the Blog section, on six social media sites, in my book *The Rescue of the Ages*, and in videos where I share what I have been hearing from the Father. My desire is to encourage participation through prayer as He gives us action items of strategic warfare. Most of all, I want to encourage you to begin your own journey into the adventure of hearing God's voice. There is nothing in life that matches the intimacy and the joy of the God of the Universe speaking to your spirit. Be sure to check out the five-video series, "Hearing God's Voice," on my YouTube channel *A Watchman's Journal* under the "Playlist" tab.

A Watchman's Journal Team loves to read your comments, join you in prayer for the needs in your lives, help with interpreting your dreams, and hear your testimonies of what the Father is speaking to you and what He is doing in your lives. Contact us through the email attached to this website:

awatchmansjournal@protonmail.com.

www.ingramcontent.com/pod-product-compliance
Lightning Source LLC
Chambersburg PA
CBHW070907120626
46546CB00001B/173